Varietal Wines

Published in 2015 by Hardie Grant Books

Hardie Grant Books (Australia)
Ground Floor, Building 1
658 Church Street
Richmond, Victoria 3121
www.hardiegrant.com.au

Hardie Grant Books (UK)
5th & 6th Floors
52–54 Southwark Street
London SE1 1UN
www.hardiegrant.co.uk

All rights reserved. No part of this publication may be reproduced, stored in a retrieval system or transmitted in any form by any means, electronic, mechanical, photocopying, recording or otherwise, without the prior written permission of the publishers and copyright holders.

The moral rights of the author have been asserted.

Copyright text © James Halliday
Copyright photography © Adam Hobbs/One Idea (unless otherwise specified); Dr Stefano Dini (Durif, Tempranillo, Negroamaro, Pinotage, Tannat); Randy Caparoso (Primitivo, Carignan, Piquepoul Blanc); Kevin Miller/iStock (Pinot Gris)

A Cataloguing-in-Publication entry is available from the catalogue of the National Library of Australia at www.nla.gov.au
Varietal Wines
ISBN 978 1 74270 860 7

Publishing Director: Fran Berry
Project Editor: Rihana Ries
Editor: Sarah Shrubb
Indexer: Max McMaster
Design Manager: Mark Campbell
Designer: Philip Campbell
Typesetter: Megan Ellis
Photographer: Adam Hobbs (principal); Dr Stefano Dini, Randy Caparoso, Kevin Miller (additional)
Production Manager: Todd Rechner

Colour reproduction by Splitting Image Colour Studio
Printed and bound in China by 1010 Printing International Limited

JAMES HALLIDAY
Varietal Wines

A guide to 130 varieties grown in Australia
and their place in the international wine landscape

Table of Contents

Introduction	x
A Short History of Wine Grapes	xiv
How to Use this Book	xviii

Chapter 1
The Classic White Varietals: Chardonnay — 1

INTERNATIONAL HISTORY	1
INTERNATIONAL STYLES	3

France

Burgundy	3
Puligny and Chassagne Montrachet	4
Corton Charlemagne	5
Meursault	6
Chablis	6
Côte Chalonnaise and Mâconnais	6

Rest of Europe

Italy	7
Lesser Western Europe: Cool Regions	8
Lesser Western Europe: Warm Regions	8
Lesser Eastern Europe	8

United States

Napa and Sonoma Valleys, California	8
Carneros, California	9
Edna, Santa Maria and Santa Ynez Valleys et al., California	9
Oregon	9
Yakima Valley and Walla Walla, Washington State	9

Canada

Okanagan Valley, British Columbia	10
Ontario	10

Chile

Central Valley	11
Casablanca Valley	11
Bío-Bío and Malleco Valleys	11
Costa | Coastal	12

South Africa	12

New Zealand

Auckland	12
Waiheke Island	13
Gisborne	13
Hawke's Bay	13
Wairarapa | Martinborough	14
Marlborough	14
Nelson	14
Canterbury | Waipara	15
Central Otago	15

AUSTRALIAN HISTORY	15
AUSTRALIAN STATISTICS	17
AUSTRALIAN WINEMAKING	17
AUSTRALIAN REGIONAL STYLES	19

New South Wales

Hunter Valley	19
Mudgee	20
Orange	20
Cowra	21
Tumbarumba	21

South Australia

Adelaide Hills	22
McLaren Vale	22
Coonawarra	22
Padthaway	23
Mount Benson and Robe	23
Barossa and Eden Valleys	23

Victoria

Strathbogie Ranges and Upper Goulburn	24
Gippsland	24
Beechworth	24
Geelong	25
Macedon Ranges	25
Mornington Peninsula	26
Yarra Valley	26
Henty	27

Pan-Australian Zones	27

Western Australia

Great Southern	28
Manjimup and Pemberton	28
Margaret River	29

Tasmania — 30

Chapter 2
The Classic White Varietals: Riesling — 33

INTERNATIONAL HISTORY	33
INTERNATIONAL STYLES	36

Germany

Rheingau	36
Pfalz	37
Rheinhessen	38
Nahe	38
Mosel-Saar-Ruwer	38

Alsace, France — 39

Austria — 40

New Zealand — 42

North America — 42

AUSTRALIAN HISTORY	43
AUSTRALIAN STATISTICS	45
AUSTRALIAN WINEMAKING	45
AUSTRALIAN REGIONAL STYLES	47

South Australia

Clare Valley	47
Adelaide Hills	49
Eden Valley	49
Barossa Valley	50

Western Australia

Great Southern	50

Tasmania — 51

Chapter 3
The Classic White Varietals: Semillon — 53

INTERNATIONAL HISTORY	53
INTERNATIONAL STYLES	54

Bordeaux, France — 54

AUSTRALIAN HISTORY	55
AUSTRALIAN STATISTICS	57
AUSTRALIAN WINEMAKING	57
AUSTRALIAN REGIONAL STYLES	59

New South Wales

Hunter Valley	59
Mudgee	61
Riverina	61

South Australia

Adelaide Hills	61

Western Australia

Margaret River	62

Chapter 4
The Classic White Varietals: Sauvignon Blanc — 65

INTERNATIONAL HISTORY	65
INTERNATIONAL STYLES	66

France

Loire Valley	66

Northern Italy, Austria and Slovenia — 67

South Africa — 67

Chile — 68

New Zealand

Hawke's Bay	69
Martinborough | Wairarapa	69
Marlborough	69
Nelson	71

AUSTRALIAN HISTORY	71
AUSTRALIAN STATISTICS	72
AUSTRALIAN WINEMAKING	72
AUSTRALIAN REGIONAL STYLES	74

Western Australia

Margaret River	74
Great Southern	75
Geographe	75

South Australia

Adelaide Hills	76

New South Wales

Orange	76

Chapter 5
The Classic White Varietals: Pinot Gris | Pinot Grigio — 79

INTERNATIONAL HISTORY	79
INTERNATIONAL STYLES	80
AUSTRALIAN HISTORY	80
AUSTRALIAN STATISTICS	81
AUSTRALIAN WINEMAKING	82
AUSTRALIAN REGIONAL STYLES	82
Tasmania	82
South Australia	
Adelaide Hills	83
Victoria	
Mornington Peninsula	83
King Valley	84

Chapter 6
Second Tier White Varietals — 85

Chenin Blanc	85
Colombard	89
Gewurztraminer	Traminer	91
Marsanne	94
Muscadelle	96
Roussanne	99
Trebbiano	101
Verdelho	102
Viognier	105
Muscat Blanc a Petits Grains	107
Muscat of Alexandria	109

Chapter 7
Lesser White Varietals — 110

Aligote	110
Arneis	111
Assyrtiko	112
Aucerot	113
Biancone	113
Chasselas	114
Clairette	114
Cortese	115
Doradillo	115
Fiano	115
Furmint	Harslevelu	117
Garganega	117
Gouais Blanc	118
Greco	Greco Bianco	119
Grillo	120
Kerner	120
Malvasia	121
Malvasia Istarska	122
Montils	122
Moscato Giallo	123
Muller-Thurgau	124
Nosiola	124
Ondenc	125
Pedro Ximenez	127
Petit Manseng	127
Petit Meslier	126
Picolit	128
Pinot Blanc	130
Prosecco	131
Schonburger	132
Siegerrebe	132
Silvaner	133
Taminga	133
Verdejo	133
Verduzzo Friulano	134
Vermentino	134
Other White Varietals	136

Chapter 8
The Classic Red Varietals: Cabernet Sauvignon — 143

INTERNATIONAL HISTORY	143
INTERNATIONAL STYLES	146
Bordeaux, France	146
Italy and Spain	147
United States	
Napa and Sonoma Valleys, California	148
Washington State	148
Argentina	149
South Africa	149
Chile	150

New Zealand	
Hawke's Bay	150
Waiheke Island	151
AUSTRALIAN HISTORY	151
AUSTRALIAN STATISTICS	153
AUSTRALIAN WINEMAKING	154
AUSTRALIAN REGIONAL STYLES	156
South Australia	
Coonawarra	156
Padthaway	157
McLaren Vale	158
Barossa Valley	158
Eden Valley	159
Clare Valley	160
New South Wales	
Hunter Valley	160
Mudgee	161
Orange	161
Western Australia	
Margaret River	161
Great Southern	162
Victoria	
Bendigo	164
Goulburn Valley	164
Heathcote	164
Yarra Valley	164

Chapter 9
The Classic Red Varietals: Merlot — 167

INTERNATIONAL HISTORY	167
INTERNATIONAL STYLES	169
Bordeaux, France	
Haut Medoc	169
St Emilion and Pomerol	170
United States	
Napa and Sonoma Valleys, California	170
Washington State	171
Canada	171
Chile	172
New Zealand	
Hawke's Bay	172

South Africa	173
AUSTRALIAN HISTORY	173
AUSTRALIAN STATISTICS	174
AUSTRALIAN WINEMAKING	174
AUSTRALIAN REGIONAL STYLES	176
South Australia	
Adelaide Hills	176
Barossa and Eden Valleys	176
Coonawarra	177
Wrattonbully	177
McLaren Vale	178
Victoria	
Yarra Valley	178
Western Australia	
Margaret River	179
Manjimup and Pemberton	179
Other Regions	179

Chapter 10
The Classic Red Varietals: Pinot Noir — 181

INTERNATIONAL HISTORY	181
INTERNATIONAL STYLES	184
Burgundy, France	184
New Zealand	
Wairarapa	187
Nelson	187
Marlborough	187
Canterbury	188
Waipara	188
Central Otago	188
United States	
Oregon	189
Sonoma County, California	190
South Central Coast	Edna Valley	Arroyo Grande	Santa Barbara, California	190
Rest of California	190
Canada	
British Columbia and Ontario	191
Rest of France and Europe	191
South Africa	192

AUSTRALIAN HISTORY	192
AUSTRALIAN STATISTICS	194
AUSTRALIAN WINEMAKING	195
AUSTRALIAN REGIONAL STYLES	196

Victoria

Yarra Valley	196
Mornington Peninsula	197
Geelong	197
Macedon Ranges	198
Gippsland	198
Ballarat	198
Henty	199

South Australia

Adelaide Hills	200

Tasmania 200

Western Australia

Great Southern	201
Mount Barker	201

Chapter 11
The Classic Red Varietals: Shiraz | Syrah — 203

INTERNATIONAL HISTORY	203
INTERNATIONAL STYLES	205

France

Hermitage, Northern Rhône Valley	205
Crozes Hermitage, Northern Rhône Valley	205
Côte Rôtie, Northern Rhône Valley	206
St Joseph, Northern Rhône Valley	207
Cornas, Northern Rhône Valley	207
Southern Rhône Valley	208
Rest of Southern France	208

Spain	208
Italy	208
North America	209
South Africa	209
New Zealand	210
AUSTRALIAN HISTORY	210
AUSTRALIAN STATISTICS	213
AUSTRALIAN WINEMAKING	213
AUSTRALIAN REGIONAL STYLES	215

South Australia

Barossa Valley	215
McLaren Vale	217
Clare Valley	218
Eden Valley	219
Langhorne Creek	219
Coonawarra	219
Padthaway	220
Wrattonbully	221

New South Wales

Hunter Valley	221
Mudgee	222
Orange	223
Canberra District	223
Hilltops	224

Victoria

Heathcote	224
Bendigo	225
Goulburn Valley	226
Grampians	226
Pyrenees	227
Glenrowan and Rutherglen	228
Sunbury	228
Macedon Ranges	229
Mornington Peninsula	229
Yarra Valley	229
Geelong	230

Western Australia

Great Southern	230
Margaret River	231
Peel, Perth Hills and Swan District	231

Chapter 12
The Classic Red Varietals: Grenache | Garnacha Tinta — 233

INTERNATIONAL HISTORY	233
INTERNATIONAL STYLES	234

France

Châteauneuf-du-Pape	234
Côtes du Rhône	235

AUSTRALIAN HISTORY	236
AUSTRALIAN STATISTICS	236
AUSTRALIAN WINEMAKING	237

Australian Regional Styles — 238

South Australia
McLaren Vale — 238
Barossa Valley — 238
Clare Valley — 239

Chapter 13
Second Tier Red Varietals — 240

Barbera — 240
Cabernet Franc — 241
Chambourcin — 243
Dolcetto — 244
Durif — 245
Gamay — 247
Mourvedre | Monastrell — 248
Nebbiolo — 249
Petit Verdot — 252
Pinot Meunier — 254
Ruby Cabernet — 255
Sangiovese — 256
Tempranillo — 258
Zinfandel | Primitivo | Tribidrag — 259

Chapter 14
Lesser Red Varietals — 262

Aglianico — 262
Aleatico — 263
Alicante Bouschet — 264
Ancellotta — 264
Aranel — 264
Bastardo | Trousseau — 265
Canaiolo Nero — 265
Carignan | Mazuelo — 266
Carmenere — 267
Carnelian — 268
Cienna — 268
Cinsaut — 268
Colorino del Valdarno — 269
Corvina — 270
Counoise — 270
Dornfelder — 270
Freisa — 271
Graciano — 271
Jacquez — 272
Lagrein — 273
Lambrusco — 274
Lambrusco Salamino — 275
Mammolo — 276
Marzemino — 277
Mencia — 278
Mondeuse — 278
Montepulciano — 278
Muscardin — 280
Negroamaro — 280
Nero d'Avola — 281
Pinotage — 282
Refosco dal Peduncolo Rosso — 284
Rondinella — 285
Sagrantino — 285
Saint Macaire — 286
Sankt Laurent | St Laurent — 286
Saperavi — 287
Tannat — 287
Teroldego — 288
Tinto Cao | Tinta Barroca | Tinta Roriz — 289
Touriga Nacional — 289
Trollinger | Schiava Grossa — 291
Tyrian — 297
Zweigelt — 291

Index — 292
Acknowledgements — 308

Introduction

This book looks at the history of each variety from an international and then an Australian point of view; discusses the way the varietal wines are made here; looks at the international styles and, finally, Australian regional styles. In both the Australian and international contexts, best producers are nominated. In the section 'How to Use This Book' on page xviii, I explain a number of its features in greater detail.

When I started to become seriously interested in wine, well over 50 years ago, this book could not have been written. Only a handful of wines from the New World were accorded a varietal name or identification (back labels did not exist), while the question simply didn't arise in the Old World: what was relevant was the place the wine was made, not its varietal base.

Moreover, the varietal bank in the New World had very few deposits. Australia was the only country outside France to grow Shiraz but, like the United States, it was almost bereft of Chardonnay, Sauvignon Blanc and Merlot. In addition, the United States had only minuscule patches of Semillon and Riesling, while South Africa lingered in a sea of Chenin Blanc (which it called Steen), New Zealand in a sea of Muller-Thurgau.

France was by far the most important exporter, followed by Germany with Riesling-based wines, and Portugal with Port. Over the centuries, the British developed a lexicon of names for these wines: Claret (for Bordeaux); White Burgundy and Red Burgundy; Chablis; Hock, Riesling and Moselle (for the wines from Germany); Champagne and (very importantly) Sherry and Port. The Loire Valley, Alsace and the Rhône Valley escaped these generic names, although the endemic fraud and misuse of Châteauneuf-du-Pape in the early part of the twentieth century led Baron Le Roy to develop the Appellation Contrôlée system brought into law in France in 1936–37.

Australia happily borrowed all these names from the British, and continued to use them for the domestic market right up to the end of the twentieth century, although their use in the EU has long been proscribed. 'Phase out' dates exist for the domestic market, either in concept or in reality, under an Australia–EU Wine Agreement, although commercial practice had outpaced the ponderous inter-government negotiations, which dragged on for a decade, over the implementation of phase-out dates.

But a century ago, W Percy Wilkinson, then head of what became the CSIRO, patented a series of names which he proposed should be used by the Australian wine industry free of charge. It was simplicity itself: for Claret, Claralia; for Burgundy, Burgalia; for Hock, Hockalia; for Sauternes, Sautalia; for Port, Poralia; for Chablis, Chabalia – and so on. He was not killed in the rush; indeed, I have never seen or read of a single instance of the use of any of these names.

Instead, led by California, varietal naming has become standard practice for the New World over the past 40 years, becoming ever more entrenched as the waves of new, obscure varieties from Italy (the largest varietal storehouse in the world), Eastern Europe, Spain and Portugal have been enthusiastically planted in the wake of the French classics.

Australia, in its usual fashion, has embraced these old, often ancient, varieties. Where the varieties in question have evolved in hot, arid climates, there is every reason to experiment with them in warm, dry regions here. But cooler climate varieties have also been imported and planted here, there and everywhere. In all, 46 varieties join this book for the first time, lifting the number of lesser red varieties from 20 to 44, and lesser white varieties from 29 to 51.

This, in turn, has caused the Old World to writhe in agony as its markets have been eroded, and generational changes in attitude no longer mean the varieties used are irrelevant. If you own a slice of Grand Cru Burgundy or a classed growth Château in the Haut Medoc, you must resolutely stick to the line that what is important is the place where the grapes are grown; the only relevance of the variety is to ensure that it complies with the relevant Appellation Côntrolée. The trouble is, the new markets of the world don't see it that way.

To exacerbate the problem, the Trojan Horse has come to the south of France in a big way. Chardonnay, Shiraz, Merlot and Cabernet Sauvignon have swept aside the indigenous varieties and, for good measure, have their identities emblazoned on their labels – they are, after all, international currency. Since the first edition of this book, French appellation laws have been changed to accommodate regional blends by allowing the use of varietal names.

This change has been driven by the ever-increasing globalisation of the wine business. From the point of view of the vigneron, both domestic and international markets have been, and remain, in a state of flux. At the most basic level, consumers' demands and preferences have led to the spread of grape varieties into countries (and regions within countries) where they were previously absent or had only small plantings, regarded as insignificant.

Wikipedia, Google and individual websites have fuelled an explosion of knowledge; this is feeding on itself, increasing the rate of change with no end in sight. It is inevitable that parts of this book will be outdated by the time it is published and you come to read these words.

Research continues apace, and even the ultimate source of present-day knowledge available to writers such as myself, *Wine Grapes* by Jancis Robinson, Julia Harding and Jose Vouillamoz (Ecco/HarperCollins, 2012), will need to be updated. In some respects, a challenge has already been thrown down by Ian D'Agata in *Native Wine Grapes of Italy* (University of California Press, 2014).

For many years I have been asking research scientists, or those having lines of communication with researchers, when DNA research will be able to identify, on a reliable and ongoing basis, individual clones of a given variety. Just when I thought an answer was imminent, it turns out that the answer will require the more sophisticated and expensive DNA analysis techniques used in human medicine.

For example, using the generally accepted six to eight SSRs (simple sequence repeats) reveals that Pinot Noir, Pinot Gris, Pinot Meunier and Pinot Blanc have identical DNA, and at this level of analysis they are definitely the same variety. They are almost certainly clones of an original Pinot variety.

Even the most casual inspection by a lay person would lead to the conclusion that these four varieties are very 'different' from each other: the shape of the leaves and the colour of the bunches as the grapes ripen should end any discussion. Historically, the morphology of vines was used as the basis of both varietal and clonal identification. This involved the recording of the differences in the way the new canes grow each year (upright or droopy), the shape of the bunches, the typical berry colour and size, leaf colour, leaf shape, leaf patterns, and so forth.

D'Agata suggests that these seemingly different forms of a given variety should be described as biotypes rather than clones, but (understandably) doesn't suggest a numbering or code system. In this context biotypes and mutations occupy similar territory. From time immemorial the definition of a clone is a cell or individual genetically identical to another, and derived from one cell or individual (plant or animal) without fertilisation or by asexual reproduction. In the context of vines, cuttings from the parent will be planted and establish their own root systems. Obviously, using both DNA evidence and morphology in tandem is better than either approach in isolation.

It will be obvious that there is an Adam's Rib issue here. All cuttings planted in a short period of time – say 50 years – and in a delimited area should be genetically, morphologically and biochemically identical, the grapes they give rise to likewise.

But take the timescale out to hundreds of years, and increase the area, and things change. With each cell division errors can occur, leading to mutations; just to complicate matters further, the resulting vine may look the same or different. It has been suggested that Pinot Noir is particularly subject to mutation, but in comparison to other vines it is not. It is just that it is one of the most ancient vines, propagated and repropagated frequently because of the quality of the wine that it makes. Less worthy grapes simply fade away.

D'Agata has the last word when he suggests that for the purposes of identification of a clone or a variety, the interaction of the two nucleic acids, DNA and RNA, may be far more important than is presently understood. It is for this reason that it is being actively studied in laboratories and universities around the world.

All of the above is only half the story of DNA. The other half is its opening of the door of Alice in Wonderland in exploring the genetic history of the grapevines of today. When, in 2000, Professor Carole Meredith of the University of California, Davis established that Shiraz was the offspring of a natural cross between Dureza (an obscure black grape that had almost disappeared) and Mondeuse Blanche (only slightly less obscure), it caused much excitement. But Pinot Noir is a likely grandparent of Dureza, meaning it is a likely great-grandparent of Shiraz.

That may be considered surprising, but if Pinot is a parent (not an offspring, which is possible but less likely) of Savagnin, it is also a grandparent of Sauvignon Blanc and a great-grandparent of Cabernet Sauvignon (even more surprising). The gatefold family tree between pages 806 and 807 of Robinson's *Wine Grapes* is fascinating, bordering on hypnotic as it throws up all these (and hundreds more) possibilities.

Throughout this book you will find frequent references to Robinson in the discussion of the parentage (certain, probable or unknown) of the varieties described. But as with the story of Pinot Noir, the parent/offspring/sibling relationships of many of the key varieties are yet to be determined with certainty.

And so it is with the future of wine.

A Short History of Wine Grapes

Although the idea must necessarily remain in the realm of fantasy (or common sense, according to your personal view) it is virtually certain that our nomadic hunter-gatherer ancestors ate the grapes from wild vines growing up trees in forests. It is not a big step to suggest that with the end of autumn coming, such people would have collected extra grapes to be eaten as winter set in and food became scarce. Nor, then, is it a larger step to suggest that these grapes may have been stored in watertight vessels, whether made from hide or clay, leading to the discovery that the grape juice, having been in such vessels for some time, had pleasurable effects. Wild yeast fermentation has become a badge of honour in Australia since 2000AD, but yeasts have always been in the atmosphere, so our hunter-gatherers beat us to the game 10 000 years ago.

Once permanent settlements began to appear, around 10 000–8000BC, collecting and storing wild grapes, along with planting crops, became part of a changed attitude to food. Wild grapevines climbed trees, and only once they had reached the sunlight at the top of the forest would they turn their energies from growing canes to producing grapes. (These vines were all *Vitis sylvestris*.) How much better, then, to plant seeds and provide some support for the growth.

It might seem obvious that planting seeds was the best solution, but the nature of the growth of the vine, the type (white or red), the amount of grapes provided and their flavour were all random. So when we discuss the domestication of vines, do we mean simply the convenient growing of the grapes, or the selection of the best vines (a more difficult problem)?

A further problem was finding vines that produced grapes reliably. Pollen fertilisation is the starting point, but by the nature of even prototype vine growing, using male vines (which don't produce grapes) to fertilise female vines (which do) was very inefficient. So one of the first steps was to identify the right vines – there are a mere 2–3 per cent hermaphrodite vines, the most useful ones, in the wild.

There is consensus among ampelographers, archaeologists, botanists and grape geneticists that the first domestication took place in the uplands between (today's) eastern Turkey, western Iran, and Georgia, Armenia and Azerbaijan. There is less agreement on the question of time. Numerous important archaeological sites across Europe and Asia Minor have yielded carbonised grape pips, evidence of collection of grapes.

The irony is that while carbonised pips positively establish domestication around 3400–3000BC, there is chemical evidence of wine in stoppered clay jars laid on their side, embedded in earthen floors, from 5400–5000BC. They were discovered in the Zagros Mountains in northern Iran, an area where wild vines still exist.

Viticulture and viniculture then spread to Lebanon, Jordan and Palestine, between 3500BC and 3000BC. At this point (3200–2700BC) significant wine export trade began between Palestine and Egypt, the latter country having no wild vines. The development of winemaking in Egypt is fascinating. We know about it thanks to painted and/or tiled frescoes in the pyramids, and amphorae emblazoned with the name of the pharaoh, the vintage year, and the name of the maker on the lid. Wine labels 4000 years ago!

The next major move was to Greece (2200–2000BC), then Italy, courtesy of Greek grapegrowers (900BC), and on to Marseille. Wine was a central point of Greek civilisation at its zenith; the word 'symposium' comes directly from Greece, meaning a conversation over wine. But it was the Roman Empire that created the wine world as we know it today. Pliny the Elder, Columella, Cato and Marcus Varro wrote practical handbooks on viticulture, while the writings of Virgil, Juvenal and Ovid all covered one or other aspect of wine. Grape varieties were named, but there is no linguistic link with those of today.

Italy's great vintages were much discussed, and Opimian, made in 121BC, was still being drunk when it was 125 years old. Likewise, Falernian was revered for its longevity. By 100AD wine was being made all over Italy, in particular around Rome and further south of the city. Rome took its considerable knowhow to the Loire Valley by 100AD, Burgundy by 200AD, and to Paris, Champagne and the Mosel Valley by 400AD. England, too, had vineyards established before the collapse of the Roman Empire in 400AD and the arrival of the Dark Ages. In France, Italy and, to a degree, Germany, the church filled the yawning gap; only Bordeaux stood on its not particularly exalted own.

An obvious issue is the origin of the grape varieties today – and of previous millennia. Throughout this book you will come across descriptions of certain varieties as very ancient; as I note in the introduction, Pinot Noir is a great-grandparent of both Shiraz and Cabernet Sauvignon. It stands alongside Gouais Blanc and Savagnin as the progenitors of 156 of the most important Western European grape varieties of today.

Pinot (without the word Noir appended) was first known as Moreillon, and is recorded as early as 1283, with various spellings thereafter until Morillon, Noirien and Auvernat came into common use. The names of grape varieties were not used in written documents until the late Middle Ages, but Pinot must surely have been propagated in France and elsewhere well before its name was documented. The word 'Pinot' (rather than Pineau, as it was spelt north of Burgundy) was not finally adopted until a meeting of wine scholars in Chalon-Sur-Saône in 1896.

In many areas, the world took close to 1500 years to catch up with Roman civilisation, and so it was with the naming of grape varieties. A variety called Allobrogica, named by Columella and Pliny the Elder in the first century AD, has often been identified as Pinot Noir, but Pinot wasn't (and isn't) grown in the area in which Allobrogica was grown.

In the broader scheme of things, linguistic barriers are of little or no importance. Far more important has been, and is, the appearance of new varieties, and the demise of others. So I come back to the chicken-and-egg question of how a new variety is created. First, two varieties must have sexually produced, through pollination, a new variety some (or many) years earlier. This new variety produces grapes, and by virtue of either being eaten by birds or simply falling to the ground, one of its seeds germinates to produce a seedling that grows, and three or four years later produces a crop. It is thus a new variety, the offspring of two parents, and grown from seed.

Charles Darwin's survival of the fittest then comes into play. A human must make a judgement: is the new variety worth persevering with? If not, it will sooner or later die. If it is of merit, a new variety is adopted, and propagated: new vines of this variety can only be achieved by taking cuttings and planting them. Thus every grape variety has two parents, and each vine of that variety is in principle identical to every other vine.

But how was the initial sexual production of the parents achieved? *Vitis vinifera* vines are all hermaphroditic, their flowers with male organs that produce pollen and a female ovary to be fertilised. Normally, the pollen will come from the same flower or an adjacent flower on the same vine, or even from an adjacent vine. This is self-pollination. The other possibility – once far more common – is natural cross-pollination, where a different variety provides the pollen, and the possibility of a new variety. Finally, there is deliberate cross-pollination, which came on the scene in the nineteenth century, for wine grapes, table grapes and hybrids (created by the crossing of a *vinifera* species variety with, say, *Vitis labrusca* or *Vitis aestivalis*). An exceptionally complex family tree (a three-page gatefold) of hybrids appears in Robinson between pages 136 and 137.

In bygone centuries field blends with different varieties cheek-by-jowl were more frequent than single variety plantings; the further back in time one goes, the more common field blends were. All the 136 varieties in the so-called Pinot tree were the result of natural cross-pollinations.

Once again, the survival of the fittest comes into play. Over the centuries, some varieties that were chosen have fallen prey to more 'attractive' (in the sense of producing more disease-resistant grapes, or bigger or more reliable yields, for instance) genetically related varieties. Thus Mondeuse Blanche and Dureza were both nearing extinction when it was discovered that they were the parents of Shiraz – the former had only 5 hectares in production, the latter existed only in a couple of nurseries (a breeding program is now full steam ahead).

Thus if you look at the family tree of Shiraz in Robinson (page 1026), eight of the ten varieties involved have only one parent identified; the other parents are all extinct. If you see this process in the time frame of the past 1000 years, the trial and error/survival of the fittest of the 1000 years prior to that must have been even more lethal.

Moreover, the arrival of DNA analysis has disproved all the suggestions that the most important varieties of Western Europe came direct from different countries. I have briefly pinpointed the move of viticulture from east to west over a period of over 3000 years, with major climatic shifts in the process. France and Italy have had greater areas of intensive viticulture over the past 2000 years than other countries. It is inevitable that they have given birth to more varieties and the knowhow to gauge their worth.

There are 10 000 varieties in the world today – wine varieties, table grape varieties, ornamental varieties: the church is a broad one. Many thousands must have been and gone, and grape breeding is continuing, and important. But the fact remains that Italy (337 varieties), France (204) and Spain (84) account for half the 1368 varieties from the 39 countries profiled in Robinson.

How to Use this Book

Statistics
The statistics for areas of grapevines and production of grapes have been sourced from the most complete and up-to-date records. Regrettably, the most recent years span 2008 to 2014. Likewise, some sources provide both hectares and tonnes; other than those for South Australia, Tasmania and New Zealand, only hectares are provided.

In Chapters 7 and 14 you will see instances where the Australian plantings are shown as <1 ha. This indicates that at least one planting is known to exist, but the area is too small to be recorded.

Providing footnotes for these statistics was considered, but rejected as too cumbersome. All except Robinson and D'Agata are online, and in some instances (particularly Anderson), even greater detail is available at no cost. Both books have been recently published, and can be purchased from specialist bookstores or online.

Australia
Australian Bureau of Statistics, *Wine Grape Varietals: Area, Production and Yield, Australia: Season 2012*, October 2012.
Phylloxera and Grape Industry Board of South Australia, *2014 South Australian Winegrape Crush Survey*.
Wine Tasmania, *About Our Wine*, winetasmania.com.au/about_our_wine.

Australia and International
Kym Anderson and Nanda R Aryal, *Database of Regional, National and Global Winegrape Bearing Areas by Variety, 2000 and 2010*, Wine Economics Research Centre, University of Adelaide, 2013 (revised 2014).
Jancis Robinson, Julia Harding and Jose Vouillamoz, *Wine Grapes*, Ecco/HarperCollins, 2012.

New Zealand
New Zealand Winegrowers, *Vineyard Register Report 2014*.
New Zealand Winegrowers, *Annual Report 2014*.

Italy
Ian D'Agata, *Wine Grapes of Italy*, University of California Press, May 2014.

Climate Data for Australian Regions

This data is that shown in my *Wine Atlas of Australia* (Hardie Grant, 2014), in turn taken from Dr John Gladstones' *Wine, Terroir and Climate Change* (Wakefield Press, 2011).

Briefly, there are four broad climate classifications, determined by the Mean January Temperature (MJT) of each region: hot (MJT 23°C–25.9°C), warm (MJT 21°C–22.9°C), moderate (MJT 19°C–20.9°C) and cool (MJT 17°C–18.9°C). This is arrived at by taking the mean temperature of each day in January, calculated by adding the minimum and maximum temperature for the day and dividing by two, then adding the accumulated daily means and dividing that total by 31.

For each region, the broad classification there is given first, followed by the exact MJT (on a 30-year average).

Next comes a second warmth measurement: E° Days. This is a refinement by Dr Gladstones of a long-used numeric of Heat Degree Days (HDD). Both E° and HDD reflect the fact that there is little vegetative growth of the vine at temperatures below 10°C, and both assume a seven-month growing season in Australia, from October to April inclusive. For the calculation of E° (biologically effective degree days) see Gladstones, page 11.

Sunshine hours per day (SH) and rainfall are collated for the seven-month growing season. Altitude requires no explanation other than that it, too, is an average.

Geographic Indications

These are legally defined Zones, Regions and Subregions of Australia registered pursuant to the provisions of the *Australian Wine and Brandy Corporation Act 1980* (Cth).

Producers | Best Producers

There is, in effect, a three-tier system: at the top, a producer with an asterisk against its name in a list headed *Best producers*. Next is a winery in the same list without an asterisk. Other producers of lesser quality status are not mentioned.

Growers | Makers

This is deliberately ambiguously linked information. Extracts from our *Wine Companion* database and from the *Wine Industry Directory* (www.winetitles.com.au) are the starting point for identifying businesses that grow and/or make the variety in question. However, it isn't feasible to determine whether, for example, a grower supplies multiple wineries, but is not itself a winemaker, or whether a winemaker makes wine for itself as well as selling wine or grapes to other winemakers.

Chapter 1

The Classic White Varietals
Chardonnay

199 632 ha of Chardonnay is grown worldwide in 35 countries, with as little as 1 ha each in Myanmar and Peru. Those with over 500 ha are: Argentina 6473 ha, Australia 25 879 ha, Bulgaria 2457 ha, Canada 1178 ha, Chile 13 082 ha, China 738 ha, Croatia 668 ha, Czech Republic 766 ha, France 44 593 ha, Germany 1180 ha, Greece 586 ha, Hungary 2757 ha, Italy 19 709 ha, Japan 602 ha, Moldova 534 ha, New Zealand 3911 ha, Portugal 803 ha, Romania 1067 ha, Russia 1981 ha, Slovenia 1208 ha, South Africa 8278 ha, Spain 6958 ha, Ukraine 2985 ha, United States 40 846 ha.

International History

Grapegrowing and winemaking in Burgundy had been established for well over 1000 years before Chardonnay officially appeared in the records, three centuries after the first mention of Pinot Noir. (In each case I am using the first references to the two varieties using recognisable spelling: Chardonnet 1685–90, Pinot in 1375.)[1] DNA research has established that its parents were Pinot Noir and Gouais, but its birthplace is still unknown. It is, of course, quite possible it had been grown alongside other grapes, notably Pinot Gris, then called Fromenteau, which may have produced much of the white wine of Burgundy in the middle ages. Indeed, Robinson[2] says that Pinot Noir, Pinot Gris and Pinot Blanc are mutations of Pinot Noir, all three having the same DNA, and hence are genetically one and the same variety.

---

1 Jancis Robinson, Julia Harding and Jose Vouillamoz, *Wine Grapes*, Ecco/Harper Collins, 2012, pp. 221, 809.
2 ibid., p. 806.

Chardonnay was confused with Pinot Blanc until the end of the nineteenth century in France, and was often called Chardonnet Pinot Blanc or Pinot Blanc Chardonnet. While Robinson[3] says Chardonnay takes its name from the village of Chardonnay in the Mâconnais in southern Burgundy, that name did not become common until the twentieth century. Small wonder that at one stage Chardonnay was called Pinot Chardonnay; Tyrrell's clung to this incorrect nomenclature until 2000.

When it did appear, its stronghold was the Côte de Beaune, hemmed in by Pinot Noir to the north in the Côte de Nuits, and to the south by the higher-yielding Aligote. Hemmed in it may have been, but its supreme quality was recognised and revered in the form of Le Montrachet by the end of the seventeenth century. In 1728 Claude Arnoux noted that not only was Le Montrachet expensive, but it needed to be ordered a year in advance. In 1833 Cyrus Redding (in *A History and Description of Modern Wines*) wrote of 'the delicious white wine called Mont-Rachet, of exquisite perfume, and deemed the most perfect white wine of Burgundy, and even of France, rivalling Tokay itself in the opinion of many French connoisseurs'.

White Burgundy, for this purpose coextensive with Chardonnay, was unchallenged as the greatest French dry table wine by the start of the nineteenth century, but, given its adaptability to a wide range of climate and soil, it was surprisingly slow to establish itself elsewhere (other than in Champagne, for sparkling wine).

A small amount went to California prior to Prohibition; 8 hectares were established by Wente Brothers in Livermore, but other records are scant. In 1948 the University of California was advising prospective vignerons that it was difficult to grow and to set. Prior to 1959 there was less than 80 hectares in the state, but the growth through to 1980 might have been considered spectacular were it not for more recent history. In 1980 there were 7200 hectares; by 2010 there were 38 555 hectares, making it by some distance the most widely planted white variety.

It was in the 1970s and 1980s that the variety spread like wildfire around the Old World and New World alike, led by France in the first instance. In 1958 there were 7325 hectares planted, mainly in Burgundy and Champagne; by 2009 the area had risen to 44 593 hectares, surpassing that of all other countries. But only 2120 hectares were planted in the Côte d'Or, a fraction of the 9781 hectares established in Champagne.

These figures do not compute until you factor in the 12 156 hectares planted in Languedoc Roussillon, making it the dominant white variety in this large region. The headline to Robinson's chapter on Chardonnay describes it as 'Hugely popular, versatile

---

3   ibid., p. 223.

and widely planted international white variety equally capable of extreme mediocrity and regal splendour'.[4]

This is true wherever Chardonnay is grown, and it is grown in more parts of the wine world than any other single premium white variety. (Premium is the operative word: in 2008 Spain had 284 623 hectares of the white grape Airen planted, down from over 300 000 hectares, as the EU took steps to reduce the excess production of wine grapes in its member states.)

So while Chardonnay is planted throughout Eastern and Western Europe, the Americas and South Africa, its importance is best measured by the best wines it produces in its innumerable regional homes.

International Styles

FRANCE
44 593 ha

Burgundy

I have long likened the role of the Burgundian makers of Chardonnay to sculptors who have large masses of clay to work with in creating their sculptures. They can hack away pieces of clay without imperilling the final work, make mistakes which can easily be corrected, and only need to be really careful as the clay starts to dry out and they are adding the final touches.

If, however, they start with a small amount of clay, and seek to make a work of similar proportion and style – if not size – they must jealously guard every gram of clay, precisely determine every scoop and cut. If they don't, their sculpture will be full of holes, and with a propensity to fall over.

Winemakers around the world who seek to imitate the techniques of their Burgundian counterparts often seem oblivious to the fact that their lump of clay – their grapes – is of much smaller dimension, making the techniques required much finer and more considered.

So White Burgundies are made from hand-picked grapes which are usually crushed and then immediately pressed; whole-bunch pressing is uncommon in Burgundy, but may become an option in warmer vintages. The juice is left to settle overnight before being taken to barrel (still milky) for fermentation in ambient cellar temperatures (admittedly very cold) and usually allowed to start fermentation without the addition of cultured

---

4   ibid., p. 221.

yeast. Malolactic fermentation may not commence until the following spring; in the meantime, the wine will have been protected against oxidation as much by lees contact and lees stirring as by SO_2.

It will remain in barriques for around 16 months before being racked for the final time and bottled. Grand Cru wines receive the highest percentage of new oak (100 per cent is not uncommon); village wines are given either none or 10 per cent to 20 per cent. The choice of forest and cooper is in fact more important than the percentage of new oak; the degree of toasting and the method of toasting (dry or wet staves) is also important.

If for no other reason than propinquity, there are usually long-term relationships between the vigneron and the cooper; common sense will tell you that the Burgundian makers will receive the best barrels in their chosen style. This does not mean there is no active quality control: the best producers may select the trees before they are felled, or select their own oak, pay for it, and then leave it for up to four years of air-drying before having it coopered using agreed techniques.

The exact style will (or should) first and foremost reflect the terroir (Grand Cru, Premier Cru or Commune) and its location, but the philosophy and skill – the artistry – of the maker will also have a profound influence.

Arguably, the most significant change in Burgundy since the early 1990s has been the arrival of organic and biodynamic practices in the vineyards, the latter gaining most airplay because the scientific pathways of biodynamic practices are very tenuous. Those who practise it simply say they believe the quality of the grapes is improved. While producers such as Leflaive and Leroy (two of the leaders of the move) are adamant about its benefits, and practise it without any compromise, others say they practise biodynamics, with the spoken or unspoken qualification that in particularly wet or humid vintages, they will use systemic fungicides if it means the difference between saving or losing the crop. While the number of vignerons adopting biodynamics grows year by year, there is a suspicion that some use it for public relations reasons akin to those given for abandoning filtration or fining, or – especially so – making 'natural' wines.

Puligny and Chassagne Montrachet

It need hardly be said that the ultimate expression comes from Le Montrachet (as that half falling within Chassagne Montrachet is correctly known) or Montrachet (that half within Puligny Montrachet), with the other Grand Crus of Chevalier-Montrachet, Batard Montrachet, Bienvenues-Batard Montrachet and Criots-Batard Montrachet in such close attendance it can be easier to recognise the maker than the vineyard. The common theme is a layered richness, a profundity, an all-encompassing array of flavours of honey, nuts and stone fruit once the wines reach maturity, at five to seven years.

The subject of maturity immediately raises the scourge of random/sporadic/premature oxidation that has bedevilled White Burgundy over the past 20 years. It is a subject far too complex to fully cover here, but I am firmly of the view that the fact that no two corks are precisely the same (they are a natural product of mind-boggling complexity) is the root cause, compounded by the irregularity of the internal finish of the bottle neck. Next is the reduction of the use of copper sulphate sprays in the vineyard, hotly pursued by lower SO_2 levels in the wine, this in turn exacerbated by lower acidity and higher pH levels (the last requiring higher levels of SO_2 for the same outcome with higher pH/acid levels compared with lower levels).

It is no accident that 97.6 per cent of all Australian white wines tasted for the 2015 edition of my *Australian Wine Companion* were closed with screwcaps. Diam seemed the solution for those who for marketing or technical reasons didn't want to use screwcaps; it obviates TCA taint, and has very good oxygen barrier capacity, but as more and more Diam-closed wines with five-plus years of bottle age are tasted, discernible glue characters can start to become apparent.

Reverting to the subject of cork and White Burgundies, many commentators who think the problem of sporadic oxidation is being addressed are missing the forest for the trees: it strikes wines with five to ten years bottle age far more than younger wines. Thus there is a rolling five- to ten-year time fuse, after which some bottles of a given wine will be superb, others badly oxidised, with every shade of grey in between. So I tend to drink my cork-closed White Burgundies in the first five years of their life, albeit with some sadness that I am missing the magic of a White Burgundy at its prime of 15–20 years post vintage.

Best producers
Domaine Blain-Gagnard, Domaine Bouchard Père et Fils, Domaine Henri Boillot, Domaine Louis Carillon et Fils, Domaine des Comtes Lafon, Domaine Vincent Dancer, Domaine Gagnard-Delagrange, Domaine Leflaive, Domaine Bernard Moreau et Fils, Domaine Jean Marc Pillot, Domaine Ramonet, Domaine de la Romanée-Conti, Domaine Etienne Sauzet

Corton Charlemagne

Corton Charlemagne is the other Grand Cru, less weighty and profound but more elegant, the portion coming from the southern end next to Pernand Vergelesses (typified by Bonneau du Martray) with a flinty/steely framework for its apple and stone fruit flavours. It has hit a purple patch since 2000, consistently excellent, largely immune from the pox (as UK writers describe oxidation), and is less expensive than the other Grand Crus (other than Chablis). Indeed, until recently (2010 or thereabouts) all the wines of Corton were under-priced, but increased understanding and appreciation of their elegance and finesse have seen prices rise substantially.

Best producers
Bonneau du Martray, Bouchard Père et Fils, Chandon de Briailles, Bruno Clair, Comte Senard, Dubrueil Fontaine, Louis Latour, Pierre Yves Colin-Morey

Meursault

A substantial patchwork quilt of Premier Crus and highly regarded commune vineyards, the best five Premier Crus being Charmes, Poruzots, Genevrieres, Perrieres and (to the north) Les Gouttes d'Or. While each has its own characteristics, they share a wonderful ability to age and to increase in dimension as they do so, unfolding a totally seductive panoply of peach, butter, nut, stone fruit and honey flavours, the minerality of youth still a background echo. Comtes Lafon is the uncrowned king of the region, Coche-Dury the prince. The three great Premier Crus are Perrieres, Charmes and Genevrieres, the prices for which reflect the view that they (or at least Perrieres) should be Grand Crus.

Best producers
Michel Ampeau, Michel Bouzereau, Coche-Dury, Comtes Lafon, Domaine Francois Jobard, Remi Jobard, Pierre Morey, Roulot

Chablis

Physically disconnected from the Côte d'Or, this northern outpost of Burgundy was brought to its knees in the 1950s, when the area under vine shrank to little more than 500 hectares. The 1970s saw a massive expansion in plantings in the wake of a highly controversial move outside the traditional Kimmeridgian soil to Portlandian soil, the latter without the marine fossils of the former.

In the 1920s, Chablis was described as having the aroma of gunflint, the flavour akin to sucking river pebbles – all pointing to high SO_2 levels and fruit of modest ripeness. Since then, the style of Chablis has gone through several revolutions as some makers tried to imitate White Burgundy.

Various commentators believe that the world has tired of rich, ripe, heavily oaked Chardonnays. Whether or not this is true, the classic fresh, crisp, mineral and apple, lightly oaked style of Chablis has come back into its own. Asked whether he uses lees stirring, Michel Laroche, of Domaine Laroche, responds, 'No; I don't want to make Burgundy.'

Finally, the generally lower pH and higher acidity of Chablis seems to have joined elevated levels of SO_2 in a defence against premature oxidation.

Best producers
Jean-Marc Brocade, Rene and Vincent Dauvissat, William Fevre, La Chablisienne, Laroche, Patrick Piuze, Jean-Marie Raveneau

Côte Chalonnaise and Mâconnais

The chief virtue of the large production of Chardonnay from these southerly outposts of Burgundy is the relatively modest price most of the wines command. Chalonnaise is still awaiting a long-promised revival, leaving it to the Mâconnais to produce Chardonnay (not Aligote) of real merit. Its appellations are Mâcon, Mâcon plus village name, Mâcon-Villages, Puilly-Fuisse, Pouilly-Loché, Pouilly-Vinzelles, Saint-Véran and Viré-Clessé, covering 5639 hectares, overwhelmingly Chardonnay. Mâcon producers of particular note are Domaine Guffens-Heynen, Les Héritiers du Comte Lafon and Verget.

While Saint-Véran is a quality region, its best vineyards are owned by producers in Puilly-Fuisse, itself divided into numerous village appellations. Leading producers include Domaine Daniel Barraud (outstanding), Château de Beauregard, Domaine Cordier Père et Fils, Château de Fuissé and Domaine Valette. The common feature of all these wines is their value for money.

OTHER EUROPE

Italy
19 709 ha

Italy has some scattered old Chardonnay vineyards, historically confused with Pinot Blanc, but a massive surge in interest triggered by Australia's success, and that of other New- and Old-World fellow travellers, saw plantings increase to 11 772 hectares by 2000.[5] In typical Italian fashion, it was planted with enthusiasm in every climatic corner of the country, and equally enthusiastically smothered in oak at one extreme, or monastically fermented in stainless steel after the juice had been deliberately oxidised.

Italy's thing is red wines, and it is not excessively unkind to say its Chardonnays taste better in situ than elsewhere in the world, especially Australia. Sicily's Planeta is one exception to prove the rule, Gaja Gaia & Rey (Langhe) and Antinori Cervaro (Umbria) are other qualified exceptions.

---

5   ibid., p. 223.

Lesser Western Europe: Cool Regions
Chardonnay is grown and made with varying degrees of success in Luxembourg, Switzerland, Belgium, Austria and Alsace. It's very much a work in progress. Warmer, drier vintages, older vines, and practical experience (especially keeping new oak to a modest level) will see good wines made, some very good, perhaps.

Lesser Western Europe: Warm Regions
Spain is the main player, and there is no need of warmer vintages – in fact the converse is true: it needs cooler vintages – although Torres, in the highest parts of Penedès, and Chivite, in Navarra, have shown what can be achieved with the variety.

Lesser Eastern Europe
Moldova, Bulgaria, Romania, Slovenia, Croatia, Czech Republic, Montenegro and Ukraine have plantings (Moldova over 5000 hectares in 2009), but Hungary (over 2800 hectares in 2008) has the most advanced wine industry, and produces the best wines. Here the problem is the unpronounceable names of the producers and the regions.

UNITED STATES
40 846 ha

Napa and Sonoma Valleys, California
In my *Wine Atlas of California* (HarperCollins, 1993) I observed, 'Like Xerox, Chardonnay has passed into everyday language. You no longer ask for a glass of white wine, but for a glass of Chardonnay, for the two have become coextensive. And, at the risk of appearing unkind, that is precisely what the consumer gets from the average Napa Valley Chardonnay: a wine which is bland, inoffensive and varietally anonymous.'

I went on to include the Sonoma Valley in much the same basket, but hurriedly excluded Carneros and the Russian River, and likewise some of the producers whose names are listed below. I have to admit I have not gone out of my way to taste Napa/Sonoma Chardonnay over the ensuing years, but the wines I have tasted have given me little or no cause to change my views. Indeed, two of the most highly regarded producers, Kistler and Kongsgaard, whose wines I have tasted in recent times in blind tastings of the best of the best from France, New Zealand, California, Chile and Australia, have been actively disliked by the professional participants in the tastings.

Best producers
Napa Valley: Chateau Montelena, Cuvaison, Forman Vineyard, Grgich Hills Cellar, Kongsgaard, St Clement Vineyards, Signorello Vineyards, Spring Mountain, Stony Hill;

Russian River: Marimar Torres Estate, J Rochioli, Simi Winery; Sonoma Valley: Ancient Oaks Cellars, Gary Farrell, Flowers Vineyard, Freestone, Gallo Family Vineyards, Hanzell, Iron Horse Vineyards, Kistler Vineyards

Carneros, California

The incessant winds which sweep over Carneros every afternoon significantly slow the ripening process, and imbue the wines with a lean, crisp, appley intensity; they age with elegance and grace.

Best producers
Acacia Winery, Bouchaine Vineyards, Buena Vista, Hyde de Villaine, Kent Rasmussen, Marcassin, Patz & Hall, Saintsbury, Sonoma-Cutrer Vineyards, Truchard Vineyards

Edna, Santa Maria and Santa Ynez Valleys et al., California

The better Chardonnays of these regions have all the vibrancy, life, length and intensity which the majority of the wines from further north lack. In the hands of makers such as Jim Clendenen of Au Bon Climat they also possess all the complexity one could wish for.

Best producers
Arroyo Grande: Talley Vineyards; Edna Valley: Edna Valley Vineyards, Stephen Ross; Monterey: Chalone Vineyard, Peter Michael Winery, Talboit; San Benito: Calera; Santa Barbara: Byron Wines; Santa Maria Valley: Au Bon Climat, Villa Mount Eden; Santa Ynez Valley: Babcock Vineyards, Sanford Winery, Zaca Mesa Winery

Oregon

I include this region as much to point out what it has not achieved as what it has. There are, however, signs that the thin, featureless wines of the past will be replaced by fine, elegant, citrussy wines from the Burgundian clones (76, 95, 96 and 277) selected by Professor Raymond Bernard, which became available in the 1990s.

Best producers
Argyle Winery, Cameron, Ken Wright Cellars, King Estate

Yakima Valley and Walla Walla, Washington State

The Chardonnays tend to the lean and bony end of the spectrum, although the best have considerable complexity when malolactic fermentation and oak influences have been introduced with a gentle touch. The plantings exceed those of all the other white varieties taken together.

Best producers
Bookwalter, Canoe Ridge, Columbia Crest/Stimson Lane, Hogue Cellars, Woodward Canyon

CANADA
1178 ha

Okanagan Valley, British Columbia
In 1992, the then newly appointed winemaker of Mission Hill Estate, New Zealander John Simes (former chief winemaker of Montana Estate), made a Chardonnay, half barrel-fermented in American oak and half in stainless steel. The wine went on to win the trophy for Best Chardonnay at the International Wine & Spirit Competition in London, bringing lasting recognition to the Okanagan Valley and Mission Hill Estate alike. The fact that no other wine from the Valley has since come close to repeating the feat is unimportant. However, the compressed growing season and the high, dry summer temperature peaks seem to rob most of the wines of the richness and texture of top quality Chardonnay.

Best producers
Blue Mountain, Mission Hill Winery, Quails Gate, Red Rooster Winery

Ontario
While some unexpected varieties are bobbing up (Shiraz is one), this is Chardonnay, Pinot Noir, Riesling, sparkling and ice wine territory (actually, there are four appellations of origin) first and foremost.

Best producers
13th Street, Cave Spring, Creekside, Flat Rock, Les Clos Jordanne, Malevoire, Ravine Vineyard, Tawse

CHILE
13 082 ha

Central Valley

The improbably shaped Chile, like a cord stretching over 4000 kilometres down the western coast of South America, enjoys unique viticultural conditions: unlimited, pure, snow-melt water; stony rubble soils akin to those of Marlborough; no phylloxera; and a dependably dry summer. These Garden of Eden conditions have proved both blessing and bane: large yields of disease-free, ripe grapes are an irresistible temptation, so furrow irrigation is the order of the day, stretching right up to harvest. The consequence was smooth, soft, easy-drinking Chardonnay sold on the international markets at mouth-watering prices. Great Chardonnays they were not.

It is unfortunate that Chile's producers, new and old, have seemingly become members of the ABC (Anything But Chardonnay club), for the variety is conspicuous by its absence from the regions and producers.

Best producers
Caliterra, Calyptra, Conch y Toro, Errazuriz, Aurelio Montes, Santa Carolina, Viña Carmen

Casablanca Valley

The Maipo, Maule and Rapel valleys (of the Central Valley region) cover a considerable north–south distance, but the climate in each is nearly identical. This is the one valley uniquely open directly to the cold Pacific Ocean, with morning fogs replaced by cool, onshore breezes in the afternoon. Here, Chardonnay with greater intensity and bite can be, and is, made by those who don't over-irrigate.

Best producers
Errazuriz, Lapostolle, Villard, Viña Casablanca

Bío-Bío and Malleco Valleys

There is much discussion about these far-south regions, with some vineyards in production (grapes going in part to the likes of Concha y Toro) and some small wineries. A cross-section of these were the subject of an impromptu masterclass at the Canberra National Wine Show around 2007, and were 'interesting', not exhilarating. But the story has time to run.

Costa | Coastal

Just to complicate things (the glass-half-empty view), Chile has introduced three over-arching appellations: Costa (or Coastal); Entre Cordilleras (between the Andes and the coast, best known as the Central Valley); and the Andes. The first and the last are the coolest, thus two of the new regions gaining real traction are the Elqui and Limari valleys, well to the north of Santiago and the Central Valley (Elqui's hinterland rises to 2200 metres, hardly a valley, but still has sea breezes). Producers to gain attention include Conch y Toro, with its Maycas Chardonnay, from Limari.

SOUTH AFRICA

8278 ha

The dead hand of KWV and severe virus infection in the small amount of Chardonnay planted in the 1980s and early 1990s rendered the variety meaningless until ten years ago. When virus-free clones became available, there was a predictable fascination with skin contact and lots of generally poor quality new oak; it was not until the second half of the 1990s that the wines started to achieve acceptable international quality. Since that time, there has been a continuous learning curve.

The best wines combine subtlety and complexity; South Africa likes to see itself as a halfway house between the Old World and the fruit-forward wines of Australia, New Zealand and Chile. As long as this is achieved by positive winemaking and style decisions, and not by default, it may serve the country well.

Best producers

Ataraxia Wines, Boland, Bouchard Finlayson, Paul Cluver, de Wetshof Estate, Fairview, Groot Constantia, Hamilton Russell Vineyards, Haskell Vineyards, Neil Ellis Wines, Newton Johnson, Jordan Wine Estate, Mulderbosch, Rustenberg, Simonsig, Tokara, Vergelegen, Warwick Estate, Waterford

NEW ZEALAND

3911 ha

Auckland

On much the same latitude as Sydney, Auckland's summers are warm, humid and often rainy. Once an important part of New Zealand's viticultural plantings, it is no longer, with only 3 per cent in total. Kumeu River makes Chardonnay of world quality.

Best producers
Kumeu River, Mudbrick Vineyard, Puriri Hills

Waiheke Island
Waiheke Island is a short trip from Auckland (some people commute each day), and has a unique climate: as the summer/autumn rain which bedevils the mainland comes down from the north and reaches the Hauraki Gulf, it splits, part going west over Auckland, the remainder east over the Coromandel Peninsula. Summer temperatures are ideal, with maxima ranging between 26°C and 32°C, and the island's hills and dales offer great individual vineyard sites. While best known for its Bordeaux blend red wines, it makes high quality, complex, medium- to full-bodied Chardonnay. Unfortunately, it also comes at a high price.

Gisborne
Corresponds to Australia's Riverlands in terms of the importance and size of its Chardonnay production in the New Zealand context. Most of the wine goes to major companies; while formerly usually blended away under proprietary brands, its ability to rise above itself when vintage conditions are right has seen single region (i.e. Gisborne) Chardonnays being proudly marketed. There are also several small makers who show what can be achieved; the style is always rich and luscious, made to be drunk today or, failing that, tomorrow.

Hawke's Bay
As is the case in Gisborne, Chardonnay is the dominant white variety (with 995 hectares), but to a much lesser extent than in Gisborne. Some of the country's most complex and best structured Chardonnays are made here; they are rich but not heavy (as they once tended to be).

Best producers
Brookfields, Church Road Winery, Clearview Estate, Craggy Range Vineyards, Elephant Hill, Esk Valley, Mills Reef, Ngatarawa, Sacred Hill Wines, Sileni Estate, Stonecroft, Te Mata, Trinity Hill, Vidal Estate, Villa Maria

Wairarapa | Martinborough

While Pinot Noir plantings are twice as large as those of Chardonnay, the latter is on a par with Sauvignon Blanc – they are the two most important white varieties. At their best, the wines are at once complex, yet racy and fresh, with very good length.

Best producers
Alana Estate, Ata Rangi, Lintz Estate, Margain Vineyard, Nga Waka Vineyard, Palliser Estate, Te Kairanga

Marlborough

Frenetic planting activity (and acquisitions) running well into the new millennium still focuses on Sauvignon Blanc and Pinot Noir, but Chardonnay remains an important variety for both still and sparkling wines. Clonal selection plays a major role here, the Mendoza clone producing wines which can be uncomfortably dense, with Clone 5 and the new French clones providing better balance and elegance when blended with Mendoza, or used on their own.

Best producers
Allan Scott Wines, Cairnbrae Vineyards, Cloudy Bay Vineyards, Fairhall Downs, Forrest Estate, Foxes Island, Fromm Winery, Grove Mill, Hawkesbridge, Highfield, Huia, Hunter's Wines, Isabel Estate, Jules Taylor, Lake Chalice, Lawson's Dry Hills, Mahi, Marisco Vineyards, Saint Clair Estate, Selaks Dryland Estate, Seresin Estate, Shingle Peak, Spy Valley, Vavasour Wines, Yealands Family Estate

Nelson

Chardonnay is being run down rapidly by the ubiquitous Sauvignon Blanc, but remains the most important variety. Neudorf, in particular, demonstrates just how opulent the wines can be.

Best producers
Brightwater Vineyards, Denton Winery, Greenhough Vineyard, Moutere Hills, Neudorf Vineyards, Spencer Hill Estate

Canterbury | Waipara
A relatively small number of producers make some powerful, densely packed and complex wines.

Best producers
Bell Hill, Giesen Estate, Greystone, Main Divide, Mountford, Pegasus Bay, St Helena Wine Estate, Daniel Schuster

Central Otago
What the production lacks in size it certainly makes up for in quality. The best wines have mouth-tingling intensity and a subtle rainbow of flavour and texture.

Best producers
Bannockburn Heights, Chard Farm, Felton Road, Gibbston Valley, Hay's Lake, Mt Difficulty Wines, Nevis Bluff

Australian History

On Friday, 16 December 1831, James Busby collected cuttings of two varieties from Clos Vougeot in Burgundy, recorded in the appendix to his *Journal of a Tour*. One was Pinot Noir; the other he described as 'pinneau blanc, or chaudeny – white. Produces indifferently; is the only variety of white grape cultivated in the best vineyards [of Burgundy].'

The variety was taken to Smithfield, on the outskirts of Sydney, to Mudgee, and (one must assume) to Busby's Kirkton Vineyard in the Hunter Valley, managed by his brother-in-law, William Kelman. Thereafter it languished in semi-obscurity, partly due to the fact that it became known as Pineau or Pineau Blanc. The *Maitland Mercury* of 19 March 1898 reported that Henry de Beyer had Pineau planted; it reappeared (in a fashion) in 1908, when it was planted on the Hunter Valley Distillery (HVD) Vineyard, which was acquired by Penfolds in 1942, ownership passing to Tyrrell's in 1982. Max Lake (*Classic Wines of Australia*, Jacaranda Press, 1966) wrote at some length about the Penfolds Pinot Riesling Bin 302 of 1959, which was subsequently changed to Bin 365 (a bin number which remained constant once adopted) and which was in fact a blend of 75 per cent Semillon and 25 per cent Chardonnay. Tyrrell's Vat 61 was similarly labelled Pinot Riesling for 20 years after its first vintage in 1970.

I remember both owning and drinking the Penfolds wine, but have no more bottles. On the other hand, in a dark corner of my cellar I had several bottles of wine I had purchased in January 1978: Lindemans 1968 Show Reserve Chardonnay Semillon Bin 3480. The back label reads 'was vintaged at Ben Ean Cellars, Pokolbin, from Chardonnay and Semillon grapes grown in the district. The total quantity bottled on July 18, 1968, was 120 dozen and this particular bottle is one of 25 dozen released in January 1978; the balance being retained for further maturation and subsequent re-release. Gold medal 1976 Canberra Show.' I am as guilty as most contemporary critics in writing that 1971 was the first year in which Pinot Chardonnay [sic] appeared on Tyrrell's Vat 47, and Chardonnay on 1971 Craigmoor (Mudgee).

However, none of this alters the fact that with the introduction of the first Tyrrell's Vat 47 Pinot Chardonnay (as it was incorrectly called until 2001, when, grudgingly, Tyrrell's took the word 'Pinot' off the label), the course of Australian wine production was destined to change forever, Australia's position in the world of wine likewise.

Initially, the small production was eagerly snapped up by the domestic market, with demand far exceeding supply, and the 75 per cent rule applied with a degree of elasticity. (This was originally the percentage of one variety required if it was the only variety specified on the label; the other 25 per cent in those days was almost always Semillon.)

From a minuscule 445 tonnes in 1976, production increased steadily to 8500 tonnes in 1984. It is no coincidence that thereafter plantings soared, for the increase closely matched the phenomenal growth in Australian exports through to the new millennium. From a near-invisible blip on the radar in 1984, Australia rose to become the fourth-largest exporter (by value) in the world in 2002, when 256 300 tonnes were crushed.

Most of those tonnes were from clones I10V1 and I10V5. But there had always been Penfolds clone P58, with a mix of large and small berries, and the Mendoza clone (particularly in Western Australia), with a similar morphology. Both of these clones are considered able to provide Chardonnay with greater depth of flavour.

However, it was the arrival of four clones identified by Professor Raymond Bernard at the University of Dijon that have proved to be game changers since their arrival in the 1990s. The four clones are 76, 95, 96 and 277, and all have much to offer, preferences coming down to site and climate. Clones 95 and 96 are most frequently rated as superior, but 277 (particularly) and 76 can also produce Chardonnay of the highest quality.

Australian Statistics
25 879 ha, 348 283 tonnes, 1692 growers/makers

Chardonnay: tonnes crushed in Australia, 1976–2012

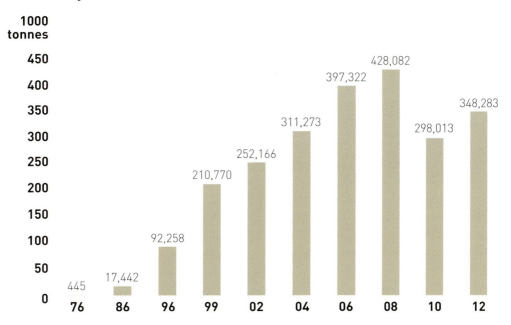

Australian Winemaking

The first Chardonnays made by Tyrrell's were cold-fermented in stainless steel, and had a generous percentage of Semillon, which served to keep some of those early wines remarkably fresh until their corks failed and the wines oxidised. Oak maturation then followed, but it was not until 1978 that Tyrrell's moved to barrel fermentation in 100 per cent new oak for all of the wine.

While barrel fermentation, lees contact and stirring, and malolactic fermentation were soon adopted by small wineries (in part for logistical reasons and in part seeking maximum complexity), big wineries went in the opposite direction, for logistical reasons of a different kind. It is far easier to ferment white wine in large stainless steel fermentation tanks, rack and filter it, then place it in barrel for maturation than to use the messy, space-wasting and labour-intensive alternative of barrel fermentation.

This was true even for the top end of the big companies' production. At the lower price points, the wine was given extensive skin contact (the grapes crushed, then the must allowed to sit at cold temperatures for up to 24 hours before being pressed), then cold-fermented in stainless steel with copious quantities of inner staves (oak planks) or oak chips.

Particularly when grown in warm regions such as the Riverina or Riverland, the result was a rapidly developing golden-yellow wine with a startlingly rich and sweet peach, honey and oak flavour, best drunk within 12 months of vintage, and certain to go downhill rapidly thereafter. After initial shock and hesitation about such a vividly flavoured wine, unlike anything that had previously been offered, the UK market fell head over heels in love with the style.

The love affair continued for the best part of ten years, but jaded palates then sought a little more restraint, and Australian winemakers were happy to oblige – indeed, they had already sensed the ten-year itch of their partner market. So skin contact times in the winery were cut right back (mechanical harvesting can result in de facto skin contact in the vineyard before the grapes reach the winery processing pad), as was the use of oak chips. Moreover, even huge volume wines such as Lindemans Bin 65 and Orlando Jacob's Creek have (or had) components of whole-bunch pressing, barrel ferment, malolactic ferment, lees contact and cool-grown Semillon or Sauvignon Blanc added for complexity. Moreover, new generation harvesters can deliver whole berries free from MOG (material other than grapes) to the winery – but not, of course, whole bunches.

Moving back up-market, by the mid-1990s all the top-quality wines from big and small makers alike were being barrel-fermented. Prior to fermentation, whole-bunch pressing had become commonplace, and deliberate use of cloudy juice likewise, particularly when pressed directly to barrel, and where wild, or indigenous, yeasts were relied on to initiate fermentation. Temperature-controlled barrel halls gave winemakers the opportunity to slow down rates of fermentation (or speed them up at the latter stages to ensure all fermentable sugar has been converted).

Increasing attention was given to every aspect of barrel-sourcing and -making techniques: which forest in France; how tight the grain is; how long the oak has been air-dried (for two or three years?); how thick the staves should be; the degree of toast and how it is done; and whether or not the heads should be toasted. The questions went on and on, but an even more important development coincided with the new millennium. Up to this point, use of the Burgundian-sized barrique of 225 litres was the automatic choice for small, quality-oriented wineries (and in larger facilities with super premium labels). Almost overnight, producers started experimenting with, and increasingly adopting, puncheons of 500 litres (bypassing the halfway house of 300-litre hogsheads), and even larger demi-muids (upright vats) of 600 litres to 2200 litres. The desire was to achieve the benefits of barrel fermentation but minimise the oak impact and give greater protection against oxidation in the maturation phase prior to bottling.

The new millennium tolled the beginning of the end of the use of cork for all Australian white wines, screwcaps becoming to all intents and purposes obligatory for wines sold in Australia. In my 2015 *Wine Companion*, 97.6 per cent of the 3269 white wines tasted during the 12-month period prior to its release in August 2014 were closed with screwcaps. Vertical tastings now mercilessly lay bare the massive difference between the performance of the screwcap (predictable, and identical for each bottle of a given vintage) and the cork (unpredictable, the difference between each and every bottle increasing as each year passes). It is said the best cork can match the performance of a screwcap, but how many bottles sealed with cork have to be opened to find the perfect one?

It is ironic to note that one of the objections to screwcaps is (or was) that they cause reductive characters to form in the wine. Ironic, because some highly regarded Australian makers of Chardonnay deliberately build in some funky (reductive) characters to increase complexity. Ironic also because screwcaps do not themselves create reductive characters; the precursors have to be there as a consequence of the winemaking. Screwcaps are only the messenger.

Australian Regional Styles

Chardonnay is the most malleable and compliant of all the great white wine grapes, giving the impression it would even grow up a telegraph pole in the centre of Sydney or Melbourne and produce a more than half decent wine. For mysterious reasons, the only major Australian region which is clearly incompatible with the variety is the Clare Valley. Necessarily, therefore, I will pass by some regions which produce sound Chardonnays, and only briefly mention others.

NEW SOUTH WALES

Hunter Valley

583 ha, 2832 tonnes, total all varieties 3380 ha

Climate: Hot, MJT 23.6°C, E° Days 1823, SH 7.3, Rain 534 mm, Alt 110 m

Since this is where it all started, I shall follow suit. The strange climate of the Hunter Valley, exceedingly warm and humid at the best of times, rain-sodden at worst, pushes Chardonnay to its limits, and it is remarkable how well the variety responds. With Tyrrell's and Lake's Folly setting the pace, the wines can achieve considerable complexity without phenolic coarseness; the fruit flavours are predominantly in the stone fruit (nectarine, white peach, yellow peach) and fig spectrum, barrel fermentation adding creamy cashew, spice and nut flavours.

The wines generally peak at between two and five years of age, although they will live longer, deepening their yellow and acquiring a strongly honeyed flavour which is more regional than varietal. If the decision to pick is perfectly timed, the alcohol in the bottled wine around 12 per cent, and the oak restrained, some striking Chardonnay can be made, with some of the characters of cool-grown wines.

Best producers
Audrey Wilkinson*, Capercaillie, First Creek*, Keith Tulloch, Lake's Folly*, Margan Family, Mistletoe, Poole's Rock, Ridgeview, Tintilla, Tyrrell's*

Mudgee
557 ha, total all varieties 3323 ha

Climate: Hot, MJT 23.3°C, E° Days 1663, SH 9, Rain 441 mm, Alt 480 m

At its best, the wine has good varietal definition, a relatively tight structure and good balance. Although quality varies with vintage conditions (here as anywhere), there are only two producers that stand out: Robert Oatley Vineyards and Robert Stein.

Orange
289 ha, total all varieties 1531 ha

Low Altitude Climate: Warm, MJT 22.9°C, E° Days 1571, SH 8.9, Rain 414 mm, Alt 670 m
High Altitude Climate: Moderate, MJT 19.6°C, E° Days 1250, SH 8.7, Rain 524 mm, Alt 950 m

Altitude means this region is cooler than Mudgee, and far cooler than Cowra. Its Chardonnay fully reflects the cool climate; it is delicate but intense, with citrus, melon and even apple aromas and flavours. Its good natural acidity offers winemakers latitude with malolactic fermentation and, coupled with the usually sensitive use of oak, the net result is finely structured and balanced wine.

Best producers
Bantry Grove, Belgravia, Bloodwood*, gilbert by Simon Gilbert, Patina, Pepper Tree*, Printhie, Swinging Bridge*, Tamburlaine

Cowra
733 ha, total all varieties 1418 ha

Climate: Hot, MJT 24.2°C, E° Days 1665, SH 9, Rain 368 mm, Alt 330 m

By far the warmest of the three Central Ranges districts, Cowra has been a major source of Chardonnay for well over 20 years. Although Brian Croser doubtless wishes people would not continuously remind him of the fact, the first Petaluma Chardonnays (1977 to 1982) came wholly or partially from Cowra. These days the use of Cowra Chardonnay is primarily in 'fighting varietal' wines, but for the ever-growing number of wineries in the region, Chardonnay is the key. The style reflects the climate: generous and soft, with yellow peach and tropical fruit, best drunk within 18 months of vintage.

Tumbarumba
93 ha, total all varieties 248 ha

Climate: Warm, MJT 21°C, E° Days 1330, SH 8.4, Rain 495 mm, Alt 650 m

For over 15 years after Ian Cowell and Frank Minutello first planted Chardonnay in 1982–83, Tumbarumba remained an obscure region (even after it was gazetted in December 1998), but in the first decade of the new millennium producers materialised at a near-frenetic pace. The pattern is strking: whether they be based in the Canberra District or Hilltops, the best Chardonnays of the most highly rated producers (of all varieties) are made from Tumbarumba grapes. Then there are producers from other parts of eastern Australia, most notably Penfolds, and virtual wineries buying grapes and having the wines contract-made. Ironically, none of the few small wineries resident in Tumbarumba makes noteworthy wines.

Best producers
Barwang*, Chalkers Crossing*, Collector Wines*, Coppabella, Echelon Armchair Critic, Eden Road*, Hungerford Hill, Moppity Vineyards*, Penfolds*

SOUTH AUSTRALIA

Adelaide Hills
830 ha, 3457 tonnes, total all varieties 3904 ha

Climate: Cool, MJT 18.9°C, E° Days 1359, SH 8.4, Rain 352 mm, Alt 500 m

The startling difference that altitude makes (the 440-metre contour line defines the boundary of the Adelaide Hills region) is vividly reflected in the excellent Chardonnays from this region. Yields are typically low, especially on a yield-per-vine basis (some of the vineyards are close-planted). This in turn gives the wines great structure, intensity and length, and allows the winemaker the full bag of winemaking options. Cellaring capacity is better than average, and should improve further as the vines age – few are much more than ten years old, only a handful more than 15.

Best producers
Anvers, Barratt, Bird in Hand, BK Wines*, Casa Freschi, Geoff Weaver, Grosset*, Henschke, Lobethal Road*, Lofty Valley, Michael Hall, Murdoch Hill*, Nepenthe, Penfolds*, Petaluma, Scott Wines, Shaw + Smith*, Tapanappa*, The Lane Vineyard, Tomich, Wirra Wirra*, Wolf Blass

McLaren Vale
470 ha, 1959 tonnes, total all varieties 7422 ha

Climate: Warm, MJT 21.3°C, E° Days 1680, SH 8.4, Rain 230 mm, Alt 130 m

This was the first region in South Australia to gain attention after Chardonnay became generally available in the state in the early to mid-1980s, although much of the Fleurieu Zone production now comes from Langhorne Creek. The style is solid but yield-dependent: nicely weighted but not riveting wines coming from those who control yields, bland and boring from those who don't.

Coonawarra
306 ha, 1662 tonnes, total all varieties 5603 ha

Climate: Moderate, MJT 19.9°C, E° Days 1379, SH 7.5, Rain 272 mm, Alt 60 m

The limestone soil and the moderately cool climate might have been expected to produce outstanding Chardonnay; in fact, it simply varies between good and very good, the outcome in part a reflection of yield, and in part how well the wine is treated in the winery (notably in the choice of oak). The wines are of mid-weight and intensity, with fruit characters oscillating between melon, citrus and nectarine. In some cases (such as Wynns) the chief attraction is price. The two producers to consistently succeed are Balnaves and Parker Coonawarra Estate.

Padthaway
987 ha, 8622 tonnes, total all varieties 4092 ha

> Climate: Warm, MJT 21°C, E° Days 1550, SH 7.8, Rain 210 mm, Alt 50 m

The region came out of the blocks fast in the late 1980s and early '90s, but the gloss has well and truly worn off. Two factors of equal importance have led to the change: first, viticultural practices aimed at maximising yield and minimising cost, and second, the emergence of the slew of high-quality vineyards in Western Australia and of Tumbarumba, Orange and Beechworth, among many.

Mount Benson and Robe
Mount Benson: 38 ha, total all varieties 504 ha. Robe: 106 ha, total all varieties 682 ha

> **Mount Benson** Climate: Cool, MJT 17.7°C, E° Days 1377, SH 7.5, Rain 272 mm, Alt 60 m

Share many of the problems confronting McLaren Vale, Langhorne Creek, Coonawarra and Padthaway, but several wines were made by the forerunners of Treasury Wine Estates that showed it was possible to produce wines with real finesse and intensity.

Barossa and Eden Valleys
Barossa Valley: 457 ha, 2062 tonnes, total all varieties 11 110 ha. Eden Valley: 265 ha, 892 tonnes, total all varieties 2264 ha

> **Barossa Valley** Climate: Warm, MJT 21.4°C, E° Days 1571, SH 8.6, Rain 199 mm, Alt 270 m
> **Eden Valley** Climate: Moderate, MJT 20.2°C, E° Days 1460, SH 8.5, Rain 275 mm, Alt 420 m

These two regions produce significant amounts of workmanlike Chardonnay, the cooler climate of the Eden Valley leading to somewhat tighter and finer wines. In both regions, other varieties – Riesling, Shiraz and Cabernet Sauvignon – do better. Mountadam's High Eden Estate and Hill Smith Eden Valley are the leaders of a small pack.

VICTORIA

Strathbogie Ranges and Upper Goulburn
Strathbogie Ranges: 85 ha, total all varieties 365 ha. Upper Goulburn: 54 ha, total all varieties 242 ha

Climate: Moderate, MJT 19.7°C, E° Days 1237, SH 7.9, Rain 440 mm, Alt 560 m

Elevation provides these two regions with a distinctly cooler climate than that of the other three regions in the zone. In vintages not affected by drought or heat, attractive wines can be made. The best producer in the Strathbogies is Fowles Wine, that in the Upper Goulburn is Delatite.

Gippsland
60 ha, 191 tonnes, total all varieties 233 ha

West Climate: Moderate, MJT 19.3°C, E° Days 1400, SH 7.2, Rain 518 mm, Alt 140 m
East Climate: Cool, MJT 18.7°C, E° Days 1360, SH 7.3, Rain 353 mm, Alt 40 m
South Climate: Cool, MJT 17.9°C, E° Days 1288, SH 6.6, Rain 446 mm, Alt 80 m

After an initial burst of activity centred around Bairnsdale and Lakes Entrance in the 1970s, the vast Gippsland Zone seemed to go into hibernation, with only Nicholson River fighting on with its then spectacularly rich Chardonnay. Apart from a handful of isolated wineries dotted across the centre, of which Narkoojee was (and is) the most important (just north of Traralgon), most of the activity occurred in the eastern half, in a rough circle around Leongatha, with an extension northwards. Then Tambo Estate popped up back where it all began. While there have been a number of casualties along the way, the present group of producers do the Zone proud.

Best producers
Bass Phillip*, Bellvale, Caledonia Australis, Cannibal Creek Vineyard, Narkoojee, Onannon, Tambo Estate*

Beechworth
10 ha, total all varieties 53 ha

Climate: Warm, MJT 21.2°C, E° Days 1435, SH 8.7, Rain 467 mm, Alt 550 m

Another region that owed its initial fame to one producer, Giaconda, whose Chardonnay scales the utmost heights of Australian style and quality, magnificently complex yet full of finesse, and with an ability to age second to none. If Gippsland is large, Beechworth is tiny, and Giaconda has played a Pied Piper of Hamelin role in attracting a bevy of top-notch micro-makers to the region. It had (or has, I'm not sure which tense I should use) a second pillar of support with Mark Walpole and Adrian Rodda's salvation of the Smith Vineyard, planted way back in 1978. The synergy between the winemakers, the climate and the variety is, without exaggeration, awesome. Every hectare produces liquid gold; the suspicion is that there may be more than 10 hectares planted.

Best producers
A Rodda*, Brokenwood*, Fighting Gully Road*, Giaconda*, Golden Ball, Savaterre, Warner Vineyard

Geelong
85 ha, total all varieties 506 ha

Climate: Cool, MJT 18.5°C, E° Days 1377, SH 7.2, Rain 319 mm, Alt 70 m

This cool coastal–region regular presents some of the most densely packed Chardonnay to come from Australia, ageworthy and gaining strong Burgundian nuances as it moves slowly to maturity.

Best producers
Banks Road, Bannockburn*, Clyde Park*, del Rios of Mt Anakie, Farr | Farr Rising*, Lethbridge, Oakdene, Scotchmans Hill, Shadowfax*

Macedon Ranges
53 ha, total all varieties 218 ha

Climate: Cool, MJT 18.2°C, E° Days 1149, SH 7.8, Rain 428 mm, Alt 500 m

A windswept and at times bitterly cool region (even in summer) takes the challenge of fully ripening Chardonnay to the extreme, a fact reflected by the number of sparkling wines (based on Chardonnay and Pinot Noir) to come from the Ranges. Citrus, apple and mineral characters dominate, and the tightly structured wines age very slowly – but surely. Bindi (with its Quartz and Composition duo) and Curly Flat (with its top wine simply labelled Chardonnay), are among Australia's most highly regarded practitioners.

Best producers
Bindi*, Curly Flat*, Hanging Rock, Lane's End, Silent Way

Mornington Peninsula
190 ha, total all varieties 732 ha

> **Mornington** Climate: Cool, MJT 18.9°C, E° Days 1428, SH 7.1, Rain 380 mm, Alt 60 m
> **Red Hill South** Climate: Cool, MJT 17.5°C, E° Days 1240, SH 6.8, Rain 400+ mm, Alt 180 m

Even for Chardonnay, site selection is of great importance on this long and (for occasional visitors) surprisingly large peninsula. Most of the vineyards are small, reflecting high land costs and the number of long-standing subdivisions, but the area over which they are spread is large, as is site-climate variation. High natural acidity, leading some to employ total or partial malolactic fermentation to ameliorate it, results in elegant wines with a distinctive and complex mix of citrus and stone fruit on the one hand, and nutty/cashew/creamy malolactic flavours on the other.

Best producers
Circe, Crittenden Estate*, Darling Park, Dexter*, Eldridge Estate of Red Hill*, Foxeys Hangout*, Garagiste, Jones Road, Kooyong*, Main Ridge Estate*, Montalto*, Moorooduc Estate*, Ocean Eight Vineyard, Paringa Estate*, Port Phillip Estate*, Red Hill Estate, Scorpo, Stonier*, Ten Minutes by Tractor*, Tuck's Ridge, Yabby Lake*, Yal Yal Estate*

Yarra Valley
663 ha, total all varieties 2408 ha

> **Lower** Climate: Moderate, MJT 19.4°C, E° Days 1463, SH 7.4, Rain 437 mm, Alt 120 m
> **Upper** Climate: Cool, MJT 18.4°C, E° Days 1253, SH 7.3, Rain 700 mm, Alt 200 m

The sheer size, and differences in altitude, rainfall and soil type, not to mention extreme climatic fluctuations between 1998 and 2002 inclusive (not restricted to the Yarra Valley, incidentally) suggest that generalisations should not be possible. Paradoxically, they are: Yarra Chardonnay is notable for its elegance and, above all else, the length of its palate and aftertaste. Restraint in the use of new oak, with low levels of toast, and larger barrels (500 litres) and cuvees (2250 litres or more). The arrival of screwcaps has already proved ten years' bottle age can be achieved with ease, 20 years around the next bend.

Best producers
Coldstream Hills*, De Bortoli, Domaine Chandon, Helens Hill, Hoddles Creek Estate*, Innocent Bystander, Mac Forbes, Medhurst, Mount Mary*, Oakridge Estate*, Punch, Serrat, Seville Estate*, TarraWarra Estate, Toolangi*, Yering Station

Henty
39 ha, total all varieties 168 ha

> Climate: Cool, MJT 17.4°C, E° Days 1213, SH 6.8, Rain 345 mm, Alt 70 m

Another southern region to push the limits of viticulture to the extreme, so cool is it. Not surprisingly, the best vintages are the warmest ones, the cooler years sometimes resulting in no vintage at all. Seppelt Drumborg was the name most likely to provoke recognition for this renamed region (it used to be known as Far South West Victoria), but ongoing brand and label changes for Seppelt mean the disappearance of the word 'Drumborg'. The style is intense, finely strung, with citrus/grapefruit at its core. A piece of wine trivia is that Dr John Gladstones classifies the climate as the coolest in Australia (hence cooler than the coolest parts of Tasmania).

PAN-AUSTRALIAN ZONES (CHARDONNAY'S ENGINE ROOM)

Lower Murray Zone, South Australia
4608 ha, 71 686 tonnes. Riverland: 4608 ha

> Climate: Hot (MJT 23°C–25.9°C)

Northwest Victoria Zone, Victoria
3457 ha, 52 089 tonnes. Murray Darling: 2542 ha. Swan Hill: 915 ha

> Climate: Hot (MJT 23°C–25.9°C)

Big Rivers Zone, New South Wales
Murray Darling: 1743 ha. Swan Hill: 47 ha. Perricoota: 192 ha

> Climate: Hot (MJT 23°C–25.9°C)

These three zones (and their regions) grow a total of 221 844 tonnes (two-thirds) of Australia's Chardonnay. The wine produced will at best be bottled and labelled South East Australia Chardonnay and sold for plus or minus $10. It may also be sold as bag-in-a-box with similar naming, or blended with other varieties to be sold in bulk to purchasers in Australia or overseas, simply described as Wine of Australia.

WESTERN AUSTRALIA

Great Southern
463 ha, total all varieties 2752 ha

> **Frankland River** Climate: Moderate, MJT 20.7°C, E° Days 1574, SH 7.6, Rain 203 mm, Alt 230 m
> **Mount Barker** Climate: Moderate, MJT 20°C, E° Days 1548, SH 7.3, Rain 280 mm, Alt 220 m
> **Denmark** Climate: Cool, MJT 18.9°C, E° Days 1512, SH 6.7, Rain 332 mm, Alt 130 m

The five subregions (Albany, Denmark, Frankland River, Mount Barker and Porongurup) all leave subtly differing marks on the Chardonnays coming from within their boundaries. The cooler Albany, Denmark and Porongurup subregions produce finer, citrus- and at times passionfruit-accented wines, the structure and density increasing as the more continental climate of Frankland River and Mount Barker comes to bear. While the region may be better known for Riesling and its powerful red wines, the sheer quality and balance of its Chardonnays should not be ignored.

Best producers
Alkoomi, Burch Family Wines*, Byron & Harold, Castelli Estate*, Castle Rock*, Forest Hill Vineyard*, Harewood Estate, Larry Cherubino*, Marchand & Burch Wines, Plantagenet, Rockcliffe, Singlefile*, Snake + Herring, Staniford Wine Co., The Lake House*, West Cape Howe, Willoughby Park*

Manjimup and Pemberton
188 ha, total all varieties 788 ha

> **Manjimup** Climate: Moderate, MJT 20.6°C, E° Days 1591, SH 7.3, Rain 269 mm, Alt 260 m
> **Pemberton** Climate: Moderate, MJT 19.2°C, E° Days 1468, SH 7, Rain 326 mm, Alt 170 m

The boundary between these two regions remained in dispute until February 2006, reflecting the ever-changing topography, soil and aspect of each. The common features are an abundance of water and relatively rich soils, the richness, however, varying considerably in degree. Increased vine age and experience have ironed out problems encountered in the early stages of development, and restrained, stylish Chardonnays are now regularly made by the best producers.

Best producers
Bellarmine*, Castelli Estate*, Evans & Tate, Houghton*, Larry Cherubino*, Merum Estate, Peos Estate

Margaret River

782 ha, total all varieties 4771 ha

Yallingup Climate: Moderate, MJT 20.5°C, E° Days 1655, SH 7.6, Rain 221 mm, Alt 100 m
Wallcliffe Climate: Moderate, MJT 20°C, E° Days 1552, SH 7.4, Rain 261 mm, Alt 90 m
Karridale Climate: Cool, MJT 18.8°C, E° Days 1497, SH 7.1, Rain 305 mm, Alt 50 m

It is easy to agree with the proposition that this is one of Australia's foremost regions for Chardonnay, so many great wines come from within its boundaries. Quite why this should be so, if the Burgundian climate model (strongly continental, freezing winters, summer daytime peak temperatures and so forth) is taken as a guide, is not obvious. The adjacent Indian Ocean provides a year-round air-conditioning system for the region; year-round surfing attests to the mild winters, and helps explain why Chardonnay tends to burst into new growth in August, barely two months after it has shed its leaves from the preceding vintage. The day/night temperature variation is likewise compressed, and there is an even accumulation of heat degree days (physiologically effective warmth for ripening) throughout the growing season, which (misleadingly) puts the Margaret River (1552 E°Days) at more or less the same level as Nuriootpa in the Barossa Valley (1571 E°Days).

Be that as it may, Margaret River Chardonnay manages to combine an almost shocking voluptuousness within an iron-clad structure, intensity with generosity, and sweet fruit with flowing natural acidity. The wines age surely, gaining in complexity while not sacrificing varietal character.

Best producers

Brookland Valley*, Burch Family Wines*, Cape Mentelle*, Clairault | Streicker*, Credaro Family Estate, Cullen*, Deep Woods Estate*, Devil's Lair*, Evoi*, Fermoy Estate, Flametree, Flowstone*, Hamelin Bay, Hay Shed Hill*, Leeuwin Estate*, Lenton Brae, Marq, Redgate, Robert Oatley Vineyards, Rosabrook, Thompson Estate, Vasse Felix*, Voyager Estate*, Windows Estate, Woodlands Estate, Xanadu*

TASMANIA

292 ha, 1780 tonnes, total all varieties 1231 ha

South Coast Tasmania
Lower Derwent Climate: Cool, MJT 18.2°C, E° Days 1268, SH 7.3, Rain 280 mm, Alt 80 m
Busby Park Climate: Cool, MJT 17.8°C, E° Days 1151, SH 7, Rain 329 mm, Alt 80 m
Hobart Climate: Cool, MJT 17.1°C, E° Days 1195, SH 7.2, Rain 345 mm, Alt 10 m
Huon Valley Climate: Cool, MJT 16.8°C, E° Days 1115, SH 6.5, Rain 458 mm, Alt 40 m
Northern Tasmania
Tamar Valley Climate: Cool, MJT 18.1°C, E° Days 1307, SH 7.5, Rain 321 mm, Alt 50 m
Pipers Brook Climate: Cool, MJT 17.6°C, E° Days 1208, SH 7.5, Rain 477 mm, Alt 120 m
North Coast Climate: Cool, MJT 17°C, E° Days 1133, SH 7.3, Rain 432 mm, Alt 60 m
Lake Barrington Climate: Cool, MJT 16.9°C, E° Days 1165, SH 7.4, Rain 496 mm, Alt 160 m
East Coast Tasmania
Climate: Cool, MJT 17.4°C, E° Days 1233, SH 7.2, Rain 388 mm, Alt 50 m

So far, Tasmania has resisted the temptation to break itself into two regions, however obvious they may be to those who make wine there or visit it as regularly as I do. So I shall pass over some differences, and concentrate on the common features. These turn largely on the minerally spine, and the very high natural acidity, both of which give the wines great length and intensity. This is one part of Australia in which unwooded (or very lightly oaked) Chardonnay of real quality and interest can be made with relative ease. A corollary is the ability of these finely strung wines to hasten slowly to maturity, and hold that maturity for some years. By way of postscript, Tasmania produces wonderful sparkling wines (almost all by the traditional method), with House of Arras providing Australia's finest examples, which are of world class. Arras, together with many other producers, led by Stefano Lubiana, uses significant amounts of Tasmania's Chardonnay and Pinot Noir (plus all its modest amounts of Pinot Meunier) in making sparkling wines.

Best producers

Bay of Fires*, Dalrymple Vineyards, Dawson & James*, Derwent Estate, Freycinet, Frogmore Creek*, Heemskerk*, Holm Oak, Josef Chromy, Ministry of Clouds, Moorilla Estate, Riversdale Estate, Stoney Rise*, Three Wishes, Tolpuddle*

Chardonnay

Chapter 2

The Classic White Varietals
Riesling

49 997 ha grown worldwide in 31 countries. Those with over 100 ha are: Australia 3893 ha, Austria 1852 ha, Canada 871 ha, Chile 367 ha, China 437 ha, Croatia 676 ha, Czech Republic 1181 ha, France 3490 ha, Germany 22 434 ha, Hungary 1304 ha, Italy 446 ha, Kazakhstan 111 ha, Luxembourg 120 ha, Moldova 1343 ha, New Zealand 784 ha, Russia 882 ha, Slovakia 605 ha, Slovenia 676 ha, South Africa 211 ha, Spain 161 ha, Ukraine 2702 ha, United States 4852 ha.

International History

The ancestral home of Riesling was today's Austria, Germany and Alsace, or, more specifically, on the northern bank of the Rhein River in Rheingau.[1] As with all the major *vinifera* varieties, the early records of Riesling are open to question (and to interpretation) because of variations in spelling. Riesling has a parent–offspring relationship with Gouais Blanc, one of the most ancient wine grapes of Western Europe, the latter having a fertile relationship with at least 80 other grape varieties, including Chardonnay and Gamay, which are either half-siblings, grandparents or grandchildren of Riesling.[2]

The first use of the term 'Riesling' was in 1552[3], but it seems the quality of the variety (under various spellings) was well known by the late Middle Ages, and had become widely planted in the Rhine and Mosel valleys by the mid-sixteenth century.

Its status grew steadily over the seventeenth and eighteenth centuries, reaching its high point in the nineteenth century. At the time, the 1855 classification of Bordeaux divided

---

1 Jancis Robinson, Julia Harding and Jose Vouillamoz, *Wine Grapes*, Ecco/HarperCollins, 2012, p. 888.
2 ibid.
3 ibid.

its 61 greatest producers into five growths (or classes), and mature German Riesling brought higher prices than First Growth Bordeaux. One of its greatest protagonists was Queen Victoria, who allowed a producer in Hochheim to rename its vineyard Konigin Victoriaberg, the distinctly ornate label including the British Royal coat of arms.

'Mature' in this context meant up to 50 years, or even more. It was quite usual for the wine to be kept in old wooden vats, the interior coated with layers of tartaric acid, which prevented any semblance of oak flavour appearing in the wine, and also made the vat impervious to oxygen through its walls.

The oldest Riesling I have tasted was the 1727 Rudesheimer Apostlewein, taken from the great tun (or vat) still held in the Bremer Ratskeller, and which comes up for auction from time to time: the bottle was purchased at Christie's in the 1970s. The wine is a curio, the vat having been repeatedly topped up over the decades in the manner of a solero Sherry, and indeed was so madeirised it had some Sherry characters.

The twentieth century brought Riesling to its knees. In 1870–79 the average yield (for all regions) in Germany was 17 hectolitres per hectare. By 1970–79 the average yield had soared to 104 hectolitres per hectare (6.5 tonnes per acre), with yields of 200 hectolitres per hectare (12.5 tonnes per acre) not uncommon. True it is that much of the increase was attributable to a legion of higher-yielding crosses bred in German research institutions, the best known being Muller-Thurgau. But there was a spillover into Riesling, both in yield and quality.

Some of the greatest German Rieslings were and are the sweet wines, ranging upwards through Kabinett, Spatlese, Auslese, Beerenauslese and Trockenbeerenauslese, with Eiswein off to one side. The sweetest wines are produced in tiny quantities; they bore no similarity to the slightly sweet, vapid, thin wines epitomised by Blue Nun, Black Tower and so on.

As the wines progressively lost appeal in both domestic and international markets, which tired of weak, sugary wines, German winemakers duly took out the sweetness (which usually had been added back by sussreserve) of these over-cropped wines and developed Trocken (dry) and Halbtrocken (off-dry) wines. To say that the cure was worse than the illness was to put it mildly: a scrawny, feeble emperor in no clothes lost his few remaining citizens in quick time.

The archaic, impenetrable German wine labelling, full of long and (in English-speaking markets) unpronounceable names and words of unknown meaning, added yet more nails to the coffin.

Then the German bureaucrats got into the act with a series of wholesale changes to the chaotic appellation contrôlée system in Germany, culminating in the seemingly precise but terminally confusing wine laws of 1971. The most famous single vineyard in Germany is Bernkasteler Doctor, equivalent (say) to Romanée-Conti. The new law stipulated a minimum size of 5 hectares for a recognised site or vineyard, almost twice that of Bernkasteler Doctor.

The bureaucrats had no problem: they simply added adjoining vineyards so that, with a stroke of the pen, Bernkasteler Doctor was now of the appropriate size. The neighbours, whose holdings were now worth infinitely more, were delighted; the Bernkasteler owners were outraged. Complex and lengthy litigation finally saw the Bernkasteler Doctor shrink to its original size of 3.3 hectares, but not before yet further damage had been done to the image of German wine.

Bad though the 1971 law was, that of 1994 (prompted by the need to align with EU wine laws) was even worse, making no attempt to provide any guide to quality, and compounding confusion. The system adopted in 1994 has been replaced with four general grades of quality. At the bottom is Wein, formerly Tafelwein. Next is g.g.A., or Geschützte Geographische Angabe, or Protected Geographical Indication, formerly Landwein. Third is g.U., Geschützte Ursprungsbezeichnung, or Protected Designation of Origin, replacing Qualitätswein's previous meaning, the word (Qualitätswein) now designating a wine that has sugar added before fermentation, but is tested for quality, and shows regional and varietal character.

Then there is the VDP group with a four-tier rating corresponding to Burgundy: Gutswein at the bottom; Ortswein (village equivalent); Erste Lage (Premier Cru); and Grosse Lage (Grand Cru). VDP is a self-selected group of 200 winemakers and their classification has no legal standing – just as well, because Grosse Lage exists under German law for the lowest category of blended wine. Confused? Yes, of course you are. The solution: pay attention to the producer's name. If that rings a bell, select on price.

A further measure of the travails of Riesling came courtesy of the planting figures for Germany in the 1970s, when Muller-Thurgau overtook Riesling as the country's most-planted variety. Riesling has since dismissed the challenge, with plantings 80 per cent greater than those of Muller-Thurgau (as at 2008).

Almost by way of postscript, Blue Nun was repackaged in a clear glass Bordeaux-style bottle, filled with Riesling, clearly labelled as a wine from Rheinhessen (and joined by a Merlot and a Cabernet Sauvignon from the Pays d'Oc of France!).

Driven to distraction, and in some instances to bankruptcy and even suicide, the best makers in the Rheingau banded together to draw up self-imposed rules for a Charta (pronounced Karta) of quality for dry Rieslings from their region. These wines, bearing the distinctive Charta logo, must be 100 per cent estate-grown, hand-picked in several tries (or passes) through the vineyard, have a minimum of 12 per cent potential alcohol, and – most tellingly – come from vines with a maximum yield of 50 hectolitres per hectare.

Where now? It is tempting to say the worst is over, and I, for one, believe that to be so. But the recovery will be slow, and the canny consumer will be the beneficiary for the foreseeable future while prices remain low.

International Styles

GERMANY
22 434 ha

Germany not only is the ancestral home of Riesling, but also has the world's largest plantings of the variety. It is also the dominant variety in Germany itself, having regained the throne it lost in the late twentieth century to Muller-Thurgau.[4] Moreover, the style varies greatly over the principal regions: the Rheingau, Pfalz, Rheinhessen, Nahe, Mosel-Saar-Ruwer and Württemberg. Tack on the differing (increasing) sugar levels of Kabinett, Spatlese, Auslese, Trockenbeerenauslese and Eiswein, and it is obvious that the German Riesling proposition is a complex one.

Rheingau
2464 ha

Historically this region was the heart and soul of German wine, albeit the smallest of the best regions. Schloss Johannisberg stands ever-so-conspicuously on the skyline as you drive in either direction along the Rhine River, and it was here that the first recorded botrytis-infected wine, a Spatlese, was made in 1775. Schloss Vollrads is another historic landmark, dating back to 1335 in the ownership of the Matuschka-Greiffenclau family. The state-owned Kloster Eberbach was built between 1150 and 1200; here Steinberger (with the German eagle emblazoned on its label) is made and matured, and education classes for international students are held throughout the year.

These, and many other estates, produced wines up to Trockenbeerenauslese level with greater regularity than any other region. Rheingau also produced Kabinett and Spatlese styles of tremendous depth, power and concentration. Insidiously, and perhaps due to

---

4   ibid., p. 890.

complacency, the great names started to lose some of their lustre, and the wines of the Mosel-Saar-Ruwer and the Pfalz shone ever more brightly.

The fightback has been led by the late Bernhard Breuer of Weingut Georg Breuer, who gathered a group of producers absolutely and totally dedicated to quality, and who have elected to work outside the cumbersome German bureaucracy.

The dry wines are firmly structured, picking up a lightly honeyed character as they age. Moving up the scale, and ultimately arriving at Trockenbeerenauslese, the wines become ever-more luscious, complex, long-lived – and correspondingly more expensive.

The villages (communes) of Rheingau are Assmannshausen, Erbach, Hattenheim, Hochheim, Johannisberg, Kiedrich, Lorch, Oestrich, Rauenthal, Rüdesheim and Winkel – a roll call of honour, if ever there was one.

Best producers
Georg Breuer of Rüdesheim and Robert Weil of Kiedrich stand at the head of a large number of high-quality producers, closely followed by: Johannishof, August Kessler, Peter Jakob Kuhn, Franz Kunstler, Schloss Reinhartshausen and J Wegeler.

Pfalz
5458 ha

The Pfalz makes full-bodied Rieslings that become honeyed and verging on outright fatness with increasing bottle age, but are balanced by acidity. Thanks to the (relatively) warm climate, the wines are fermented to dryness, and reach a level of alcohol not far short of that of Alsace or Australia.

The villages are Deidesheim, Forst, Kallstadt, Ruppertsberg, Ungstein and Wachenheim.

Best producers
Muller-Catoir of Haardt and Dr Burklin-Wolf of Wachenheim lead the honour board, closely followed by: Christmann, Georg Mosbacher, Koehler-Ruprecht, Rebholz, Von Basserman-Jordan and Von Buhl.

Rheinhessen
3769 ha

This region sprawls west and south of the Rhine. At its least it is responsible for oceans of dilute, vapid, slightly sweet Niersteiner Gutes Domtal, and – even worse – is the home of Liebfraumilch. At the other extreme, Nierstein itself, on the bank of the Rhine, has outstanding producers, and closer to the city of Mainz is the town of Nackenheim, where the amiable Fritz Gunderloch (and wife Agnes) make velvety smooth wines of the highest quality. The superbly structured dry wines of Wittmann are typical of yet another style flourishing in the southern part of the region.

Best producers
Gunderloch*, Heyl Zu Herrnsheim, Keller, Sankt Antony, Wagener-Stempel*, Wittmann*

Nahe
1200 ha

The Nahe is yet another tributary of the Rhine, which it joins near Bingen. The best wines have an almost lustrous appeal, combining the verve and raciness of the Mosel with the depth of Rheingau, never more than when made by Hermann Dönnhoff, the region's uncrowned king. The affable Helmut Dönnhoff is a relatively frequent visitor to Australia, bringing glorious Eisweins and Trockenbeerenausleses for wine professionals to taste. But only one-third of the region is planted to Riesling, Muller-Thurgau and Sylvaner occupying much of the remainder, producing bland wines of little merit. By way of postscript, there are more conflicting figures than usual for the area planted to Riesling: the figure given above is an average.

Best producers
Traisen: Dr Crusius; Oberhausen: Dönnhoff; Burg Layen: Schossgut Diehl

Mosel-Saar-Ruwer
5390 ha

This is the coolest German wine region, able to ripen Riesling on its vertiginous dark shale/slate hillsides, which can maximise sunlight interception. There are two ways of understanding the region: one is based on the three rivers (Mosel, Saar and Ruwer), the other on the division between the lower Mosel (seldom exciting), the middle Mosel (bursting at the seams with great Rieslings) and the Upper Mosel, its fame based on the cold Saar River Valley and the less visually dramatic Ruwer River (more exactly a stream).

I have to declare a strong personal preference for the wines of the Mosel-Saar-Ruwer over the other great regions of Germany. They are less weighty, but have a dazzling, diamond-like purity which sets every taste receptor in my mouth (and nose) singing. Most of the wines fall in the Kabinett and Spatlese levels, with Auslese less common, and Eiswein, Beerenauslese and Trockenbeerenauslese rare (and awesomely expensive), for they are usually made in microscopic quantities, down to 100 litres or so.

Only in some regions are top-ranked German Rieslings fermented dry (or less than 7 grams per litre). In most instances some sugar is needed to balance the naturally high acidity, and is often masked by that acidity. The consequence is low alcohol levels, down to 8.5 per cent for very sweet wines, and (for example) for Kabinett, Spatlese and Auslese wines from the Mosel.

The villages' names set my pulse racing as I remember visits to each, my mouth salivating at the thought of their wines, and (crass though the thought may be) satisfaction in knowing I have more bottles of these wines than those of any other Riesling region on earth. Those of the Mosel proper are (in alphabetical order) Bernkastel, Brauneberg, Erden, Graach, Piesport, Trittenheim, Urzig and Zeltingen; of the Saar, Saarburg, Serrig and Wiltingen; and Kasel of the Ruwer.

Best producers
Grans Fassian, Maximin Grünhaus*, Fritz Haag*, Reinhold Haart, Von Hövel, Karthäuserhof, Reichsgraf Von Kesselstatt, Dr Loosen*, Markus Molitor, Egon Müller*, Dr Pauly-Bergweiler, Joh Jos Prüm*, SA Prüm, Max Ferd Richter*, Von Schubert*, Zillikin

ALSACE, FRANCE
3382 ha

It is arguably of no consequence that Riesling cannot be grown anywhere in France other than Alsace, a by-product of the ping-pong ownership of Alsace between France and Germany during the eighteenth and nineteenth centuries – it changed hands four times in 140 years.

It is somehow appropriate that the arrival of the twenty-first century should mark a distinct crack in the wall of the desire by the winemakers of Alsace (other than those in the next paragraph) to ferment their wine to absolute dryness. Higher baumé levels have allowed the retention of some residual sugar, and neither wine law nor the disposition of those who go down this path requires any disclosure on the label.

Only a small percentage of distinctly sweeter wines – Vendage Tardive and Selection de Grains Noble – were made over the years, but the impact of apparent changes in climate has resulted in an increase in the production of these wines. They combine high alcohol and sweetness, and I remain to be convinced that the conjunction is a happy one for Riesling.

In a not dissimilar fashion, the introduction of Grand Cru vineyards in 1983 (expanded in 1992) has complicated the once-clear labelling system (vintage, variety and place), not so much by what it says, but by what it does not say. Quite apart from the inevitable arguments with producers who feel entitled to Grand Cru status for their vineyards, there are those vineyards within a declared Grand Cru site (Rosacker) that do not mention either Rosacker or Grand Cru on their label; Trimbach's Clos Ste Hune is the most obvious, but far from sole, example, arguing that the larger surrounding Grand Cru does not have the same terroir as its own. (Shades of Château Mouton-Rothschild's motto before it was elevated to First Growth status in Bordeaux.)

The basic Alsace style is, as I say, dry; the bouquet is powerful, initially with lime and hints of mineral and smoke, then growing in complexity and depth as the wine develops in bottle over 20 years. As Alsace Riesling makers progressively move to screwcap, as they surely will, that 20 years will become 40 or more.

Best producers
Paul Blanck, Marcel Deiss, Dopff et Irion, Hugel & Fils*, Josmeyer*, Kuentz-Bas, René Muré*, Domaine Jean Sipp*, Pierre Sparr et Ses Fils, Trimbach*, Domaine Weinbach*, Zind-Humbrecht*

AUSTRIA
1852 ha

Riesling accounts for only 4 per cent of Austria's total plantings, but is considered the country's most important variety for international markets; Gruner Veltliner is inevitably the king, with 13 519 ha, but the numbers have to be treated with circumspection.

Austria's best Rieslings come from the Wachau, Kamptal and Kremstal regions. They are normally fermented dry, although in the warmer, drier vintages sweeter wines are made, ranging up to Spatlese level. In many ways, the style of the dry wines is closer to that of Australia's Clare and Eden valleys than to that of either Germany or Alsace;

the difference (compared to Clare and Eden valleys) lies in its higher natural acidity. The wines age well (I have tasted wines from the 1940s and '50s which were still full of life) and are certainly in the food-friendly category.

In the spectacularly beautiful Wachau and Kremstal regions, with steep slopes running down to the Danube (Donau in Austria), Riesling occupies the steeply terraced vineyards established on the highest parts of the slopes, Gruner Veltliner the lower parts.

Austrian wine law is a great deal easier to understand and, in one respect at least, immeasurably better than German law: it limits yields to 60 hectolitres per hectare for whites and 75 hectolitres per hectare for reds. (Strangely, the opposite of what we might expect in the New World, but no matter.) Wine is graded by 'Pradikat', the first true quality level being Kabinett, which must have 84 oechsle (the Austrian measure of sweetness, which is also used in Germany) – this converts to a minimum of 12.7 per cent alcohol. Dry wines must have less than 9 grams of residual sugar per litre and balancing acidity.

Thereafter one moves up the scale with Spatlese (94 oechsle), Auslese (105 oechsle), Eiswein and Beerenauslese (127 oechsle), Ausbruch (138 oechsle), an Austrian specialty from the Rust area adjacent to Neusiedlersee, where botrytis occurs every year, and finally Trockenbeerenauslese (156 oechsle).

Just to confuse the issue, the Wachau has its own system for Riesling and Gruner Veltliner: Steinfeder, with an oechsle of 73–83.5 and a maximum alcohol of 11 per cent; Federspiel, with an oechsle of 83.6–90 and a maximum alcohol of 12.5 per cent; and top-of-the-range Smaragd, with an oechsle of over 90 and alcohol of more than 12 per cent.

The Steinfeders are often the most attractive in the two or three years following vintage, with a racy, tingling freshness. At the other extreme, the Smaragds can seem heavy, and demand at least five years' cellar age, preferably ten or more. It is not unlike the contrast between a top Mosel wine and a top Rheingau.

Best producers

Wachau: Leo Alzinger*, Franz Hirtzberger*, Josef Högl, Josef Jamek, Emmerich Knoll*, Karl Lagler, FX Pichler*, Rudi Pichler, Franz Prager*, Weingut Schmelz, Friei Weingärtner Wachau*; Kremstal: Winzerhof Dockner, Weingut Malat, Mantlerhof, Martin Nigl*, Weingut Proidl, Salomon Undhof*; Kamptal: Weingut Bründlmayer*, Schloss Gobelsburg, Weingut Hiedler, Weingut Hirsch, Fred Loimer*

NEW ZEALAND
784 ha, 6013 tonnes

At the start of the 1980s, New Zealand was awash with Muller-Thurgau, made in various off-dry versions, united by their boring, bland flavour. Riesling, on the other hand, was barely on the radar.

All that has changed: Muller-Thurgau is in fast retreat, and while Riesling is never going to challenge Sauvignon Blanc, its growth – particularly in Marlborough – has been impressive, rising from 2200 tonnes in 1993 to its present (2014) level of 6013 tonnes. Marlborough (309 hectares) and Waipara (266 hectares) are the two most important regions.

Its basic taste profile is determined by the winemaker's decision on the best balance between acidity and residual sugar. If the wine is not de-acidified, it will very likely require at least 7 grams per litre of residual sugar (and sometimes more) to balance the high level of natural acidity. 'Dry' is a comparative term in this context; certain it is that New Zealand Riesling carries a certain amount of residual sugar more easily than all other New World producers. It is also more perfumed than any of its New World counterparts, Australia included. Whether this makes it better is another question.

Like Australia, New Zealand produces small quantities of high quality, highly botrytised Riesling, travelling under various names. These can have spectacular intensity, but develop more quickly than their German counterparts (possibly due to the lower SO_2 levels in the New Zealand wines).

Best producers
Canterbury: Giesen Estate, Waipara Hills; Central Otago: Chard Farm, Felton Road*, Mount Maude, Pegasus Bay, Peregrine, Rippon Vineyard; Hawke's Bay: Ngatarawa; Marlborough: Allan Scott Wines, Drylands, Forrest Estate*, Framingham Wines*, Fromm Winery, Grove Mill*, Hunter's Wines, Isabel Estate, Jackson Estate*, Lawson's Dry Hills*, Saint Clair Estate, Seresin Estate, Spy Valley, Te Whare Ra; Martinborough: Nga Waka Vineyard; Nelson: Kahurangi Estate, Neudorf Vineyards*, Seifried Estate; Wairarapa: Dry River Wines*, Mission Estate, Muddy Water, Winslow

NORTH AMERICA
5723 ha

Riesling is grown in Ontario and British Columbia in Canada (871 hectares), in Washington State (2258 hectares), in Oregon, and in California. A striking achievement is in the Ice Wines of Canada (Iniskillin the undisputed leader) and (to a lesser degree) the botrytised wines of California (Chateau St Jean and Joseph Phelps to the fore).

When it comes to dry or near-dry Rieslings, Washington State has made vast strides in the new millennium, plantings rising from 769 hectares in 1999 to 2258 hectares in 2011, the peripatetic Dr Ernst Loosen joining forces with Chateau Ste Michelle (the largest winery in the state) to produce some excellent Rieslings.

Australian History

Both James Busby (1832) and Willam Macarthur (1838) listed Riesling in their official records of the varieties imported. Busby named his 'Rischling' (procured from 'the Garden of the Luxemberg [sic]' at Paris), while Macarthur named the 'Bas-Rhin' as the source of his vines. Dr AC Kelly wrote (in 1868) that 'Riesling was imported by Messrs Macarthur from the Rheingau, 1838, and it has established its character as one of the most valuable wines in the Colonies.'

Given that most development of viticulture in South Australia was courtesy of Silesian immigrants (from part of today's Germany), it is not surprising that one of the first specific references to Riesling comes in Ebenezer Ward's *Vineyards and Orchards of South Australia*; here he records that Mr Joseph Gilbert of Pewsey Vale had Riesling wine from both the 1842 and 1844 vintages, and that the latter had been tasted by experts in Adelaide, who pronounced it to be very good. It quickly became entrenched in the Barossa Valley, recognised and enthusiastically adopted by the Lutheran Silesians.

Before long, however, its name was adopted by other varieties. In the Hunter Valley, the local nurseryman Shepherd supplied vines which were called Shepherd's Riesling in the 1850s; in due course the name was changed to Hunter River Riesling, and thereafter shortened simply to Riesling. No problem, except that the variety was in fact Semillon, and only McWilliam's had a small planting of true Riesling.

In the Clare Valley, ironically destined to become the foremost region of the variety in Australia, the altogether inferior variety Crouchen was called Clare Valley Riesling. But worse was to come: in the midst of all this confusion, Riesling was used to denote a (very loosely defined) style, and 'Rhine' was tacked onto the front to denote a wine made from true Riesling.

Nowhere was this better demonstrated than in the Hunter Valley, where Lindemans waved their magic wand over Semillon to produce Riesling, Hock, Chablis and White Burgundy, the difference lying in slightly different picking dates, vineyard plots and/or alcohol.

Nonetheless, in the white wine boom of the late 1960s and '70s, true Riesling became Australia's leading white variety, rising from 1900 tonnes in 1966 to an all-time high of 44 000 tonnes in 1986. It was not until 1992 that Chardonnay overtook it, and thereafter the two varieties went in opposite directions, Riesling declining until 2002, increasing to 2008, and falling again until 2012, Chardonnay consistently soaring upwards.

A group of very determined Clare Valley vignerons, led by Jeffrey Grosset, began a campaign in 1994 to have the use of the generic name Riesling abolished, and to drop the technically incorrect 'Rhine', limiting the name to the true variety. It was opposed by the big companies, in particular those who were heavily involved in the cask market, where generic terms (Riesling, Chablis, Claret, Burgundy, etc) were used, and varietal names were not. (The casks were typically an unholy blend of lesser varieties, with Trebbiano, Sultana and others in the white wines.)

The campaign finally succeeded in 2000, partly because of the negotiations for an Australian–EU wine agreement (finally signed in 2010), but more to get those pestilential Clare Valley makers off corporate backs. In 2000 that same group decided to abandon the use of corks, and to move en masse to Stelvin screwcaps.

Little could they have imagined that by 2014, 97.6 per cent of the 3269 white wines submitted for tasting for my annual *Australian Wine Companion* would be sealed by screwcaps. Little would anyone have imagined that almost all vertical tastings of Australian Rieslings would commence with the first screwcapped wine, leaving those finished with corks to moulder away in the corner of the cellar.

Australian Statistics

3893 ha, 32 317 tonnes, 710 growers/producers

Riesling: tonnes crushed in Australia, 1976–2012

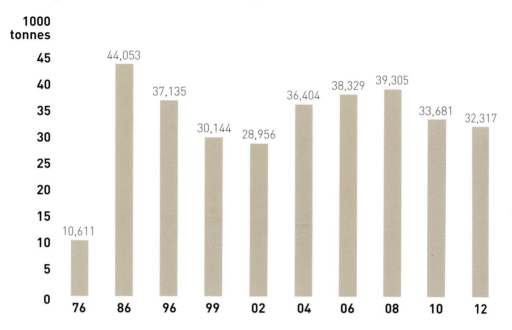

Australian Winemaking

The year 1953 was a watershed in white winemaking in Australia. In the wake of World War II all imported goods had to have an import licence, and Colin Gramp of Orlando managed to beat Yalumba for permission to import the first stainless steel pressure-fermentation tanks from Germany.

The tanks had originally been developed to store fresh grape juice in bulk for long periods by saturating it with carbon dioxide under high pressure. After the war, the German wine scientist W Geiss developed the use of the tanks as fermentation vessels to retain the primary aromas and flavours of Riesling.

Orlando achieved outstanding results almost immediately. The 1955 Orlando Barossa Rhine Riesling won first prize at the 1955 Adelaide Wine Show, causing a sensation because it was so different from the prevailing, bottle-aged Hock-style Rieslings.

Back in Europe, Professor Salter of Kloster Neuburg in Austria sought to achieve the same results by a different method: refrigeration to strictly control the fermentation temperature. Within a few years Australian winemakers followed suit, using the pressure tanks instead for the production of such delicacies as Barossa Pearl (a semi-sweet sparkling wine which was launched in 1956 and achieved huge success).

The mainstream Australian techniques for making Riesling have changed little over the past 50 years, sharing much with Hunter Valley Semillon. If hand-picked, the grapes are whole-bunch pressed (i.e. without crushing, the one change facilitated by the development of horizontal presses with inflatable inner bags) and the resultant juice is either cold-settled at very low temperatures, centrifuged, or cross-flow filtered. The objective in each case is to have star-bright juice with absolutely no phenolics.

The juice will then be inoculated with a neutral cultured yeast and fermented at a low temperature (12°C to 15°C). Once fermentation is finished, the wine will be racked off its lees, sterile-filtered, and taken to bottle as quickly as possible, usually within three or four months of vintage.

Brian Croser and Jancis Robinson argue that this essentially simple winemaking path makes Riesling the most noble grape of all, able to express its varietal character and terroir without elaboration. Contrast, if you will, the winemaking inputs required for Chardonnay.

But wait. The six-monthly diaspora of Australian Flying Winemakers to Europe, the globalisation of wine knowledge at all levels via the internet, and the curiosity of the typical Australian have led to experimentation (on a commercial scale) with many techniques previously regarded as unthinkable.

Use of wild yeast was the first step, retention of solids in the juice next, fermentation on skins (as if it were a red wine) third (and most radical). Where undertaken by skilled Riesling makers – *not* natural winemakers – these techniques have produced valid alternatives, without causing any substantial move away from conventional wisdom.

The less radical change has come with the rehabilitation of the reputation of off-dry through to fully sweet Rieslings, the former typically achieved by picking the grapes at normal maturity (or slightly earlier) and stopping the fermentation at between 7 and 18 grams per litre of residual sugar, balanced by slightly elevated acidity.

Then there is cane-cutting, resulting in the dehydration of the grapes, thus increasing both sugar and acidity. Freeze concentration of the juice achieves a similar result, working particularly well in cool climates. If taken to extremes, it can result in wines with the intense sweetness of German Eisweins or Beerenauslese and above.

Botrytis is the usual agent for the greatest Beerenauslese and Trockenbeerenauslese styles, investing the wines with levels of complexity that elude any of the wines made by the techniques discussed above.

Australian Regional Styles

SOUTH AUSTRALIA

Clare Valley

1164 ha, 5567 tonnes, total all varieties 5339 ha

Climate: Warm, MJT 21.4°C, E° Days 1493, SH 8.9, Rain 248 mm, Alt 450 m

Long considered the monarch of Australia's Riesling regions, the Clare Valley is under attack from two very different forces. The first is the continuing refusal by consumers to understand and appreciate the magnificence of the variety, an issue which affects all regions more or less equally. The second is the rapidly growing number of cooler climate Rieslings, led by Western Australia's Great Southern, Victoria's Henty and Tasmania.

In typical vintages, Clare Valley Riesling commences life in bottle with a pale, almost watery, yet brilliant, straw green colour. The aroma will be spotlessly clean, as much minerally as floral, with hints of spice, citrus, apple and/or passionfruit in the background. The flavour tracks the bouquet, which is crisp, flinty and bone dry, the fruit seldom more than a promise for the future, but a promise easily recognised by those who have watched the development of these wines over a decade or more.

Whether maturity is reached in five, ten, or more years, the colour is an immediate guide to the quality of the wine. The best are a brilliant yellow-green, lit from within by an invisible light source (and in this respect similar to Hunter Semillon of like age and quality). The tinge of green is the key: without it the quality may be lesser, and if there is the faintest hint of orange or brown, the wine (and the taster) is in trouble.

The fruit aromas will have intensified, the minerally notes diminished. Now there will be an array of some or all of lime, lemon, ripe apple and tropical/pineapple fruit aromas. At some point along the way – usually later rather than earlier – a whiff of lightly browned toast will appear; this is another character which Riesling shares with Semillon, and it is unequivocally desirable.

The flavour development closely tracks that of the bouquet: remember that there are no confounding influences of oak, malolactic fermentation, lees contact or the like. The weight of the wine increases, the mouthfeel becomes softer and rounder, but the finish remains clear and dry (unless the wine was originally made with more than 6 or 7 grams per litre of residual sugar, or, if you prefer, in a Spatlese style).

One character that can develop during the years after the wine is bottled is akin to kerosene or petrol. It sharply divides opinions, some rejecting the wine, others seeing it as but one of a number of aromas and flavours of mature Riesling, quite probably linked to lightly browned toast and/or honey. It is usually abbreviated to TDN, understandable when you find that its (full) name is *trimethyl dihydronapthalene*. There is some research suggesting a precursor of TDN comes through sunburnt fruit, which is seldom an issue with German or Austrian-grown grapes. Deliberately shading the canopy is an answer, but the cure can be worse than the illness. I should go on record by saying I don't like the character at all.

It is a very complex subject, difficulties arising even before the intricacies are discussed, as opinions are split on the threshold question of whether TDN is or is not a terpene. It's arguably a purely academic question, because Riesling has six terpenes that produce its aromas once it has finished fermentation.

The ultimate life of these wines is strongly influenced by the type of closure used and storage conditions. A typical potential life of at least 20 years has frequently been cut well short by the failure of natural one-piece cork in Australian storage conditions. It is this, as much as the issue of cork taint, which led the winemakers of the Clare Valley to adopt (en masse) the Stelvin screwcap, a move enthusiastically accepted by retailers, sommeliers and the wine-buying public.

A bottle finished with a screwcap will not be entirely unaffected by poor storage conditions, but will suffer less. It does provide an impervious seal, but does not (contrary to the belief of some) prevent the wine from moving through all the normal phases of maturation, albeit at a slightly slower pace. The maturation process uses the dissolved oxygen in the wine and in the headspace, but there are also changes with age which are anaerobic – in other words, that do not require the presence of oxygen to take place.

Best producers
Annie's Lane, Clos Clare, Greg Cooley, Grosset*, Jim Barry Wines*, Kilikanoon*, Knappstein, Leasingham*, Leo Buring, Mitchell, Mount Horrocks, O'Leary Walker*, Paulett*, Petaluma*, Pikes*, Skillogalee, Taylors, Tim Adams, Wilson Vineyard*, Wines by KT*

Adelaide Hills

79 ha, 287 tonnes, total all varieties 3904 ha

Climate: Cool, MJT 18.9°C, E° Days 1359, SH 8.4, Rain 352 mm, Alt 500 m

As is obvious, the climate of the Adelaide Hills is very much cooler than that of the Clare Valley. The consequence is that the wines have greater fragrance and finer fruit definition than those of the Clare Valley. The explanation for the plantings lagging so far behind Chardonnay, Sauvignon Blanc and Pinot Gris – and, even more obviously, behind those of the Clare Valley – is a timing issue. By the time the development of the Adelaide Hills of today got underway, the decline in the fortunes of Riesling was ancient history.

Best producers

Bird in Hand, Geoff Weaver*, Henschke*, Kersbrook Hill, La Linea, Mayhem & Co., Mt Lofty Ranges Vineyard, Shaw + Smith*, Wirra Wirra*

Eden Valley

546 ha, 1917 tonnes, total all varieties 1921 ha

Climate: Moderate, MJT 20.2°C, E° Days 1460, SH 8.5, Rain 275 mm, Alt 420 m

The aroma and flavour of Eden Valley Riesling tends to develop more positively fruit-oriented characters early in the piece, with lime/citrus the key. Mouthfeel, too, starts to flesh out a touch more rapidly, and these wines often approach their peak at five to seven years of age. However, the greatest examples live for just as many years as those of the Clare Valley.

Best producers

Bethany*, Brockenchack*, Cooper Burns, Echelon, Eden Hall*, Elderton, Forbes & Forbes, Grant Burge, Heirloom Vineyards*, Henschke*, Hentley Farm, Leo Buring, Mayhem & Co.*, Penfolds, Peter Lehmann*, Pewsey Vale*, Poonawatta, Radford*, St Hallett*, Saltram, Sons of Eden*, Two Hands, Woods Crampton

Barossa Valley

240 ha, 1314 tonnes, total all varieties 11 110 ha

> Climate: Warm, MJT 21.4°C, E° Days 1571, SH 8.6, Rain 199 mm, Alt 270 m

The Barossa was once the heartland of the variety, but Riesling has been banished to the elevated country of the Eden Valley and Adelaide Hills, with only scattered plantings of old vines, and only a handful of Rieslings carrying the Barossa Valley designation (as opposed to the ambiguity of the Zone Appellation).

WESTERN AUSTRALIA

Great Southern

265 ha, 1482 tonnes, total all varieties 2752 ha

> **Frankland River** Climate: Moderate, MJT 20.7°C, E° Days 1574, SH 7.6, Rain 203 mm, Alt 230 m
> **Mount Barker** Climate: Moderate, MJT 20°C, E° Days 1548, SH 7.3, Rain 280 mm, Alt 220 m
> **Denmark** Climate: Cool, MJT 18.9°C, E° Days 1512, SH 6.7, Rain 332 mm, Alt 130 m

Without the rich history of the Clare and Eden valleys, and without the 60- to 100-year-old vines of those regions, Great Southern is very much the new kid on the block. There are also its five subregions to consider: Albany, Denmark, Frankland River, Mount Barker and Porongurup. There is among them, however, a central core of highly fragrant yet delicate aromas, a finely chiselled and structured palate, and a whistle-clean finish. Frankland River often produces wines with strong passionfruit aromas, Porongurup the finest, with a long, minerally finish. All, however, have proved their ability to develop for at least ten years, and may well pass their 21st birthday full of life.

Best producers

Albany: Kalgan River, Willoughby Park*; Denmark: Burch Family Wines*, Harewood Estate; Frankland River: Alkoomi, Ferngrove Vineyards, Frankland Estate*; Great Southern: Byron & Harold, Estate 807, The Partners; Mount Barker: 3 Drops, Capel Vale, Gilberts; Porongurup: Abbey Creek*, Castle Rock*, Duke's Vineyard*, Robert Oatley Vineyards*; All subregions: Larry Cherubino*

TASMANIA

106 ha, 592 tonnes, total all varieties 1611 ha

South Coast Tasmania
Lower Derwent Climate: Cool, MJT 18.2°C, E° Days 1268, SH 7.3, Rain 280 mm, Alt 80 m
Busby Park Climate: Cool, MJT 17.8°C, E° Days 1151, SH 7, Rain 329 mm, Alt 80 m
Hobart Climate: Cool, MJT 17.1°C, E° Days 1195, SH 7.2, Rain 345 mm, Alt 10 m
Huon Valley Climate: Cool, MJT 16.8°C, E° Days 1115, SH 6.5, Rain 458 mm, Alt 40 m

Northern Tasmania
Tamar Valley Climate: Cool, MJT 18.1°C, E° Days 1307, SH 7.5, Rain 321 mm, Alt 50 m
Pipers Brook Climate: Cool, MJT 17.6°C, E° Days 1208, SH 7.5, Rain 477 mm, Alt 120 m
North Coast Climate: Cool, MJT 17°C, E° Days 1133, SH 7.3, Rain 432 mm, Alt 60 m
Lake Barrington Climate: Cool, MJT 16.9°C, E° Days 1165, SH 7.4, Rain 496 mm, Alt 160 m

East Coast Tasmania
Climate: Cool, MJT 17.4°C, E° Days 1233, SH 7.2, Rain 388 mm, Alt 50 m

This is another region to only recently stake its claim in the top echelon, although Moorilla Estate has been making fine Riesling (and the occasional stellar Botrytis Riesling) since 1958, and Pipers Brook likewise since 1974. Between them, Andrew Hood and Julian Alcorso (wearing their contract winemaking hats) produced a disproportionately large number of the outstanding Rieslings to come from Tasmania in recent years. All of the wines have naturally high levels of acidity (every bit as high as those of New Zealand), resulting in brilliantly focused, crisp, intense palates and a lingering finish. Balancing the acidity with discreet residual sugar is the primary challenge for the winemaker, but make no mistake, these are stellar wines.

Best producers

Bream Creek*, Craigow*, Derwent Estate, Devil's Corner, Freycinet*, Frogmore Creek, Heemskerk, Josef Chromy*, Kate Hill Wines, Moorilla Estate*, Morningside, Pipers Brook Vineyard, Pooley Wines*, Pressing Matters*, Stargazer Wine, Stefano Lubiana, Tamar Ridge*, Third Child, Waterton Vineyards

Chapter 3

The Classic White Varietals
Semillon

22 047 ha of Semillon is grown worldwide in 18 countries, the area ranging from 1 ha in China to France's total of 11 693 ha. Those with over 100 ha are: Argentina 855 ha, Australia 6112 ha, Chile 846 ha, France 11 693 ha, New Zealand 201 ha, South Africa 1182 ha, Turkey 547 ha, United States 436 ha.

International History

Perhaps due to a lack of interest (outside Australia) in the variety as a single-grape table wine, there has been relatively little conjecture about its origins. Or perhaps its presence in Bordeaux, but nowhere else of significance in Europe, was deemed to be a sufficient answer.

It has been grown there for well over 300 years, first appearing in the forests or islands of the Gironde around the sixteenth century.[1] Once domesticated, it seems very likely it was grown alongside – or, more probably, interplanted with – Sauvignon Blanc and Muscadelle.

DNA studies suggest Semillon and Sauvignon Blanc are genetically very close, supporting all the other evidence of its genesis, but not a parent–offspring relationship.[2] Sauvignon Blanc, Semillon and Muscadelle are blended to make both a dry white wine, known generically as White Bordeaux, and the luscious, sweet botrytis-infected Sauternes. There is still some controversy about the starting point for the making of Sauternes in the style we recognise today, and (by default, as much as anything else) tacit agreement that the dry wine has a longer history.

---

1   Jancis Robinson, Julia Harding and Jose Vouillamoz, *Wine Grapes*, Ecco/HarperCollins, 2012, p. 984.
2   ibid.

France grows more Semillon than any other country, with 11 693 hectares in 2009. Within France it is the fifth most planted white grape variety, comfortably in front of Sauvignon Blanc. Given the current four-to-one proportion of Semillon and Sauvignon Blanc respectively in Sauternes, this lead seems likely to continue, although Sauvignon Blanc has a greater presence in dry White Bordeaux wines.

It remains an important grape in Monbazillac (as a contributor to the sweet, botrytis wines of that region) and is still widely planted through Bergerac, though of declining importance. It is planted elsewhere (in the Lot-et-Garonne department) but is usually anonymously blended in vin ordinaire, its cause not helped by its even less noble bedfellows. Thanks to its low natural acidity, it is largely ignored in Provence and Languedoc, although it is technically allowed to be grown there. It has also failed to make any impression elsewhere in Eastern or Western Europe.

For no obvious reason, it was widely propagated in the southern hemisphere in the early nineteenth century. In the 1820s, over 90 per cent of all South Africa's vineyards were planted to Semillon, known as the green grape.

It was also an early arrival in Chile, surviving there because of its ability to produce large yields, and the lack of autumn rain and humidity which might otherwise have rendered it susceptible to rot, both noble and ignoble. Its 2010 plantings of 846 hectares only gain label recognition with the late harvest sweet wines of Viu Manent and Valdivieso.

California has had minor plantings for a considerable time, but only in scattered, small pockets. The most important was the Livermore Valley, where Wente Bros produced small quantities of good quality wine.

More recently it was established in the Columbia and Yakima valleys of Washington State, but it is now in retreat, hanging on by its fingernails with 90 hectares in 2011.

International Styles

BORDEAUX, FRANCE
7384 ha

Here, blended with Sauvignon Blanc and decreasing amounts of Muscadelle, Semillon makes the two internationally known and respected wines, dry White Bordeaux (sometimes called Graves), and Sauternes.

The traditional ratio of Semillon and Sauvignon Blanc was four to one, but there was always the feeling that – apart from Semillon's propensity to harbour botrytis – it was Sauvignon Blanc which was the noble partner. And the fact is that Semillon plantings in Bordeaux are diminishing, even if much of the decrease occurred in the Entre-Deux-Mers. That said, there were still 7384 hectares in production in 2009.

Its Jekyll and Hyde personality is evident in its concurrent reputation (which Australians will well understand) of giving the dry wines of Graves their longevity and honeyed fruit flavours when fully mature, at 30 years of age. Its contribution to Sauternes is no less critical: it readily falls prey to the *Botrytis cinerea* mould which is the base building block for this style of wine.

The once exceedingly sulphurous and rank generic White Bordeaux has benefited enormously from New World winemaking skills. But high yields, low prices and lack of pride has left the variety with a thoroughly chequered reputation at home base.

Best producers
Graves – dry: *Château Haut Brion (Grand Cru), Château Bouscaut, Château Carbonnieux, Domaine de Chevalier, Château Laville Haut Brion, Château La Louviere*
Sauternes and Barsac – sweet: *Château d'Yquem (Grand Cru), Château Climens, Château Coutet, Château Guiraud, Château Lafaurie-Peyaguey, Château La Tour Blanche, Château Rabaud-Promis, Château Rayne Vigneau, Château Rieussec, Château Sigalas-Rabaud, Château Suduiraut*

Australian History

Semillon arrived in Sydney in 1831 as part of the Busby collection, and went shortly thereafter to the Hunter Valley. It seems highly likely that it would have also arrived in Perth ex South Africa around the same time, given its then overwhelming hold on South African viticulture.

In the Hunter Valley, it was propagated by a nurseryman called Shepherd, and quickly became known as Shepherd's Riesling. With the passage of time, the name Shepherd disappeared, and the variety became known as the Hunter River Riesling.

This did not help the cause of Semillon, however. Lindemans was one of the chief culprits, developing variously rated Rieslings (Cawarra, Private Bin and Reserve Bin) and Hocks, Chablis and White Burgundies (all with similar differentiations). All were in fact made from the one grape (Semillon) and simply picked at slightly different levels of ripeness, and sold in different bottle shapes, the Riesling bottle for Hock and Riesling, the Burgundy bottle for Chablis and White Burgundy.

Tyrrell's also called its Semillon 'Riesling', and packaged it in the slender Riesling bottle; its ultimate contribution to the confusion pot was its Bin 63, called Pinot Riesling (read

Chardonnay Semillon), and likewise sold in the slender bottle. McWilliam's, with the largest volume stake of all, followed along with Elizabeth Riesling. Although the word 'Semillon' replaced 'Riesling' over 20 years ago, and a Burgundy bottle (why not a Bordeaux bottle? one wonders) replaced the Riesling bottle, it was common to find McWilliam's Elizabeth listed in the (otherwise true) Riesling section of restaurant wine lists. (There was – and is – only one planting of Riesling in the Hunter Valley: Pokolbin Estate.)

Between 1976 and 1996 the tonnage of Semillon and Riesling was roughly the same, oscillating either side of 40 000 tonnes according to vintage conditions. Since 1996 there has been much talk of a Riesling revival, and absolutely none about Semillon. Yet between 1996 and 2012, the Riesling crush decreased by 13 per cent, while that of Semillon increased by over 72 per cent, albeit with a sharp fall since 2002.

The Semillon conundrum is explained when you look at the places in which it is grown, and the uses to which it is put. While demand for quality Semillon in the Hunter Valley is undiminished, the surge in plantings has principally taken place in the Riverina, Sunraysia and the Riverland. Here its generous yields – not often threatened by rain as it ripens – provide a very useful filler (or blender) for casks (and as a budget-priced varietal in bottles). The decline in plantings is but a microcosm of the surplus and consequent vine removal of all the major varieties in the irrigated regions sustained by the Murrumbidgee and Murray River systems. Ironically, surplus grape production has gone hand in hand with much higher prices for water.

Australian Statistics

6112 ha, 77 800 tonnes

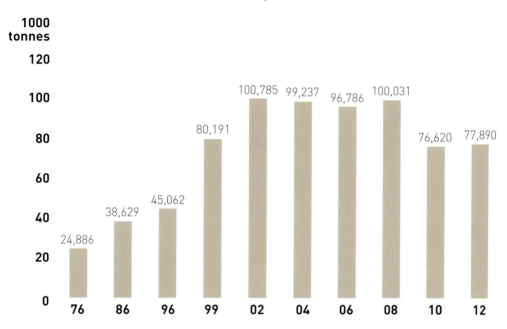

Semillon: tonnes crushed in Australia, 1976–2012

Australian Winemaking

Whether or not anyone raised elsewhere than Sydney has any empathy with (young) Hunter Valley Semillon is beside the point: the greatest Semillons are made in the Hunter Valley by treading a very narrow path. The grapes will be picked with a potential alcohol of between 10 per cent and 11 per cent; they will (usually) be whole-bunch pressed, and the juice cold-settled, or centrifuged to total clarity. A neutral cultured yeast will be used for the fermentation, which will take place at low temperatures (15°C to 18°C) in stainless steel tanks. As soon as the fermentation is finished, the wine will be racked off its lees, sterile-filtered and bottled as soon as possible, usually mid-year.

For wine that is to be held in bottle for around five years prior to release, the level of free sulphur dioxide and of carbon dioxide at bottling will be significantly higher than it is for a wine destined for release in the year of its vintage.

At the opposite end of the spectrum is (or was: mercifully, it is in fast retreat) the Barossa Valley approach of crushing the grapes and giving the must extended skin contact prior to pressing, then barrel fermenting the wine in German or American oak. The fat, oily, coarse, rapidly ageing wine which resulted was, to say the least, unfortunate, and did nothing to raise the reputation of the variety.

One Barossa maker of Semillon stopped to ponder the magic transformation of Semillon in the Hunter Valley: Andrew Wigan, then chief winemaker of Peter Lehmann Wines. Why not try the Hunter Valley techniques by picking far earlier, eliminating skin contact and oak, cold fermenting and early bottling? The result was Peter Lehmann Margaret Semillon, its first vintage in 2002 – it won the trophy for Best Semillon in the Sydney Wine Show when five years old, upstaging all the illustrious Hunter Semillons.

However, in various parts of Australia (notably the Adelaide Hills and the Margaret River) Semillon picked at the same potential alcohol as the Barossa Valley (around 13 per cent), whole-bunch pressed and then partially barrel-fermented in French oak, and often blended with Sauvignon Blanc in the manner of White Bordeaux, makes an excellent wine.

Australia briefly flirted with Semillon Chardonnay blends, but not for any noble purpose. On the contrary, in the 1970s and '80s, when Chardonnay was in desperately short supply, the 'Sem-Chard' (a name as nauseating as 'Cab Sav', and invented in California) was a marriage of convenience, sanctified – if that be the right word – for the sole purpose of making the Chardonnay stretch further. The acceptance of the blend in the United States resulted in a brief revival of its fortunes, but did little for its quality: the wine sells on price point (low) and shelf position.

Then there are the Semillon Sauvignon Blanc blends, led by Hunter Valley Semillon but coupled with Sauvignon Blanc from Orange, Hilltops, Adelaide Hills or other cool regions (even as far afield as Marlborough in New Zealand, meaning they cannot be labelled Wine of Australia).

Finally, there is Botrytis Semillon, every bit as luscious as (French) Sauternes, and made in a similar fashion, barrel-fermented and aged for up to 12 months in French oak.

Australian Regional Styles

NEW SOUTH WALES

Hunter Valley
587 ha, total all varieties 3380 ha

> **Pokolbin** Climate: Hot, MJT 23.6°C, E° Days 1823, SH 7.3, Rain 534 mm, Alt 110 m
> **Upper Hunter** Climate: Hot, MJT 23.6°C, E° Days 1799, SH 8, Rain 446 mm, Alt 190 m

Semillon's transition from youth to maturity is the most remarkable in the whole world of wine. When bottled, the colour of the wine will be little different from water; apart from free SO_2, there will be variable aromatic levels of citrus, grass, lanolin and/or herb; the palate will likewise offer a mix of citrus and mineral; and it will only be the surprising length of the wine, riding on minerally acidity, which will give a glimpse of the future.

Careful selection of cultured yeast, of SO_2 use, of screwcaps and of grapes grown on alluvial soil can give rise to significant increase in the aromatic and flavour profile of a young Semillon compared with the wines of yesteryear.

After five years the wine will start to open up, the colour moving to pale green-gold, the bouquet releasing lemon-citrus, herb and a hint of toast, the palate starting to gain weight and depth, building on the aromas of the bouquet. With the passage of another ten years, the colour will intensify, glowing green-gold as if lit from within by a tiny unseen light bulb. The bouquet will now have all the complexity of a barrel-fermented white wine such as Chardonnay, with a mix of honey, grilled nuts and lightly browned toast. The palate will be a magical combination of honey, fig and buttered toast on the one hand, and of lively acidity on the other.

The universal adoption of screwcaps has resulted in what Bruce Tyrrell describes as the golden age of Semillon. Development is leisurely but predictable, and each bottle of a given vintage of a given producer will be identical to every other bottle. It has been a case study on a grand scale of the impact of premature/random/sporadic oxidation, its clarity of colour and transparency of flavour showing any imperfection in high relief. One unopened case of ten-year-old Brokenwood Semillon (predating the use of screwcaps) was returned by a customer on a new-for-old swap. When opened, the labels were in pristine condition, the bottles and capsules likewise. The colour of the wine was a different matter, ranging from pale straw-green to brown, each bottle different.

What, you may ask, has changed? Very little in the vineyard or winery, but everything in the attitude of the consumer. In the days of innocence, the English wine trade saying

'There are no great old wines, only great old bottles' was accepted as a self-evident truth, so – in the seeming absence of an alternative – you shrugged your shoulders, and made the best of a bad thing. Anything short of brown was a sign of madeirisation, bringing with it exaggerated flavours politely described as honeyed or nutty.

When I was inducted into the mysteries of wine show judging at the Royal Sydney Wine Show in the second half of the 1970s, there were classes for Hock, Chablis, Riesling and White Burgundy that happened to coincide with the Reserve Bin examples made by Lindemans between 1961 and 1968. The managing director of Lindemans, the late Ray Kidd, was chair of the wine show committee which allowed these classes to exist in Sydney (they did not exist in other shows).

The wines, from old vines on the Sunshine Vineyard, were superb and, given the classes in which they were entered, unmistakable. So if one of these wines didn't show well, another bottle would be called for, occasionally a third, and it would then duly receive the highest points in the class.

Along with other top golds, it would proceed to the Trophy judging on the last day, and the same call would as like as not go up: another bottle, please. Thus anyone who paid top dollar for this all-triumphant wine had a 50 per cent chance at best of getting a 'good' bottle.

It was many years later when I realised why the senior Lindeman winemaker, Raymond Chan, spent a long time minutely analysing the colour of the wines in front of him. Forty years after his premature freak death (run over by a car while mowing the nature strip outside his house) the Australian Wine Research Institute has developed a protocol for analysing the precursors of premature oxidation long before they are visible to the eye – but Ray Chan's? We shall never know.

Best producers:
Briar Ridge, Brokenwood*, De Iuliis*, Hart & Hunter, Keith Tulloch, Lindemans, McLeish Estate, Meerea Park*, Mount Pleasant*, Mount View Estate, Pepper Tree, Thomas Wines*, Tower Estate, Tyrrell's*

Mudgee
158 ha, total all varieties 3323 ha

Climate: Hot, MJT 23.3°C, E° Days 1663, SH 9, Rain 441 mm, Alt 480 m

This region lives in the shadows of the Hunter Valley in many ways, none more so than in the case of Semillon, yet the character of the wine in its youth, and as it matures, is similar to that of the Hunter Valley. A little more expression when young, and a slightly shorter lifespan, is no bad thing.

Best producers
Bunnamagoo Estate, Huntington Estate

Riverina
4576 ha, total all varieties 19 757 ha

Climate: Hot, MJT 24°C, E° Days 1719, SH 9.2, Rain 223 mm, Alt 130 m

Semillon destined for dry table wine is normally picked around mid-February. That dedicated for Botrytis Semillon will have to wait for late autumn/early winter rain in the second half of May to early June. If the rain does not arrive, or an ignoble form of rot takes over, the crop will be lost. If all goes well, a yellow-gold hued wine of intense lusciousness, the sweetness balanced by acidity, will be the result. While relatively quick-maturing, this is by far the best and most complex Botrytis Semillon made outside Bordeaux. De Bortoli is the leader, but McWilliam's and Nugan Estate are also adept at making the style. Ultra rich and generous when young, their lifespan is far, far shorter than that of Sauternes.

SOUTH AUSTRALIA

Adelaide Hills
70 ha, total all varieties 3659 ha

Climate: Cool, MJT 18.9°C, E° Days 1359, SH 8.4, Rain 352 mm, Alt 500 m

Sensory (or physiological) ripeness occurs at much higher – and more conventional – sugar levels than in the Hunter Valley or Mudgee. Even without partial barrel fermentation (often used) the wines have significantly greater richness and mouthfeel at all stages of their development over the first few years of their life. The impact is heightened with the blending of a portion of Sauvignon Blanc. Grosset's Clare Valley Adelaide Hills Semillon Sauvignon Blanc is in a class of its own.

WESTERN AUSTRALIA

Margaret River
572 ha, total all varieties 4771 ha

Yallingup Climate: Moderate, MJT 20.5°C, E° Days 1655, SH 7.6, Rain 221 mm, Alt 100 m
Wallcliffe Climate: Moderate, MJT 20°C, E° Days 1552, SH 7.4, Rain 261 mm, Alt 90 m
Karridale Climate: Cool, MJT 18.8°C, E° Days 1497, SH 7.1, Rain 305 mm, Alt 50 m

If the Hunter Valley has a mortgage on Semillon (except for Peter Lehmann), the grip of Margaret River Semillon Sauvignon Blanc and Sauvignon Blanc Semillon blends is of a similar strength. The variables come through the percentage of contributions of the two varieties, the percentage of new oak in the barrel fermentation, the percentage (if any) fermented in stainless steel, and the time the wine spends in barrel and/or tank prior to bottling. I somewhat arbitrarily list the producers of blends with Semillon the dominant partner here (and the handful of 100 per cent Semillons), those with Sauvignon Blanc dominant on page 74.

Best producers
Amelia Park, Burch Family Wines, Chapman Grove, Clairault | Streicker, Credaro Family Estate, Cullen*, Forester Estate, Happs, Hay Shed Hill, Juniper Estate, Larry Cherubino*, Lenton Brae, Miles from Nowhere, Rosily Vineyard, Stella Bella Wines*, The Alchemists, Vasse Felix, Windows Estate

Semillon

Chapter 4

The Classic White Varietals
Sauvignon Blanc

111 549 ha of Sauvignon Blanc is grown worldwide in 31 countries, with China accounting for 1 ha and the United Kingdom for 3 ha at the bottom, France in the lead with 27 931 ha. Those with over 500 ha are: Argentina 2296 ha, Australia 6803 ha, Austria 845 ha, Chile 12 159 ha, Czech Republic 804 ha, Germany 516 ha, Hungary 907 ha, Italy 3744 ha, Moldova 8151 ha, New Zealand 20 029 ha, Romania 4157 ha, Russia 951 ha, Slovenia 1061 ha, South Africa 9551 ha, Spain 4011 ha, Ukraine 3123 ha, United States 6584 ha.

International History

Anyone who has tasted partially ripe Cabernet Sauvignon grapes will not be the least bit surprised that in 1997 Sauvignon Blanc was identified as one of the two parents of Cabernet Sauvignon (Cabernet Franc is the other). That taste is a mix of crushed herbs, grass and asparagus, with a minerally acid framework.

The first mention of Sauvignon Blanc (under an old synonym, Fiers) was in 1534, in Rabelais' *Gargantua*[1], its first appearance as Sauvignon Fume in 1783–84 in Sancerre and Pouilly in the Loire Valley. This was its birthplace, not – as is commonly believed – Bordeaux.

DNA analysis carried out since 1997 has shown it has a parent–offspring relationship with Savagnin; since the latter is a very ancient variety, it is highly likely that it was the parent, a sibling (inter alia) of Gruner Veltliner and Verdelho, and a grandchild of Pinot Noir.

---

1 Jancis Robinson, Julia Harding and Jose Vouillamoz, *Wine Grapes*, Ecco/HarperCollins, 2012, p. 952.

Sauvignon Blanc is a dominant variety in the upper (or eastern) Loire Valley. Grown on the limestone soils of Sancerre (2961 hectares) and Pouilly Fume (1317 hectares), it reaches its ultimate varietal expression in Europe: razor sharp, pungently dry, with an intense mix of mineral, lemon, herb, gooseberry, grass and asparagus, occasionally with a more tropical, passionfruit-accented bouquet.

It is the third most planted white wine grape variety in France (after Ugni Blanc and Chardonnay), with 27 931 hectares in 2010. Bordeaux accounts for 7117 hectares of the total, and is always blended with some Semillon, and (less) Muscadelle.

There are those who thoroughly dislike the intensity of the wine, which they regard as rank and coarse, giving rise to the oft-repeated description of it smelling like cat's pee under a gooseberry bush. As often as not, such critics dislike the goat's cheese which comes from the same region.

One does not need to look outside Europe to work out that Sauvignon Blanc needs a genuinely cool climate to give a fine wine, but the lessons of Europe have certainly been repeated elsewhere across the New World. The moment the climate becomes a little bit too warm (as it is in Languedoc Roussillon, with 7357 hectares), the variety loses focus and the wines become bland at best, degenerating into oily coarseness at worst.

Taking it south in Italy out of the northern band of Fruili, Alto Adige and Collio (most of the 3744 hectares is in these regions) has been similarly unconvincing, the earnest attempts of Pierro Antinori notwithstanding; and Miguel Torres's attempts to find high-altitude sites in Spain's Penedes have been more brave than successful.

All of this activity, and that of the New World, has been of relatively recent origin (post-1960), which points to the commercial rewards of getting it right, for the wine can be a cash cow of considerable fecundity if handled correctly.

International Styles

FRANCE
27 931 ha

Loire Valley
4278 ha

With the odd notable exceptions, such as the complex barrel-fermented wines of the late Didier Dageneau, the simple, straightforward fermentation in inert vessels – stainless steel, epoxy or old oak – at often uncontrolled temperatures relies on the strength of character of the fruit. Indeed, Loire Valley winemakers generally regard red wine vinification as more demanding than that of white wine.

Sancerre and Pouilly Fume are the big names, Sancerre a little more lively and precise, Pouilly Fume more sturdy and complex. Both wines are best drunk when young, but bottles of Pouilly Fume in a forgotten corner of the cellar can provide a major surprise ten or 20 years later. (I can personally attest to that.)

Always made dry (in contrast to the Loire's Chenin Blanc), these are the ultimate food-friendly white wines at an affordable price, particularly in French restaurants. Moreover, the quality of the wines from the better-known makers is utterly reliable.

Best producers
A compressed list from (literally) hundreds of producers. Pouilly Fume: Henri Bourgeois, Jean Claude Chatelaine, Didier Dageneau*, Grebet & Fils, Château du Nozet (de Ladoucette); Sancerre: Henri Bourgeois*, Domaine Cotat, Francois Crochet, Lucien Crochet, Andre Dezat*, Alphonse Mellot*, Vincent Pinard, Christian Thirot

NORTHERN ITALY, AUSTRIA AND SLOVENIA
5650 ha

Sauvignon Blanc from the main areas in these countries is crisp and minerally, often with teeth-chattering acidity, and without any of the sweeter fruit characters of the Loire Valley or New Zealand. But they are admirable partners for cold seafoods and salads.

I find the dauntingly austere, searingly acidic wines of Austria's Steiermark region hard to admire, let alone love. Yet they are much in fashion, particularly in the Austrian domestic market. The one outstanding exception is Manfred Tement, who crafts beautifully proportioned Sauvignon Blancs with a carefully controlled amount of barrel ferment. The other producer of undoubted quality is Sattlerhof, with flowery, fragrant wines.

SOUTH AFRICA
9551 ha

South Africa's success with Sauvignon Blanc impressed me greatly when I first visited the Cape region in 1989. At the time I attributed it to what I assumed to be a much better clone than any we had in Australia. The climate of most of the sites seemed too warm for such success, so I reasoned that it had to be the clone(s). Next came the isolation of a yeast that heightened the varietal characters – this yeast is used in both South Africa and Australia to this day. But there turned out to be a third, far more sinister, reason: the illegal use of a synthetic essence, a practice unmasked by the bravery of Mr Wine in South Africa, Michael Fridjhon. It is no longer used.

The cool Elgin, Walker Bay, Elim and Hermanus regions are clearly well suited to Sauvignon Blanc, and have helped restore the reputation of the variety. While Sauvignon Blanc Semillon blends are not common, Vergelegen, Cape Point Vineyards and Delaire Graff show they can succeed impressively.

Best producers
Altydgedacht, Cape Point, Cederberg Private Cellar*, Paul Cluver, Dellaire Graff Estate, De Grendel Wines, Diemersdal Estate, Eagles Nest, Flagstone*, Hamilton Russell Vineyards, Hillcrest Estate, Iona*, Jordan Wine Estate*, Kaapzicht Wine Estate, Klein Constantia*, Kleine Zalze Wines*, Long Mount, Lord's Wines, Meinert Wines, Mulderbosch*, Nederburg Wines, Neil Ellis Wines, Rustenberg, Saxenburg, Steenberg*, Tokara*, Vergelegen, Villiera Wines, Warterkloof

CHILE
12 159 ha

Chile has had its problems with Sauvignon Blanc. One was the confusion with the distinctly lesser variety Sauvignonasse, an offspring of Sauvignon Blanc. Replanting and/or grafting has followed recognition of the issue, but in *Alice in Wonderland* tradition, Sauvignon Blanc now is a legal synonym for Sauvignonasse (and, of course, vice versa). The other was, and remains, the high yields; intriguingly, when visiting Chile it is always the vineyard down the road which has the high yields (of up to 20 tonnes per hectare).

On the other hand, it has enormous natural advantages: unlimited, pure water courtesy of the Andes; a gravelly soil not unlike that of Marlborough; no phylloxera; and a dry, low-humidity climate with minimal disease pressure.

Most of the wines are (sensibly) made in a no-frills fashion, cold-fermented in stainless steel and early-bottled. They appeal for their price and their softness of flavour, and are best drunk within 12 months of vintage. Viña Casablanca, from the cooler region from which it takes its name, is especially good, as is Villard, from the same region.

Best producers
Amayna, Arboleda*, Bisquertt, Calyptra*, Canepa*, Casa Marin, Casas del Bosque, Concha y Toro*, Montes*, O Fournier*, Santa Carolina, Santa Rita, Tekena*, Villard, Viña Casablanca, Viu Manent*

NEW ZEALAND
20 029 ha, 310 240 tonnes

The area planted to Sauvignon Blanc increased from 5897 hectares in 2004 to 20 029 hectares in 2014; it is improbable that it will become the largest grower of Sauvignon Blanc in the world, but it quite certainly offers unbeatable value for money.

Hawke's Bay
937 ha, 13 101 tonnes

While better known for other varieties, Hawke's Bay produces distinctive Sauvignon Blanc which has clear-cut varietal character, but is quite different from that of Marlborough. Without necessarily becoming flabby or phenolic, the wines carry a little more flesh and fruit-sweetness. They are also amenable to the same bag of winemaking tricks as are used in Marlborough to add subtle complexing nuances at the one end of the spectrum, and full barrel fermentation at the other end.

Best producers
Clearview Estate, Kim Crawford, Mission Estate, Sileni Estate*, Te Mata*

Martinborough | Wairarapa
318 ha, 2625 tonnes

At least within its original boundaries, this is a small region, and revered for the quality of its Pinot Noir and Chardonnay. But at one stage in the 1990s the trophy for Best Sauvignon Blanc at the Air New Zealand Wine Awards went to this region more frequently than to Marlborough. In my view the fruit characters and structure are closer to those of Hawke's Bay than Marlborough, but not everyone would agree with that. Whichever be the truth, these can be seriously good wines with excellent balance.

Best producers
Alana Estate, Borthwick Estate, Dry River Wines*, Gladstone Vineyard*, Johner Estate, Murdoch James Estate, Nga Waka Vineyard, Palliser Estate*

Marlborough
17 725 ha, 282 608 tonnes

As the stampede for Marlborough vineyard land gathered pace through the 1990s, all on the back of Sauvignon Blanc, wise industry observers shook their heads, saying the market was already oversupplied, that the variety wasn't a true classic in any event, and that the cascade of brands all tasted much the same. But then, as the new millennium arrived and screwcaps became de rigueur, an astonishing thing happened: notwithstanding California's totally successful efforts to stamp out the varietal character of Sauvignon Blanc (too aggressive, not food friendly), the United States discovered that Marlborough Sauvignon Blanc did not start and finish with Cloudy Bay, and fell in love with the razor-sharp fruit and tingling acidity of unadorned Marlborough Sauvignon Blanc.

While Pinot Noir joined Sauvignon Blanc in the race to plant ever more, the latter remains the symbol of Marlborough. Its high aromatics range through the herbaceous group of cut grass, green bean, capsicum and snow peas to the midway fruit group of gooseberry and green apple and the citrus group (grapefruit, lime and lemon), thence to tropical passionfruit, pineapple and even banana. Usually, the palate faithfully reproduces the flavours promised by the bouquet, with the variable in the mainstream stainless steel, early-bottled style provided by the texture, balance and mouthfeel.

Here the role of subtle winemaking techniques comes in; these techniques are designed not to alter or diminish the varietal fruit flavour but to add a degree of complexity. A small percentage may be barrel-fermented; a touch of Semillon may be added; part may be taken through malolactic fermentation; and, in high acid years, a small amount of residual sugar may be retained.

Several features help the low cost of production: the vast flat plains of Marlborough, created by rivers running backwards and forwards over many centuries; the round stones trapping just enough soil; the ideal climate; the generous yields; and the ease of mechanical harvesting.

Almost from the word go, Cloudy Bay has proved exceptionally skilled in its use of these techniques in response to the basic character of the vintage, rather than in a purely formulaic approach. Other makers have watched and learnt, and the high-acid, razor-sharp, teeth-chattering Sauvignons of cooler years are far less common these days.

Then there are the completely different barrel-fermented styles. Once again, Cloudy Bay has gone further than any other maker with its Te Koko, which is almost Californian in style, with masses of oak and malolactic influence. Others are more restrained, but there is still a gulf between the mainstream and the oaked styles. Given that exceptions prove the rule, I believe the mainstream approach suits the Marlborough fruit character more than the oaked style does, Dog Point the exception to the rule. Those who simply don't like the face of Sauvignon Blanc without make-up will have the opposite view.

Having swept all before it in the Australian market, there are signs that the infatuation with the wines may be set to cool somewhat. But the quality of Marlborough Sauvignon Blanc, its vivid flavours and its low cost all mean it will be here to stay.

Best producers
Allan Scott Wines, Ara, Astrolabe Wines*, Auntsfield Estate*, Bladen Wines, Brancott Estate*, Clos Henri*, Clos Marguerite, Cloudy Bay Vineyards*, Dog Point Vineyard*, Drylands, Forrest Estate*, Foxes Island, Framingham Wines*, Giesen Estate*, Grove Mill, Hunter's Wines, Jackson Estate*, Lawson's Dry Hills*, Mount Riley Wines*, Nautilus Estate*, Oyster Bay, Palliser Estate*, Saint Clair Estate*, Selaks Dryland Estate*, Seresin Estate*, Spy Valley, Staete Landt, Stoneleigh, Ten Sisters*, Vavasour Wines*, Villa Maria*, Whitehaven, Wither Hills Estate*, Yealands Family Estate*

Nelson
540 ha, 6107 tonnes

This is an isolated enclave, with its vineyards split between hillsides and stony, sandy flats. Higher rainfall can pose a vintage threat, but it is still a quality region. The basic style is a little fuller than that of Marlborough, and correspondingly slightly less racy.

Best producers
Brightwater Vineyards*, Kina Cliffs Vineyard*, Richmond Plains, Riwaka River Estate, Sunset Valley Vineyard

Australian History

The surprising – and consistent – growth of Sauvignon Blanc plantings seems utterly counterintuitive given the tsunami of Marlborough Sauvignon Blanc that, all on its own, has had a major impact on the national sales of all Australian white wines. The domestic plantings have been driven by the overall image of the variety, although Australian producers should watch the growth of the Pinot Gris/Grigio production.

The elephant in the South Australian room is the Lower Murray, where 500 hectares produce 16 588 tonnes, or 55 per cent of the state total. This is used to make low-cost wine, with only a faint degree of varietal expression. The Barossa Zone has 148 hectares producing 1037 tonnes, with rare exceptions to a nondescript style.

The Fleurieu Zone, with 333 hectares providing 1986 tonnes, and the Limestone Coast, with 494 hectares yielding 3311 tonnes, occupy the middle ground, producing wines that do have varietal character, especially in cooler years.

Australian Statistics

6803 ha, 81 442 tonnes, 1027 growers/makers

The production graph provides the clearest possible proof that Australian production has benefited from the Marlborough invasion, not been harmed by it. Those harmed are Riesling and Semillon.

Sauvignon Blanc: tonnes crushed in Australia, 1976–2012

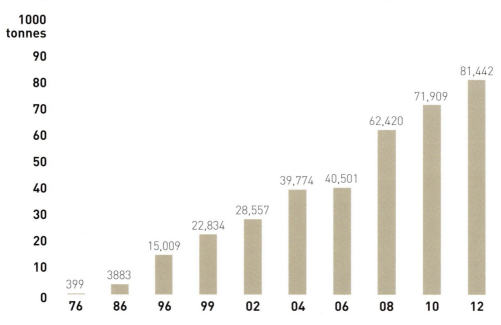

Australian Winemaking

The fastest way to the tryline (and to financial reward) is to treat Sauvignon Blanc in much the same way as Riesling or Semillon: either whole-bunch press it, or crush it, chill it by passing it through a heat exchanger, press it immediately and then either cold-settle or filter the juice before taking it to stainless steel for a cold, carefully controlled fermentation through to dryness. Aromatic yeasts are an advantage; wild yeasts have no part in this winemaking approach. Having taken this path, the wine is then racked, filtered and taken to bottle (with a screwcap) as quickly as possible, and put onto the market with the minimum delay.

This approach works well if the vines have been planted in an appropriately cool climate, the unruly canopy of the vine has been kept under control by trimming and/or leaf plucking, and the yield has likewise been controlled.

Even here, though, there is room for finesse. There is a range of philosophies and practices which are employed and which determine style: multiple pickings at different levels of ripeness and the use of different clones in the vineyard, for example. The choices in the winery are to crush and then press, or to go direct to the press with whole bunches; to ferment star-bright juice, protected by ascorbic acid and SO_2 at low temperatures in stainless steel, or to partially ferment in barrel under either controlled or ambient temperatures; to lees stir in tank or in barrel; to use partial malolactic fermentation or not; and to incorporate small amounts of Semillon, or move to a full blend, or bypass Semillon completely.

However, there is also an altogether different path available, particularly (though not exclusively) in climates such as the Margaret River or the Adelaide Hills. Here the winemaking model moves away from the Loire Valley to that of modern-day White Bordeaux – although there is a major question of which is the chicken and which is the egg in this equation.

This involves full barrel fermentation in French oak followed by barrel maturation, blending with Semillon that is similarly made, and partial (or even total) malolactic fermentation to produce a wine of radically different style. A subset alternative is to ferment the Sauvignon Blanc in stainless steel, leave it on lees, and then blend it at the end of the barrel maturation of the Semillon.

A problem can arise with cold fermentation of clear juice, followed by early racking and bottling, at all times excluding oxygen with the use of inert gas. This approach maximises the retention of varietal aroma and flavour, but can be linked with reduced, sweaty/burnt match aromas.

There is debate as to whether this is simply a varietal by-product of careful fermentation or a form of sulphide liberated by yeast during fermentation. At low levels it can be a valid way of achieving greater complexity with Chardonnay, but it doesn't suit Sauvignon Blanc. By contrast, an element of minerality can add a dimension to the structure and mouthfeel of Sauvignon Blanc. Paradoxically, it is an illusion: there are no minerals per se in the wine – the character simply reflects a low pH (sub 3.0) wine.

Australian Regional Styles

While Sauvignon Blanc is ubiquitous across Australia's wine map, there are two regions that can claim the variety as their own, even if their interpretations are very different: Margaret River and Adelaide Hills. Western Australia's Great Southern, Pemberton and Geographe regions also produce quality Sauvignon Blanc and Sauvignon Blanc blends.

WESTERN AUSTRALIA

Margaret River

798 ha Sauvignon Blanc, 572 ha Semillon, total all varieties 4771 ha

Wallcliffe Climate: Moderate, MJT 20°C, E° Days 1552, SH 7.4, Rain 261 mm, Alt 90 m

While 100 per cent Sauvignon Blanc is made with success, blends of Sauvignon Blanc and Semillon are equally numerous and sometimes more successful. Semillon in the Margaret River is itself distinctly herbaceous, to the point where its flavour merges seamlessly with Sauvignon Blanc. Its contribution comes through its minerally acidity, which tightens up the blend and assists its ability to age.

Whether straight or blended, the wine lends itself to a degree of barrel fermentation; a subtle nudge from French oak works well, and few makers have been tempted to overplay the oak.

The strong maritime influence on the climate seems to endow the wines with an extra dimension of mid-palate flesh without compromising their structure and acidity. On the other hand, intense tropical aromas of the kind found with Marlborough Sauvignon Blanc are seldom encountered. The trade-off between complexity and structure on the one hand and estery tropical aromas on the other is no cause for regret.

Best producers

Amelia Park, Brash Vineyard*, Burch Family Wines, Cape Mentelle*, Chapman Grove, Clairault | Streicker, Credaro Family Estate, Cullen*, Domaine Naturaliste, Evans & Tate, Flametree*, Flowstone*, Forester Estate, Happs*, Hay Shed Hill, Jane Brook Estate, Juniper Estate*, Knee Deep, Larry Cherubino, Leeuwin Estate, Lenton Brae, Miles from Nowhere, Preveli, Rosily Vineyard, Stella Bella Wines, The Alchemists, Thompson Estate, Umamu Estate*, Vasse Felix, Warner Glen Estate, Watershed Wines, Windance, Windows Estate*

Great Southern

444 ha Sauvignon Blanc, 25 ha Semillon, total all varieties 2752 ha

Frankland River Climate: Moderate, MJT 20.7°C, E° Days 1574, SH 7.6, Rain 203 mm, Alt 230 m
Mount Barker Climate: Moderate, MJT 20°C, E° Days 1548, SH 7.3, Rain 280 mm, Alt 220 m
Denmark Climate: Cool, MJT 18.9°C, E° Days 1512, SH 6.7, Rain 332 mm, Alt 130 m
Albany Climate: Cool, MJT 18.9°C, E° Days 1556, SH 7.0, Rain 285 mm, Alt 70 m

The climate of Great Southern's subregions of Albany and Denmark is maritime (courtesy of the Southern Ocean), that of Porongurup is intermediate, and that of Mount Barker and Frankland River is continental. No other region of Australia has such a diverse range. That said, the overall style of both single varietal and blends is largely homogenous, differentiated from that of Margaret River by its extra edge of minerally acidity.

Best producers
3 Drops, Alkoomi*, Harewood Estate*, Oranje Tractor, Singlefile, The Lake House, West Cape Howe, Wignalls, Willoughby Park, Yilgarnia

Geographe

152 ha Sauvignon Blanc, 114 ha Semillon, total all varieties 506 ha

Inland Climate: Warm, MJT 22.6°C, E° Days 1661, SH 8.2, Rain 222 mm, Alt 140 m
Coastal Climate: Warm, MJT 21.7°C, E° Days 1718, SH 8.4, Rain 185 mm, Alt 10 m

Willow Bridge Estate is the largest and best producer, using estate-grown fruit, and is situated on the inland part of the region. Its Sauvignon Blanc Semillons, one barrel-fermented, the other made in tank, are of exemplary quality.

SOUTH AUSTRALIA

Adelaide Hills

788 ha Sauvignon Blanc, total all varieties 3659 ha

> Climate: Cool, MJT 18.9°C, E° Days 1359, SH 8.4, Rain 352 mm, Alt 500 m

Adelaide Hills provides the best South Australian Sauvignon Blanc, capable of standing tall when compared to that of Margaret River. This comes as no surprise, but what is most surprising is the size of its plantings: only 10 hectares less than Margaret River.

It can blend well with Semillon, and both varieties have an extra measure of depth, texture and structure; on the other hand, Sauvignon Blanc needs both careful site selection and a cool to normal (not warm) growing season if it is to retain varietal character and intensity. In the better (cooler) vintages, the aromas have some or all of passionfruit, sweet pea, gooseberry and other tropical fruit, with the palate following a similar path. In the lesser (usually warmer vintages) these characters diminish, and more masculine, minerally notes become dominant.

Best producers

Arete, Barratt, Bird in Hand, Chain of Ponds, Geoff Weaver*, Guthrie, Hahndorf Hill, Karrawatta, Murdoch Hill, Nepenthe*, Shaw + Smith*, Sidewood Estate, Tomich**

NEW SOUTH WALES

Orange

Sauvignon Blanc 100 ha, total all varieties 1531 ha

> **Low Altitude** Climate: Warm, MJT 22.9°C, E° Days 1571, SH 8.9, Rain 414 mm, Alt 670 m
> **High Altitude** Climate: Moderate, MJT 19.6°C, E° Days 1250, SH 8.7, Rain 524 mm, Alt 950 m

Orange is the only region of note in the Central Ranges Zone. The higher elevation of the upper hillsides of Mount Canobolas have proved particularly well suited to the variety, producing attractive tropical notes and a relatively soft mouthfeel that has wide appeal.

Best producers

Bimbadgen, Brangayne of Orange, gilbert by Simon Gilbert, Orange Mountain, Philip Shaw, Ross Hill, Tamburlaine*

Sauvignon Blanc

Chapter 5

The Classic White Varietals
Pinot Gris | Pinot Grigio

43 687 ha of Pinot Gris is grown worldwide in 25 countries, China with 2 ha, the United States with the largest plantings of 5231 ha. Those with over 100 ha are: Argentina 297 ha, Australia 3767 ha, Austria 1914 ha, Canada 549 ha, Croatia 219 ha, Czech Republic 706 ha, France 2674 ha, Germany 4517 ha, Hungary 1624 ha, Italy 17 281 ha, Luxembourg 146 ha, Moldova 2042 ha, New Zealand 2451 ha, Romania 1301 ha, Slovakia 211 ha, Slovenia 501 ha, South Africa 261 ha, Switzerland 216 ha, Ukraine 685 ha.

International History

With the utmost reluctance, I have elevated Pinot Gris from the Second Tier status it occupied in the first edition of this book to Classic. I do so simply because of the volume of production: its 2012 Australian crush of 50 426 tonnes placed it ninth overall (both red and white grapes). By contrast, in 2004 the ABS did not list it, simply because its production was too small. Moreover, Australia seems certain to overtake Germany by 2017–18 and become the second largest producer in the world, leaving the United States in first place.

Pinot Gris is a colour mutation of Pinot Noir that occurred at different times in different places in Burgundy, and in the Pfalz and Baden-Württemberg regions in Germany.[1] The story of its spread across the old Austro-Hungarian Empire would have pleased Agatha Christie, as would the absolute plethora of names under which it travels.

It was called Fourmenteau/Fromenteau Gris in the Middle Ages (as was Savagnin), so a reference to a 'vin fourmentel' in 1283 could have been to either Pinot Gris or Savagnin;

---

1 Jancis Robinson, Julia Harding and Jose Vouillamoz, *Wine Grapes*, Ecco/HarperCollins, 2012, p. 817.

the first reliable reference to Pinot Gris came in 1711. Malvoisie is another synonym for Pinot Gris which appeared in the Middle Ages, and is still used in some parts of France, Italy and Switzerland. It need hardly be said that Pinot Grigio is the name most commonly found in Italy.

International Styles

The plethora of names are mirrored in the finished wine style. Alsace has had to rename Tokay d'Alsace, first as Tokay Pinot Gris, and since 2007 simply as Pinot Gris. In a warm vintage it is typically the most powerful of all the Alsace wines, which is saying something. Hugely floral, with an almost viscous palate of hyper-ripe peach or apricot fruit flavours, and high alcohol, it demands food as trenchantly as any Italian red.

Pinot Grigio from Italy's north and northeast, made in the traditional Italian fashion, and which was responsible for the flood of Pinot Grigio into the United States that began in the 1980s, is water-white, devoid of aroma and has barely any taste. It is the perfect example of what a New Zealand winemaker had in his mind when he said, 'Making Pinot Grigio is like painting a picture with white paint.' Jancis Robinson's pithy evaluation also demands to be quoted: 'Italy's Pinot Grigio has been the somewhat unfathomable success story of the early 21st century … as export markets such as the UK and US have flourished thanks to the generally fresh but anodyne style of these inexpensive wines.'[2]

Yet another manifestation is the Hungarian Szurkebarat, which takes up where the Vendage Tardive of Alsace stops. In a country which produces the most exotic late-harvest wine in the world (Hungary's Tokaji, which has absolutely nothing to do with Pinot Gris, however named), Szurkebarat stands tall as a wine with enormous extract.

Thanks to its naturally low acidity, the variety has to be grown in a cool climate if it is to provide a convincing wine. Thus its adoption by New Zealand is logical, and as at 2013 it was the third most widely planted white variety, its 2477 hectares producing 22 042 tonnes. Quite clearly, there will be no shortage of white paintings from New Zealand.

Australian History

Pinot Gris' emergence in the cooler regions of Australia made sense, and created such interest in the variety that it became a cult wine. The four key regions were (and are) Adelaide Hills, King Valley, Mornington Peninsula and Tasmania. The rush to plant the variety also extended to utterly unsuitable warm to hot regions such as Murray Darling (a whopping 695 hectares) and Riverina (a massive 1042 hectares). Their plantings of 1834 hectares are well over half of Australia's plantings, producing an average well in

---

2 ibid.

excess of 14 tonnes per hectare. The question is, will the demand for cheap, bland wine, with even less character than Italy's Pinot Grigio, continue to increase, or even stabilise at today's levels?

After getting that off my chest, there is in fact more to be said. First, the variety travels under two names in Australia: Pinot Grigio and Pinot Gris. In one of its less successful forays into the arcane world of marketing, the Australian Wine Research Institute sought to retrofit the difference between the two names by measuring the amount of extract in the wine. Reduced to the bare bones, wines with higher levels of extract could/should be labelled Pinot Gris, those with less extract Grigio.

On the face of it, this made sense. Grigio is the Italian model, and should be cheaper than Gris, the more expensive Alsatian version. There were, and are, three problems with this. First, the distinction has no legal or regulatory foundation. Second, many producers either didn't understand the protocol or decided not to use it. Third, only the top-end Gris versions were/are purchased by those consumers who are wine knowledgeable.

Australian Statistics
3767 ha, 50 426 tonnes, 470 growers/makers

Pinot Gris: tonnes crushed in Australia, 2004–2012

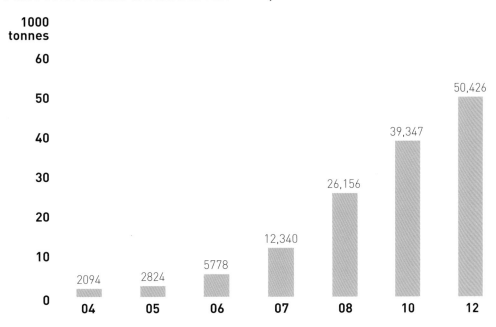

Australian Winemaking

The subtext is the vinification of top-end Pinot Gris, often involving some barrel fermentation (in used oak) compared with the no-frills cold fermentation in stainless steel, and early bottling, of Pinot Grigio. The best Grigios come from the coolest climates, which help preserve natural acidity. Thus Tasmania, the Mornington Peninsula and Adelaide Hills are the best credentialled. My problems with many, although not all, Grigios are first, the level of residual sugar left in the wine to bolster its flavour, second the price compared to that of commercial Riesling or Semillon, third, the amorphous varietal/flavour expression, and last, the fact that there is no hope of their evolving with bottle age into a wine even remotely comparable to Riesling, Semillon or Marsanne.

The evanescent flavours of Grigio/Gris stem from the ability of the vine to produce large crops which dilute the tree-fruit – headed by nashi pear – varietal flavour spectrum. The best Pinot Gris wines come from low to moderate crops, and use wild ferment of cloudy juice in predominantly used oak. They can be wholly satisfying wines, with a year or two of cellaring capacity.

Australian Regional Styles

TASMANIA

81 ha, total all varieties 1231 ha

South Coast Tasmania
Lower Derwent Climate: Cool, MJT 18.2°C, E° Days 1268, SH 7.3, Rain 280 mm, Alt 80 m
Huon Valley Climate: Cool, MJT 16.8°C, E° Days 1115, SH 6.5, Rain 458 mm, Alt 40 m
Northern Tasmania
Tamar Valley Climate: Cool, MJT 18.1°C, E° Days 1307, SH 7.5, Rain 321 mm, Alt 50 m
East Coast Tasmania
Climate: Cool, MJT 17.4°C, E° Days 1233, SH 7.2, Rain 388 mm, Alt 50 m

Tasmania larger than Mornington Peninsula? I won't be the only wine professional to be surprised by that. The climate is such, and the age of the vines is such, that embroidering Pinot Gris with barrel fermentation, etc, isn't necessary; pure varietal fruit with plenty of natural acidity (Pinot Gris has relatively low natural acidity) is all that is needed, some skin contact the main choice.

Best producers

Bay of Fires, Derwent Estate, Frogmore Creek, Gala Estate, Ghost Rock, Holm Oak, Moorilla Estate, Pipers Brook Vineyard, Stefano Lubiana, Tamar Ridge

SOUTH AUSTRALIA

Adelaide Hills
179 ha, total all varieties 3659 ha

Climate: Cool, MJT 18.9°C, E° Days 1359, SH 8.4, Rain 352 mm, Alt 500 m

The quiet achiever, producing more creditable Pinot Gris than any other region, a little fuller of varietal fruit and flesh than that of the other regions, and hence with broad appeal to most consumers prepared to pay for good Pinot Gris.

Best producers
Arete*, Bleasdale, Casa Freschi, Deviation Road, Hahndorf Hill, Heirloom Vineyards, Henschke, Petaluma, Pike & Joyce, Scott Wines

VICTORIA

Mornington Peninsula
89 ha, total all varieties 732 ha

Mornington Climate: Cool, MJT 18.9°C, E° Days 1428, SH 7.1, Rain 380 mm, Alt 60 m
Red Hill South Climate: Cool, MJT 17.5°C, E° Days 1240, SH 6.8, Rain 400+ mm, Alt 180 m

Arguably, it was this region, led by T'Gallant, that started the juggernaut, winemaker Kathleen Quealy always seeking new boundaries, and using striking, ever-changing labels. And today the region makes some of the most sophisticated Pinot Gris (as most of them are, rather than Grigio) on the market – but in very small volume.

Best producers
Baillieu Vineyard, Foxeys Hangout, Garagiste, Jones Road, Kooyong, Montalto*, Moorooduc Estate, Ocean Eight Vineyard, Paradigm Hill*, Paringa Estate, Quealy Balnarring Vineyard, Scorpo*, T'Gallant, Yabby Lake*

King Valley

151 ha, total all varieties 1255 ha (Alpine Valleys 46 ha, total all varieties 682 ha)

Milawa Climate: Hot, MJT 23.4°C, E° Days 1618, SH 8.9, Rain 309 mm, Alt 160 m

The higher the elevation of the vineyard, the more generous yields King Valley achieves, and Pinot Gris is inherently a large-yielding variety. If crop levels are controlled, and the site climate is correct, good wines are the result. The same applies to Alpine Valleys.

Best producers
Brown Brothers*, Chrismont, Dal Zotto, Gapsted, King River Estate, Pizzini, Symphonia

Chapter 6

Second Tier White Varietals

Chenin Blanc

World: 35 315 ha. Australia: 520 ha, 7308 tonnes, 149 growers/makers

General Background

The mix of historical research and DNA analysis that so illuminates Robinson's *Wine Grapes* places Chenin Blanc in the Loire Valley prior to 1496, the first confirmed reference to it via its specific birthplace of Anjou. What we don't know is how many years the vine had already been domesticated. DNA profiling shows that Sauvignon Blanc and Chenin Blanc are most likely siblings, the offspring of Savagnin and an unknown parent, making Chenin Blanc an uncle/aunt of Cabernet Sauvignon.[1]

In various parts of the Loire Valley around Anjou and Touraine it is used to make sparkling wine, dry white wine, and wines all the way from slightly off-dry to incredibly luscious and sweet. Chenin Blanc grown in the Loire Valley has very high natural acidity, which gives the sweet wines, in particular, great longevity (up to 100 years), but also tends to partially mask whatever sweetness is present, and makes the dry wines an unnerving experience for the uninitiated.

The great appellations within Anjour-Saumur are Bonnezeaux, Coteaux du Layon, Quarts-de-Chaume, Saumur, Savennières and the celebrated single-vineyard appellation of Coulée-de-Serrant. Within Touraine the top appellations are Jasnières, Montlouis and Vouvray.

---

[1] Jancis Robinson, Julia Harding and Jose Vouillamoz, *Wine Grapes*, Ecco/HarperCollins, 2012, p. 236.

The variety arrived in South Africa in the seventeenth century, where it was called Steen and was not identified as Chenin Blanc until 1965, by which time it was the dominant variety in the country. There, in California, in South America and everywhere else it has been grown, it produces a bland, neutral white wine bearing little or no resemblance to the great wines of the Loire Valley. There is at least one simple explanation for this: in the Loire Valley, the maximum yield is 50 hectolitres per hectare (2.5–3 tonnes per hectare) for the most modest appellation (and in practice much lower for the best wines, and even lower for the sweet wines), whereas its average yield in Australia, for example, is 14 tonnes per hectare (near enough to 100 hectolitres per hectare) if planted in a nice warm climate and given unlimited water to drink. And that, give or take a bit, is precisely how it has been grown and used outside the Loire Valley.

Australian Regional Styles

WESTERN AUSTRALIA

255 ha, 2854 tonnes

Chenin Blanc is to be found across the length and breadth of viticultural Australia; the only state without it is Tasmania. Its stronghold is Western Australia, where it was almost certainly brought by travellers arriving via the Cape of Good Hope. It has kept a position of importance in the Greater Perth Zone and its Peel, Perth Hills and Swan District/Swan Valley regions, but is also propagated throughout the South West Australia Zone regions.

It has always been an important component of what was once called Houghton White Burgundy (now called White Classic), and Houghton showed what could be achieved with 100 per cent Chenin Blanc by barrel fermentation and five to ten years' bottle age. Chenin Blanc also provided the template for the prolific Classic Dry White style of the Margaret River region, where it is blended with Semillon, Chardonnay and/or Sauvignon Blanc, its primary purpose being to reduce the production cost per bottle.

That said, the average quality of Western Australia's Chenin Blanc/Chenin Blanc blends is distinctly better than those of South Australia, and most of the wine is sold in branded bottles.

Best producers

Greater Perth: Paul Conti Wines; Margaret River: Amberley Estate, Aravina Estate, Cape Grace, Devil's Lair, Island Brook, Plan B, Stormflower, Swings & Roundabouts, Voyager Estate; Swan Valley: Coward & Black, Heafod Glen, Peel Estate, Sittella, Swan Valley Wines, Willow Bridge Estate

Chenin Blanc

SOUTH AUSTRALIA, VICTORIA AND NEW SOUTH WALES

South Australia: 148 ha, 2969 tonnes. Victoria: 39 ha, 646 tonnes. New South Wales: 63 ha, 830 tonnes

The difference between the quality, cost and end use of Chenin Blanc from Western Australia and those of these three other states is encapsulated in one word: yield. In Western Australia, it is 11.2 tonnes per hectare, and in the other three states (cumulatively) it is 17.8 tonnes per hectare. While there are exceptions (identified in the best producers for Western Australia), Chenin Blanc from Eastern Australia ends up in anonymous blends sold either as soft packs or in bulk, with the following exceptions.

Best producers
Barossa Valley: Kalleske, Schwarz Wine Company; King Valley: John Gehrig; McLaren Vale: Coriole, Dowie Doole; Rutherglen: Anderson

The future for the variety is encapsulated in the following chart.

Australian Statistics

Chenin Blanc: tonnes crushed in Australia, 1976–2012

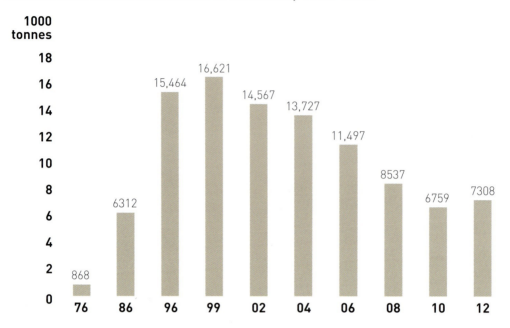

Colombard

Colombard

World: 32 944 ha. Australia: 2012 ha, 52 936 tonnes, 42 growers/makers

General Background
Colombard is one of the three varieties used in France to make Cognac and Armagnac. DNA has established that it was the result of a natural cross between Chenin Blanc and Gouais Blanc. Its plantings in France halved between 1968 and 1979, but has since made a minor comeback there, courtesy of its use to make fresh, crisp and light table wines, much as it has been used in Australia. Its home away from home is California, at one stage being California's most planted variety with 36 420 hectares before sanity (and Chardonnay) prevailed.

Australian Background
Colombard was first reported in the national crush in 1979, with 1680 tonnes. It disappeared for a while, and reappeared in 1987 with a little over 11 000 tonnes, progressing through to 30 000 tonnes in 1998, and reaching a peak of 77 500 tonnes in 2005. It has

retreated from that level, but its prodigious yield (26 tonnes per hectare in 2012) underwrites its future as a component of large-volume low-priced blends.

The ever-innovative Brown Brothers was the first company in Australia (to my knowledge) to release a varietal Colombard in 750-millilitre bottles. It was – and is – in the Riverland that so much Colombard was grown. It has consequently become the fifth most important white variety in Australia (ranked by volume), the handful of producers making varietal wines attesting to the fact that Colombard is the spine to be found in the millions of litres of generic soft-pack white wine and bulk wine.

There is one producer, however, which has performed an annual miracle of the kind generally restricted to Lourdes. It is Primo Estate, where winemaker/proprietor Joe Grilli somehow invests the wine with a racy, herbal tang one normally associates with Sauvignon Blanc (and a percentage of which was in fact blended in from time to time).

Australian Statistics

Colombard: tonnes crushed in Australia, 1976–2012

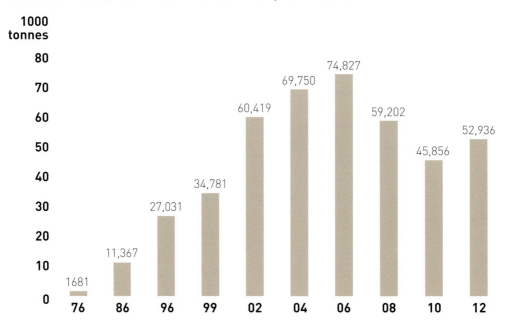

Gewurztraminer | Traminer

World: 14 355 ha. Australia: 902 ha, 10 540 tonnes, 163 growers/makers

General Background

This variety is barely entitled to second tier status in the Australian context, but it is a significant grape in Alsace, and is grown in 23 countries around the world. Moreover, as one of the most important clones of Savagnin, it has a rich and ancient history. As soon as the phrase 'ancient' is used, facts and myths collide. As has been pointed out in numerous parts of this book, assumptions or suggestions of the grape varieties of today having a demonstrable ancestry pre-1000 AD have no scientific basis.

While Robinson treats Traminer/Gewurztraminer/Savagnin as one and the same, both the ABS and Anderson's world planting records treat Gewurztraminer (and Traminer) as separate from Savagnin.

Indeed, the first recorded use of the name 'Gewurztraminer' was in 1827, and the circumstances of the use of the name suggest it was a mutation near Oppenheim, in Germany's Rheingau. The name was not used in France until 1886, but – thanks to Alsace – this is now its major domicile. Of France's total of 3168 hectares, Alsace accounts for 2928 hectares. Here it makes one of the most distinctive and recognisable of all white wines, with exotic aromas of lychee, rose petal, musk and warm spices. Its Achilles heel is its propensity to develop an oily, phenolic and bitter aftertaste.

Australian Background

The ABS statistics simply use 'Traminer', and local research suggests there may have been several importations. James Busby lists Savagnin du Jura, and this variety was first planted by George Wyndham at Dalwood in the Hunter Valley in 1839. Its name was soon corrupted to Sa-van-ah, and much later, at Penfolds' Minchinbury Vineyard at Rooty Hill on the north-western fringe of Sydney, to Tramea. This corruption is interesting for two reasons: first, it suggests knowledge of the correct name, and second, my personal tastings of the Michinbury Tramea in its youth left no doubt that it was Gewurztraminer.

South Australia may have received Savagnin Rose, the non-aromatic clone, as well as Gewurztraminer. Whatever be the case, its production in the generally stormy period between 2006 and 2012 was more stable than other second tier white varietals.

Orlando was one of the earlier producers to make Gewurztraminers with serious intent from its Eden Valley vineyards; much more recently Henschke has followed suit in the

Gewurztraminer | Traminer

Adelaide Hills, while the Macedon Ranges, Central High Country and the Yarra Valley are the logical places on the mainland.

This leaves Tasmania, where in the appropriate vintages all of the glorious qualities of perfectly balanced Gewurztraminer come to the fore: intensely fragrant rose petal, lychee and spice aromas, a similar array of intense yet delicate flavours on the palate, and a crystal clear finish. But it's on a typical micro-scale, 16 hectares producing 27 tonnes (with 14 growers/makers).

Indeed, outside the Big Rivers Zone of New South Wales, and the Lower Murray Zone of South Australia, all the players are in short pants. These two areas account for 627 hectares and 9140 tonnes. The wine may or may not be blended with similarly sourced Riesling, and either way, it will have palpable sweetness. Much is sold for plus or minus $10 a bottle (or in soft pack at an even lower price per standard drink) and has a devoted following. Chinese takeaway (or in house) is a natural match.

Best producers
Adelaide Hills: CRFT, Ochota Barrels*, Riposte; Eden Valley: Henschke; Margaret River: Flowstone*; Mount Barker: Castelli Estate*; Tasmania: Heemskerk*, Milton Vineyard*, Pipers Brook Vineyard*; Upper Goulburn, Victoria: Delatite*, Ros Ritchie*; Yarra Valley: De Bortoli

Australian Statistics

Traminer: tonnes crushed in Australia, 1976–2012

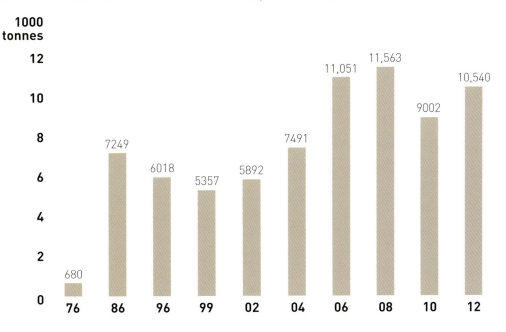

Marsanne

World: 1762 ha. Australia: 192 ha, 1709 tonnes, 111 growers/makers

General Background

DNA analysis of Marsanne points to a parent–offspring relationship with Roussanne; both varieties were mentioned by name in 1781, and all the evidence points to a birthplace in the eponymous commune near Montélimar in the Rhône Valley.[2] Here it is the variety which goes to make White Hermitage, and the small amounts of White St Joseph and White Crozes-Hermitage. Chapoutier is the foremost exponent of this relatively rare variety, making its Chante-Alouette, Ermitage de l'Oree, Ermitage le Meal and sweet Vin de Paille (straw-dried) wines. At a less exalted level, it is one of the six varieties permitted in white Cotes du Rhone. Varietal Marsanne wines from Languedoc are also gaining some traction.

There is a divergence of opinion as to whether the European plantings produce light, neutral wines or extremely heavy ones, and whether they need to be drunk when very young, or aged for 20 years or more. The one point of agreement is that Roussanne can be a synergistic blend-mate for Marsanne.

Australian Background

Marsanne was almost certainly brought to the Yarra Valley by the Swiss retinue of Charles Latrobe's wife, Latrobe being the first governor of Victoria. It was grown at Yeringberg and Chateau Yering, and it was the Yarra Valley which supplied Tahbilk with the cuttings that eventually led to Tahbilk's planting of 35 hectares, which, until a resurgence of the variety in France, was the largest single planting in the world (and undoubtedly the oldest, with the vines over 80 years old).

Mitchelton once employed substantial oak inputs, but (mercifully) has backed away from that approach, and has now blended the Marsanne with Roussanne and Viognier, backed by a 100 per cent Marsanne.

Yeringberg has returned to its former glory with the variety, and also lends strong support to the argument that the wine develops over a long period of time; here a roughly 50/50 per cent blend with Roussanne has established itself as one of Yeringberg's best wines.

The advent of the screwcap has proved beyond doubt the ability of Marsanne – particularly when made in a similar fashion to Hunter Valley Semillon or cool-climate

---

2   ibid., p. 601.

Marsanne

Riesling – to richly repay extended cellaring. The outstanding show success of Tahbilk's 1927 Vines Marsanne, hitting its stride when ten years old, leaves little more to be said. (1927 is the year of planting.)

Best producers
Barossa Valley: Hemera Estate*, John Duval, Smallfry; Geelong: del Rios of Mt Anakie; Goulburn Valley: McPherson*, Mitchelton, Tahbilk*; Margaret River: McHenry Hohnen; Orange: Tamburlaine; Rutherglen: All Saints Estate*; Yarra Valley: Ben Haines, Bird on a Wire, TarraWarra Estate, Yeringberg*

Muscadelle

World: 1637 ha. Australia: 82 ha, 602 tonnes, 45 growers/makers

General Background

This is a somewhat schizophrenic variety, relevant in only two countries, but used to make three very different styles, and – despite its name, first recorded in 1736 – unrelated to any Muscat variety. Rather it has a parent–offspring relationship with the ubiquitous Gouais Blanc.

In France it is blended with Semillon and Sauvignon Blanc to make dry table wines in the greater Bordeaux area and in the Bergerac region of the Dordogne. It is the luscious botrytised sweet wines of Sauternes, Loupiac and Monbazillac (the last in Bergerac) that are the most highly regarded wines, but Muscadelle's contribution to both dry and sweet wines has plunged from 6257 hectares in 1958 to 1589 hectares (2012).

Australian Background

In Australia only one producer uses the three-varietal blend (in the fashion of White Bordeaux) to make a dry table wine, but that wine is a very highly regarded one: Mount Mary in the Yarra Valley with its Triolet, a three-way blend with Sauvignon Blanc and Semillon. The contribution of Muscadelle averaged 9 per cent over the first 27 years of production.

The massive decline in production since the 1980s has come from the Riverland and other regions in which the variety has been used to produce table wine. Many years ago Orlando experimented with a number of varietals released in a wooden box, and Muscadelle was one of them. However, the limitations of the variety for dry white wine are all too obvious.

Muscadelle's other, and far better known, use is as the sole varietal grape to make the extraordinarily complex fortified wines of Northeast Victoria. Until the final ratification of Australia's Wine Agreement with the EU in 2010, the wine was called 'Tokay'. That use has been terminated, leaving makers with the choice of using 'Muscadelle' or the newly created name 'Topaque'. As with the other great fortified wine of the region, Muscat, there is a voluntary, but carefully monitored, use of four grades, beginning with (say) Rutherglen Muscadelle (or Topaque) as the entry point, then Classic, next Grand, and finally Rare. Each reflects greater average age and complexity. (For more detail see Muscat Blanc a Petits Grains.)

Muscadelle

When first made, it is a pale gold colour, and has a distinct varietal aroma, variously described as being like cold tea, malt extract, butterscotch or (occasionally) fish oil. Over the next 20 years the colour gradually turns to a dark, burnt sienna brown, with a tell-tale olive-green rim. The wine becomes steadily more viscous as the 'angel's share' evaporates through the cask. The amazing array of aromas, to which Christmas cake (rather than Christmas pudding) is added, are further complexed by the development of rancio. This is a character which is exceedingly difficult to describe but, once recognised, is never forgotten. It derives partly from aldehydes and partly from volatile acidity, and gives the fortified wine the cleansing cut which prevents it from cloying.

If forced to make a choice between Topaque and Muscat, many aficionados of the style (myself included) will opt for the more elegant Topaque over the voluptuous richness of Muscat.

Best producers
Barossa Valley: Seppeltsfield*; Glenrowan: Baileys of Glenrowan*; King Valley: Brown Brothers; Rutherglen: All Saints Estate*, Buller, Campbells*, Chambers Rosewood*, Morris Wines*, Pfeiffer*, Stanton & Killeen*

Australian Statistics

A word of caution when looking at the chart: the decline from its 1986 peak to 2006 is totally attributable to the waxing and waning of the export boom over this 20-year period, during which Muscadelle was used as a blend component in low-priced generic white table wine.

Muscadelle: tonnes crushed in Australia, 1976–2012

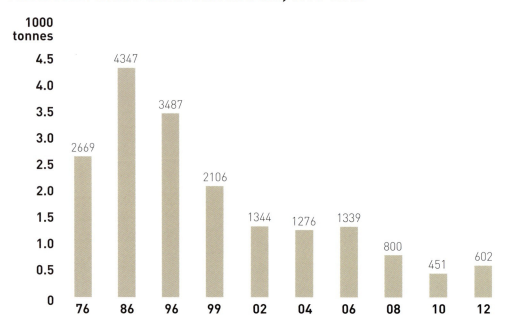

Roussanne

Roussanne

World: 1851 ha. Australia: 83 ha, 398 tonnes, 58 growers/makers

General Background

Roussanne has a parent–sibling relationship with Marsanne, its place of origin the northern Rhône Valley, and it is primarily used to provide Marsanne with more spine and perfume. The blend of these two varieties (there are no regulations specifying the percentage of each) produces the white wines of Hermitage, Crozes Hermitage and Saint Joseph. Like Viognier, were it not for its unpredictable yield, and susceptibility to powdery mildew, botrytis bunch rot and insect attack, its presence might well be greater. It is also found in the southern Rhône, where its natural acidity enables it to perform much better than Marsanne. In the 1960s its French plantings were a perilous 71 hectares, but by 2010 there were 1457 hectares, much of the growth in Languedoc-Roussillon. Italy ranks third, but with a mere 110 hectares.

Australian Background

It may seem barely warranted to treat the variety as important in the Australian context, but I justify this treatment because of its links with Marsanne and with some of the outstanding white wines from the northern Rhône Valley, and because of the love its handful of Australian exponents have for it.

The wines made by Yeringberg, where it is blended with Marsanne, are outstanding. A ten-year-old wine tasted recently looked to be no more than two years old. An increasing number of producers are also making a three-way blend including Viognier. St Huberts annually produces the most consistent 100 per cent varietal (and an occasional late-harvest botrytised version).

Best producers

Barossa Valley: John Duval, Turkey Flat, Yelland & Papps; Beechworth: Castagna; Grampians: The Story Wines; Margaret River: McHenry Hohnen; Nagambie Lakes: Tahbilk; Pemberton: Lillian; Yarra Valley: Bird on a Wire, St Huberts*, TarraWarra Estate, Yering Station, Yeringberg*

Trebbiano

World: 110 786 ha. Australia: 86 ha, 971 tonnes, 15 growers/makers

General Background

The first mention of Trebbiano appeared in 1303, but which type of Trebbiano isn't known. DNA research[3] has identified six varieties of Trebbiano that are all genetically distinct, as they do not share a common ancestor. They are Trebbiano d'Abruzzo, Trebbiano Giallo, Trebbiano Modenese (used mainly for vinegar!), Trebbiano Romagnolo, Trebbiano Spoletino and Trebbiano Toscano, planted all over the world.

It is grown so widely in Italy because of the high yields effortlessly achieved wherever it is grown there (and that is almost everywhere). In France, where the grape is known as Ugni Blanc, it is the most important base wine for Brandy/Cognac; in both countries its high natural acidity is its principal virtue. Thus in Italy it has historically been made to produce white wine with even less aroma, flavour and character than Pinot Grigio, which is saying something.

Australian Background

Trebbiano has all but disappeared off the statistical map in Australia, an amazing decline given that in 2004 its 689 hectares produced 7356 tonnes.

It may safely be assumed that only a tiny proportion of the Trebbiano crushed each year finds its way through to 750-millilitre bottles carrying the varietal name and sold by the five producers. Indeed, they almost certainly account for less than 5 per cent of the total. The remaining 95+ per cent is used as a neutral component in generic white wine casks, or as a base wine for the ever-shrinking production of Australian Brandy.

Best producers
Barossa Valley: Torzi Matthews; Beechworth: Amulet Vineyard; Glenrowan: Taminick Cellars; Heathcote: Stefani Estate; Rutherglen: Campbells

---

3   ibid., p. 1075.

Verdelho

World: 2005 ha. Portugal/Madeira: 397 ha. Australia: 1339 ha, 12 012 tonnes, 383 growers/makers

General Background

The genetic ancestry of Verdelho isn't certain, but it is most likely to have a parent–offspring relationship with Savagnin.[4]

Verdelho's home was Madeira, where it accounted for two-thirds of the island's plantings. In the wake of the dramatic shrinkage in the island's plantings of premium varieties following phylloxera, the annual crush decreased to little more than 100 tonnes per year. The modest increase in the interest in Madeira, particularly with the Port-based Symington family taking control of the major part of the island's production, has seen a modest increase in plantings to 47 hectares in 2010, dwarfed by the 350 hectares planted in the Douro Valley of Portugal.

Verdelho

---

4 ibid., p. 1119.

Australian Background

The success of Verdelho as a table wine in Australia is an extraordinary phenomenon without any obvious explanation. It is grown in 40 regions across the country, the three most important (at least in terms of producer numbers) being the Lower Hunter Valley, Margaret River and the Swan District of Western Australia – the latter two in more or less equal second place. Queensland's Granite Belt is a fellow traveller.

It was an early arrival in the Hunter Valley, but I can find no mention of it in James Busby's *Journal of a Tour*, which lists all the varieties he brought here. There was a crush of 272 tonnes in 1976; it was only in 1989 that it scraped over the 1000-tonne mark. Its extravagant growth has all occurred in the latter part of the 1990s; between 1998 and 2002 its tonnage trebled, putting it on a growth path similar to that of Merlot. It reached its high point around 2008, with a significant decline in plantings since then.

It is no easy matter to describe the varietal fruit aroma and flavour of Verdelho, although its texture and mouthfeel are distinctive, with a gentle viscosity and soft finish. Early-picked examples have a citrus/grass/lemon array of flavours, but most are picked fully ripe, when the wine has a mix of tropical fruit salad and honeysuckle aromas and flavours. Because it has a certain degree of presence, most makers have (quite rightly) come to the conclusion that it does not need oak. Most of it is consumed, as the maker intends, within days of purchase, but if you like a full-bodied wine, with ample helpings of honey, butter and toast, cellaring for up to ten years is more likely than not to repay the investment.

The plantings chart suggests the bell may have tolled for this variety in Australia, and it's not going to worry most consumers, who are busy tracking down the alternative varieties. It is striking that only one or two producers try to build structure or complexity in what is an easygoing, seldom exciting style.

Best producers

Geographe: Patritti; Granite Belt: Robert Channon, Sirromet, Symphony Hill; Heathcote: Flynns; Hunter Valley: Audrey Wilkinson, First Creek, Tallavera Grove, Tamburlaine, Tulloch, Two Rivers; Langhorne Creek: Bremerton; Margaret River: Ashbrook Estate, Sandalford, Wise; Swan Valley: Faber Vineyard, Garbin, John Kosovich, Mandoon Estate

Australian Statistics

This is a similar boom export-distorted picture.

Verdelho: tonnes crushed in Australia, 1976–2012

1000 tonnes

Year	Tonnes
76	272
86	983
96	2802
99	7290
02	16,121
04	18,979
06	19,857
08	20,464
10	14,247
12	12,012

Viognier

World: 11 847 ha. Australia: 1194 ha, 9031 tonnes, 515 growers/makers

General Background

The discovery (through DNA) that there is a parent–offspring relationship between Viognier and Mondeuse Blanche has overtones of vinous incest, for it makes Viognier either a half-sibling or grandparent of Shiraz, with which it can be so successfully co-fermented.

Given the messianic zeal with which Viognier is now promoted around the world, it seems inconceivable that in 1968 the only existing plantings, in the northern Rhône Valley, had shrunk to a mere 14 hectares. Its tenuous hold on life was in Condrieu, and the minuscule Château Grillet appellation contrôlée. There are now 4395 hectares in France, grown enthusiastically in the Northern and Southern Rhône valleys and (among other parts of the south of France) in Languedoc.

The reason for its near-disappearance was its extremely unreliable fruit set, and its sensitivity to powdery mildew. When the so-called Rhône Rangers appeared on the Californian scene in the mid-1980s, the interest in all things Rhône increased, and this included, in particular, Viognier. Unlike Marsanne and Roussanne, Viognier is vividly coloured, highly aromatic and strongly flavoured; I have always associated it with fruit pastilles, with its mix of apricot, honey, orange blossom, orange peel and peach aroma and flavour.

Its propensity to develop maximum aroma and flavour at relatively high alcohol levels means that its natural full-bodied structure is easily accentuated, and, while it is flooded with positive character, it is not an easy wine to pair with food. This, coupled with its diminished acidity and varietal expression if over-cropped or grown in overly warm climates, is causing some regions and/or winemakers to think again.

Australian Background

There is no question about the suitability of cool to temperate Australian regions for Viognier; some of the oldest plantings in the country are to be found at Elgee Park in the Mornington Peninsula. So it is no surprise that some of the most interesting wines have come from the Goulburn Valley, the Central Victorian High Country and various parts of the Adelaide Hills, including the Eden Valley.

The problem with the variety is the need to pick it at precisely the right moment in its ripening cycle and treat it with kid gloves in the winery. Unless all the right decisions

Viognier

are made the wine will either be bland, soft and lacking varietal distinction, or oily, flabby and phenolic. Thus some may argue its best use is as a co-fermented component of Shiraz, aping the Northern Rhône. A rapidly increasing number of top Shiraz wines from cooler regions are using 5 to 7 per cent Viognier for this purpose. Clonakilla has consistently been the leading producer of this blend, while Yalumba has quixotically sought (with success) to make Viognier its varietal standard bearer via its Virgilius, at the head of its Viognier family.

Best producers
Adelaide Hills: Fox Gordon, Ngeringa; Barossa Valley: Kaesler; Beechworth: Castagna, Indigo Wine Company; Canberra District: Clonakilla*, Jeir Creek; Eden Valley: Tim Smith, Yalumba*; Geelong: Farr | Farr Rising; Heathcote: Merindoc Vintners, Vinea Marson; Margaret River: Stella Bella Wines; Orange: Orange Mountain; Sunbury: Craiglee; Yarra Valley: Soumah, Yarra Yering, Yeringberg

Muscat Blanc a Petits Grains

World: 31 183 ha. Australia: 847 ha, 12 115 tonnes, 244 growers/makers

General Background

This is a very old variety grown in many parts of the world (at least 27 countries). It has a huge number of synonyms and is the parent, grandparent or great-uncle/aunt of 23 varieties with greater or lesser amounts of distinctive grapey flavours. It happens to be the smallest-berried member of the Muscat family, and makes the finest wines, whether dry or sweet. And to (partially) clear the air for Australian readers or producers, due to its ancient lineage, an unequalled number of variations in its skin colour can be found: from white (i.e. yellow) to orange, to gold, to pink, to red, to brown (though not to black), all without any change in the DNA.

Muscat of Alexandria was created as a natural cross between Muscat Blanc a Petits Grains and an ancient black table grape, Axina de Tres Bias, grown on Mediterranean islands; it is called Muscat Gordo Blanco in Australia.

Muscat Blanc a Petits Grains is the dominant Muscat (of any and all types) in France, most planted (in increasing amounts) to make fragrant, light-bodied wines in the south, notably Languedoc-Roussillon. Its use in sweet wines – so-called Vins Doux Naturel (fortified to stop the latter part of fermentation, and anything but natural) – is declining, in parallel with the move away from this style by consumers. It is also used in the sparkling wine Clairette de Die, which is grapey and lightly sweet.

Australian Background

In Australia it is used to make fruity, usually off-dry table wines that are pleasant, best chilled icy cold and consumed within months of coming onto the market (in their year of production). There was a time when a judicious amount was added to commercial Rieslings to bolster their taste – but that was in the far-off days when demand exceeded supply. Whether the wines are named after the colour of the skin of the grapes (notably Orange Muscat) or after Frontignac, which may or may not be white, the grape is the same.

Its most notable use is making the fortified Muscats (from the brown-coloured grape, also known as Brown Frontignac) of Northeast Victoria.

These wines use the following four-tier system. The precise words – and they are equally applicable to Topaque (except for the single reference to 'fresh raisin') – are:

Rutherglen Muscat – is the foundation of the style; displaying the fresh raisin aromas, rich fruit, clean spirit and great length of flavour on the palate which are the mark of all the Muscats of Rutherglen.

Classic Rutherglen Muscat – displays a greater level of richness and complexity, produced through the blending of selected parcels of wine, often matured in various sizes of oak cask to impart the distinctive dry 'rancio' characters produced from maturation in seasoned wood.

Grand Rutherglen Muscat – takes the flavour of Rutherglen Muscat to a still higher plane in development, displaying a new level of intensity, depth and concentration of flavour, mature rancio characters, and a complexity which imparts layers of texture and flavour.

Rare Rutherglen Muscat – is rare by name and nature. These are the pinnacle of Rutherglen Muscats, fully developed and displaying the extraordinary qualities that result from the blending of selected parcels of only the very richest and most complete wines in the cellar. Rare Rutherglen Muscats are only bottled in tiny quantities each year, but for those privileged to taste them, these are wines of breathtaking complexity, texture and depth of flavour.

The quality of these wines can only be understood by tasting them: they are utterly sublime, the heady ambrosia of the bouquet, the intensity of the mouthfeel, and the explosive complexity of the palate beyond all other wines.

Best producers
Table wine: *Barossa Valley: Grant Burge, Peter Lehmann, Rockford; Greater Perth Zone: Paul Conti Wines; Langhorne Creek: Lake Breeze Wines; McLaren Vale: Maxwell Wines; Rutherglen: Pfeiffer, St Leonards, Stanton & Killeen; Regional Blend: Primo Estate*
Fortified: *Glenrowan: Baileys of Glenrowan; King Valley: Brown Brothers; Riverina: McWilliam's; Rutherglen: All Saints Estate, Buller, Chambers Rosewood, Morris Wines, Pfeiffer, St Leonards, Seppeltsfield, Stanton & Killeen, Warrabilla; Swan Valley: John Kosovich*

Muscat of Alexandria

World: 26 515 ha. Australia: 2221 ha, 54 155 tonnes, 94 growers/makers

General Background

This offspring of Muscat Blanc a Petits Grains is very old, but there is no evidence to support the prior assumption that it originated in the Egyptian city of Alexandria.[5] Robinson observes that there is far more historical and genetic evidence to show that it originated either from southern Italy/Sardinia/Sicily or from Greece. Its curious pseudonym, Zibibbo (itself with various spellings), emanated from Sicily. DNA analysis shows it to be a cross between an ancient black table grape grown on the Italian island of Sardegna (Sardinia) and Muscat Blanc a Petits Grains. It has much larger berries than the latter, and much is grown for the table.

It has, from time to time, been made in precisely the same way as it is in the southern Rhône, notably by Jaboulet: into a lightly fortified wine which the French are pleased to call Vin Doux Naturel, which is entirely unnatural.

Wherever grown in Europe, and however made, Muscat of Alexandria is a powerful but coarse variety, with more total flavour and aroma than Muscat Blanc a Petits Grains, but without the finesse or subtlety.

Australian Background

In Australia the variety is officially known as Muscat Gordo Blanco (and appears as such in all the statistical records), but is also known as Lexia (by Brown Brothers in particular) and under its correct name, Muscat of Alexandria. It is chiefly grown in the Riverland; its average yield of 24 tonnes per hectare speaks for itself. But though its yield is limited, it can produce an intensely grapey wine which retains some elegance. Most of it, however, is used to provide a fruity punch to blends from altogether duller varieties, such as Trebbiano and even Riverland-grown Semillon.

Best producers

Clare Valley: Crabtree Watervale Wines; King Valley: Brown Brothers; Mudgee: Mansfield Wines; Riverina: Lillypilly; Swan Valley: Sittella; Southern Highlands: Southern Highland Wines

---

5   ibid., p. 684.

Chapter 7

Lesser White Varietals

The following varieties are grown in Australia. Some are more likely to disappear than to flourish, others are likely to become more important as their virtues in Australian conditions are better evaluated. The overall number of varieties seems certain to increase, with those that have proved their worth in the hot, dry regions of Italy and Spain to the fore.

Aligote

World: 36 120 ha. Australia: <0.5 ha, 1 grower/maker

This is the result of a natural cross between Pinot Noir and Gouais Blanc, first named in 1780.[1] Its plantings in France (1953 hectares) are dwarfed by those of Eastern Europe, which is mainly responsible for the global total of 36 120 hectares. It is by far the least of the Burgundian grapes, except for one small appellation based on the town of Bouzeron, where Bourgogne Aligote-Bouzeron is grown and made by notables such as Aubert de Villaine, co-owner and director of Domaine de la Romanée-Conti. Its lower yield (the maximum permitted is 45 hectolitres per hectare, or around 2.5 tonnes per acre) gives the wine the substance it lacks elsewhere in Burgundy and, even more, in the prolific plantings through Eastern Europe. Even at its best, it produces a rather austere, distinctly flinty, bone-dry wine.

Producer

Hickinbotham of Dromana (blended with Chardonnay)

---

1 Jancis Robinson, Julia Harding and Jose Vouillamoz, *Wine Grapes*, Ecco/HarperCollins, 2012, p. 34.

Arneis

Arneis

World: 1123 ha. Australia: 153 ha, 652 tonnes, 50 growers/makers

The variety was first mentioned in various records in northern Italy in the fifteenth century, its principal region being Piedmont. Local terminology described it as 'the little rascal', and also suggested it was interplanted with Nebbiolo to attract birds to its grapes, thus protecting Nebbiolo. Where part of the Arneis crop was left, it was used by some makers to soften Nebbiolo. Not surprisingly, it was also called Nebbiolo Bianco, but it is not genetically related to Nebbiolo.

Because it was difficult to grow, it had all but disappeared by the 1960s, when only Vietti and Bruno Giacosa bottled it. Then a single wine, beautifully made and labelled – Ceretto Blangé – took Italy by storm, becoming the country's most popular wine.[2] But this did not ameliorate the bunch-rot challenges caused by its tightly compact bunches, nor its general propensity to downy mildew.

---

2   Ian D'Agata, *Wine Grapes of Italy*, University of California Press, 2014, p. 182.

For obscure reasons, Australia is the only other country to have recorded plantings, and it has done so with enthusiasm. D'Agata says it has been planted in California and Oregon[3], but those plantings are clearly very small.

Arneis in Australia has the citrus/lemon floral notes in the cool-climate regions, the warm-region versions sharing the almond/honeysuckle/nougat/pear characters found in Piedmont. The better producers include Bird in Hand, Chrismont, Crittenden Estate, Dal Zotto, Holm Oak, Millbrook, Oakridge Estate, Pizzini, Port Phillip Estate, Sam Miranda, Tertini, Thick as Thieves and YarraLoch.

Assyrtiko

World: 902.5 ha (Greece). Australia: <0.5 ha, 1 grower/maker

A fascinating variety, linked with the island of Santorini for a very long (albeit not precisely known) time. As the modern Greek wine industry has taken shape, other regions in the country have taken note of Assyrtiko's qualities, and it is now being grown in a number of regions. Its greatest endorsement comes courtesy of Konstantinos Lazarakis MW who, in his definitive work *The Wines of Greece*, says, 'Arguably the finest Greek white grape variety today, Assyrtiko has the rare ability of balancing breadth and power with high acidity and steely austerity.'[4] In its stronghold of Santorini, it is largely trained by laying the canes in a circle around the centre of the vine, the result resembling a giant bird's nest. The reason for this approach is the relentless, scorching winds of summer. Also, attempts to train it on a low trellis have not succeeded. It is not, as Robinson suggests[5], pruned back to its roots; it does form a permanent trunk, albeit a unique one, curled rather than straight.

While it is not a variety that needs oak fermentation and/or maturation, the best producers on Santorini (Domaine Sigalas, Gaia, Thalassitis, Argyros Winery and Boutari) do make limited quantities of barrel-fermented wines. On Santorini it represents around 70 per cent of the vineyard area, but the total plantings are still relatively small; Anderson has global plantings at 902 hectares, although the split between Santorini and the other Greek regions growing and producing the wine isn't known. As at 2014 there was a single Australian producer, Jim Barry Wines, which imported cuttings, patiently waited for the quarantines process to be completed, and then had the vines propagated by Yalumba in its nursery. The first experimental wine (15 litres) was made in 2014, and

---

3   ibid., p. 183.
4   Konstantinos Lazarakis, *The Wines of Greece*, Mitchell Beazley, 2005, p. 56.
5   Robinson, Harding and Vouillamoz, *Wine Grapes*, p. 62.

commercial production is expected in 2016. It is thus prophetic that Robinson should conclude the entry on Assyrtiko by writing, 'It is surely only a matter of time before this exciting variety goes travelling.'[6]

Aucerot

World: 2785 ha. Australia: <1 ha

This is the Australian name for Auxerrois, one of the numerous offspring of Gouais Blanc and Pinot Noir, and hence a sibling of Chardonnay. Most of France's plantings (2360 hectares) are in Alsace, but Aucerot is rarely acknowledged on labels. Germany has 285 hectares and Luxembourg 184 hectares.[7] It is a low-acid variety, best suited to cool regions. William Macarthur wrote about it in the 1840s (spelling it Aucarot) and in March 1898 the *Maitland Weekly Mercury* had this to say on visiting Tyrrell's: 'A deal more land will be planted with a new grape of which Mr Tyrrell possesses a small area named Aucerot, given by Mr Lindeman and described as the king of white grapes.' Mount Pleasant, too, had plantings, and Maurice O'Shea made celebrated, long-lived wines from it.

It also gained a foothold in Victoria, and was replanted after phylloxera. It is presumably the source of the Aucerot now made by Ciavarella (in the King Valley); it is also sometimes blended with Semillon. The King Valley is a more logical place than the Hunter Valley, for it's an early-ripening variety, and rapidly loses its acidity in warm climates.

Producer
Ciavarella

Biancone

World: 7 ha. Australia: <1 ha, 2 growers/makers

Biancone is correctly called Biancone Gentile, a very rare Corsican variety (6 hectares). Australia is its other main habitat. It is described by AJ Antcliff (of the CSIRO) in his monograph *Major Wine Grape Varieties of Australia*, published in 1979. There were 44 hectares of the variety then in production, with a yield regularly reaching 30 tonnes per hectare, but it has all but disappeared since. Antcliff comments that in the Riverland

---

6   ibid.
7   ibid., p. 68.

Biancone is regarded as a variety for distillation, but there is some evidence that it can produce a distinctive dry white wine in cooler areas.

Producers
Mount Anakie (prior), Lake Moodemere (late harvest)

Chasselas

World: 13 119 ha. Australia: <1 ha, 2 growers/makers

One claim to fame of Chasselas is its astonishing number of synonyms, reflecting the fact that it is an old variety. Another is that it is grown from Spain to Luxembourg. It is France's most common table grape, but in Switzerland (where it is known as Fendant) it is regarded as a high-quality wine grape. Its most likely birthplace was Lake Geneva.[8] It is propagated in various parts of Europe under its innumerable obscure synonyms, but its high vigour and generous yield means its reputation will never be great.

Kerridge and Antcliff recorded 100 hectares in production in Australia in 1996[9]; the Grampians in Victoria was home to most, with both Seppelt and Montara then making varietal wines (called Chablis by Seppelt). It now has a more ephemeral presence.

Producer
Cathcart Ridge Estate (previous)

Clairette

World: 2820 ha. Australia: <1 ha, 4 growers/makers

This low-acid, easily oxidised wine was once endemic in the south of France, and is one of the official grapes for Châteauneuf-du-Pape, but is of rapidly declining importance, down from 14 099 hectares in 1958 to 2820 hectares in 2010. Relatively speaking, it is an old variety, first identified between 1490 and 1575.[10] Known also as Blanquette in the Hunter Valley, it was once quite widely planted there and made by Penfolds (among others), who relied on early picking to retain some fresh acidity.

---

8   ibid., p. 232.
9   George Kerridge and Allan Antcliff, *Wine Grape Varieties*, CSIRO, 2000, p. 43.
10 Robinson, Harding and Vouillamoz, *Wine Grapes*, p. 250.

Producers
Honeytree Estate, jb Wines

Cortese

World: 2953 ha. Australia: <1 ha, 3 growers/makers

An obscure Italian grape, its parents unknown, mainly associated with Piedmont, but also grown elsewhere. D'Agata chronicles its heyday in the 1960s and '70s, and its abrupt fall from grace in the '80s[11], with too much neutral, tart and meagre wine made from overcropped vines – a flavour description similar to that of its Australian wine. Indeed, its survival in Italy is due to its superior qualities as a table grape.

Producers
Ceravolo, Lost Valley

Doradillo

World: 39 812 ha. Spain: 39 741 ha. Portugal: 148 ha. Australia: 71 ha, 2 growers/makers

The correct name of this Spanish/Portuguese variety is Cayitana Blanca, with Jaén Blanco a synonym. It is not related in any way to Doradilla, but what's in a name? It's a grape of indifferent quality, but is a substantial producer of cannon fodder for fortified wines. Commonly known in Australia as Dora, it is in fast retreat; in 1981 there were over 1900 hectares in production, producing 33 300 tonnes of grapes. Now the plantings are in freefall into extinction. Whatever grapes are left are used either for distillation or for the lowest quality bulk table wine. Its Spanish plantings are all used for Sherry, its Portuguese ones for fortified wine.

Fiano

World: 1377 ha. Australia: 88 ha, 340 tonnes, 50 growers/makers

An old – possibly very old – variety from Campania in Southern Italy, specifically mentioned in 1240.[12] It has been suggested that both Pliny the Elder and Columella wrote about it in Roman times, but it is impossible to be certain: these and other authors often used the same name for any number of varieties. Fiano was widely planted until the

---

11 D'Agata, *Wine Grapes of Italy*, pp. 259–60.
12 Robinson, Harding and Vouillamoz, *Wine Grapes*, p. 350.

Fiano

arrival of phylloxera in the early 1900s, and was teetering on the edge of extinction until that champion of forgotten varieties, Antonio Mastroberardino, revived it in the 1970s. New plantings since that time have lifted the amount to over 1300 hectares.[13] D'Agata writes, 'I think Fiano may well be Italy's greatest native wine grape: only Verdicchio can lay a similar claim to that title.'

The CSIRO imported the first vines for Australia in 1978 (followed by Chalmers in 1998), and there has been considerable interest in the variety for its flowery bouquet and lively acidity underlying notes of citrus, apple and pear; barrel fermentation has also been used to good effect. Plantings in South Australia increased, from 10 hectares in 2006 to 28 hectares in 2010, and in 2014 to 43 hectares.

Producers
ArtWine, Beach Road, Bremerton, Chalmers*, Coriole*, Ducks in a Row*, Ekhidna, Fox Gordon, Galli Estate, Geoff Hardy, Jericho, Larry Cherubino, Mount Eyre Vineyards, Oliver's Taranga Vineyards, Rosemount Estate*, Rutherglen Estates*, Savina Lane, Scott Wines, Sutton Grange, Symphony Hill

---

13   D'Agata, *Wine Grapes of Italy*, p. 285.

Furmint | Harslevelu

Furmint – World: 5276 ha. Harslevelu – World: 1856 ha

Furmint is the major partner in the great dessert wine of Hungary, Tokaji, the junior partner being Harslevelu. It is also grown in Burgenland in Austria, where it also goes to make rich dessert wines. The late octogenarian Lesley Fritz grew Furmint and Harslevelu in the cool and relatively dry climate of Sutton Forest in the Southern Highlands region of New South Wales to make table wines, but the winery ceased making the wines after his death. The Perth Hills region is its current haven.

Producer
Briery Estate

Garganega

World: 15 402 ha. Australia: 2 ha, 9 growers/makers

While some researchers suggested this variety was of Greek origin, DNA profiling establishes that it is an ancient Italian variety first mentioned in the thirteenth century[14], and with a number of genetic relatives spread through Italy all the way down to Puglia. Its most important role is as a minimum 70 per cent component of the ubiquitous Soave of the Veneto region of northeast Italy, Trebbiano di Soave making up most of the remainder, albeit with a dash of Chardonnay, to build the flavour profile. Unless the normal high yield of Garganega is kept under tight control, the wine is decidedly anaemic; if controlled, the result is a fresh, feather-light wine with intriguing nuances of lemon and nashi pear combining with strong minerally acidity on the finish. Anselmi and Pieropan are among the best producers of Soave imported into Australia.

Producers
Domain Day, Politini, Primo Estate, Redbank, Scott Wines

---

14 Robinson, Harding and Vouillamoz, *Wine Grapes*, p. 392.

Garganega

Gouais Blanc

World: 1 ha. Australia: 0.2 ha, 1 grower/maker

A former inhabitant of the Jura in France, but no more. Chambers Rosewood of Rutherglen has a small patch of 100-year-old vines, and nicknames the wine 'gooey'. Once a single varietal, but now usually blended. Only three plantings in the world.

Gouais Blanc is a case study illustrating why the vines and grapes of Roman, Greek or Egyptian times (let alone the dawn of viticultural time) have long since become extinct. It is described by Robinson et al. as one of 'Western Europe's most ancient and prolific grape varieties'[15], yet the first reliable references to it were in 1539 and 1540. Moreover, claims that it originated in Eastern Europe have no DNA or other evidence to support them: on the contrary, its origins have been pinpointed in central northeastern France and (adjoining) southwestern Germany.

DNA analysis has established that Gouais Blanc is the parent of at least 81 varieties in Western Europe, yet (like its bedmate Pinot Noir) its parents are unknown, and it is virtually extinct.

---

15   ibid., p. 419.

The ultimate indignity has befallen it in France, where it has been banned – only a single small vineyard remains, and the wine is not commercially bottled.

Producer
Chambers Rosewood

Greco | Greco Bianco

World: 1762 ha. Australia: <1 ha, 3 growers/makers

These two varieties provide endless confusion and ongoing assertions of conflicting DNA analysis of Greco (claimed by some, denied by others, to be genetically the same as Asparinio) and Greco's finest wine, Greco di Tufo – the name is simply that of the DOCG in which it is made.

Greco was at one time believed to have been introduced to southern Italy in the sixth or seventh century BC.[16] Even more romantic is the notion that it is a descendant of a variety described by the Roman authors as coming from Mount Vesuvius. Mastroberardino is one of its champions. Its wines are full-bodied but minerally, with faint apricot kernel

Greco

16 ibid., p. 434.

Grillo

aromas plus notes of herb. In Australia, flavours of custard apple, pink grapefruit and white peach are framed by bony minerality.

Greco Bianco is a different variety altogether, not a clone or biotype of Greco. D'Agata says, 'There are few more confusing Italian grape varieties than Greco Bianco', and goes on to observe that Calabria is awash with Greco Biancos of all sorts.[17] Because of its (so far) extreme rarity in Australia, I shall pass on.

Producers
Beach Road (Greco), Chalmer (Greco), Swan Valley Wines (Greco Bianco)

Grillo

World: 6295 ha. Sicily: 5590 ha. Australia: <1 ha, 2 growers/makers

An important Sicilian white variety, also grown in mainland Italy. It is a relatively new variety, a natural cross between Catarratto and Muscat of Alexandria[18], which found

---

17   D'Agata, *Wine Grapes of Italy*, pp. 54–55.
18   Robinson, Harding and Vouillamoz, *Wine Grapes*, p. 439.

its way to the northwestern coast of Liguria, where it is called Rossese Bianco. It was widely planted after the arrival of phylloxera in the 1880s, but – until recently – was in turn replaced by more productive varieties. In Sicily it is one of the main components of Marsala; its use in this luscious fortified wine is far removed from its other role as a full-bodied Sicilian white wine, slightly herbaceous or floral, but not as aromatic as its Muscat parent might suggest. By Jingo!'s 2012 Murray Darling Grillo, tasted in January 2013, had attractive grainy acidity and a savoury flavour.

Producer
By Jingo!

Kerner

World: 4070 ha. Australia: <1 ha, 1 grower/maker

A German-bred cross between the Austrian red grape Trollinger and Riesling, released in 1969. Notwithstanding its recent birth, it is regarded as the best of the innumerable German crossings, simply because its taste is closest to that of Riesling, and it has similar longevity.

Producers
Kabminye, Robinvale

Malvasia

This 'variety' turns the usual pattern on its head. Usually, different (sometimes many) names are used for what is the same variety, sometimes to the dismay of those who cherish 'their' grapes as superior to others. Robinson uses the shorthand 'Pinot something' where the 'somethings' cover many different manifestations which are in fact genetically the same.

Here the situation is reversed: Robinson lists 17 Malvasia 'somethings' that are not genetically related[19], many having synonyms which make what is already a nightmare of complexity even more challenging. One issue is cleared up: the supposed Greek origin of the Malvasias is contradicted by the diversity of the DNA.

---

19 ibid., pp. 575–86.

Malvasia Istarska

Malvasia Istarska

World: 2740 ha. Croatia: 1705 ha. Slovenia: 740 ha. Italy: 296 ha

The variety propagated by Chalmers Nurseries, Malvasia Istarska, pithily described by Robinson as the emphatic white wine grape of Croatia's Istria Peninsula.[20] She adds, 'It seems like a variety that could be of real interest elsewhere, hence Chalmers' interest in it.'[21]

Montils

World: 1312 ha. Italy: 360 ha. Australia: <1 ha

A minor variety used in the production of Cognac, but only just hanging in there, with 165 hectares in France. Robinson says it is most likely a progeny of the omnipresent Gouais Blanc[22], and old vines in Bordeaux's Entre-Deux-Mers in 1960 suggested it may

---

20 ibid., pp. 386–87.
21 ibid., p. 587.
22 ibid., p. 655.

once have been used in making table wine. It seems likely that it was introduced into Australia in the nineteenth century, and some vines made their way to the Hunter Valley, and in particular to Mount Pleasant, where a tiny amount is still grown and recently has been used in a co-fermented blend with Shiraz, continuing the use made of it by Maurice O'Shea. The planting (two rows) is being increased by Mount Pleasant, but is only intended for co-fermentation. However, it is not listed as one of the varieties imported by James Busby.

Moscato Giallo

World: 1312 ha. Australia: >1 ha, 5 growers/makers

D'Agata points out that in contrast to Malvasia, most of the Moscatos are related.[23] DNA analysis shows that Moscato Giallo has a parent–offspring relationship with Muscat Blanc a Petit Grains[24] and is therefore related to at least five other Muscat varieties. This analysis disproved the long-cherished idea that Moscato is of truly ancient Greek parentage. In Italy it is mainly grown in the north – for varietal wines in Trentino and

Moscato Giallo

---

23 D'Agata, *Wine Grapes of Italy*, pp. 150–51.
24 Robinson, Harding and Vouillamoz, *Wine Grapes*, p. 668.

Alto Adige – but is also used for sparkling and passito (dried grape) wines. In Australia it is used in Moscato (the wine style) either as a straight varietal (with lemon gelato flavour) or blended. Robinson notes only that it is grown in Switzerland, whereas Anderson notes significant plantings in a number of countries: Italy (1127 hectares), Brazil (126 hectares) and Croatia (59 hectares).

Producers:
Chalmers, Dos Rios, Ducks in a Row (blend), Gracebrook Vineyards (blend), Stefano de Pieri (blend)

Muller-Thurgau

World: 22 753 ha. Australia: 5 ha, 11 growers/makers

Muller-Thurgau arrived on the scene in 1883, a fully grown adult without any childhood. It was a crossing of Riesling and Sylvaner bred by Dr Muller, and was promoted as having the best features of those two varieties. After a short pause (until 1938), it became Germany's most widely planted grape variety, the foundation of the New Zealand wine industry's move away from hybrids, and the most important variety in England.

Plantings in those countries have reduced dramatically, but Germany is still by far the largest grower, with 13 480 hectares; New Zealand has shrunk to a derisory 79 hectares. Austria (2044 hectares), the Czech Republic (1572 hectares), Hungary (2098 hectares), Italy (1312 hectares) and Slovakia (932 hectares) all find a use for the variety. Even though its high yield will ensure that it never disappears altogether, its Achilles heel is obvious enough: it makes boring white wine. Australia's 5 hectares is an approximate figure.

Producers
Bress, Galafrey, Herons Rise

Nosiola

World: 79 ha. Australia: <0.5 ha, 1 grower/maker

This extremely rare grape is grown in the Trentino–Alto Adige region of northern Italy, with only 193 hectares planted in 2000. Anderson's 2010 figure is even less, at 79 hectares. Its long-term use has been to make high quality Vin Santo.[25] The total area dedicated to

---

25 ibid., pp. 737–38.

Nosiola

Vin Santo is said to be only 10 hectares. The remainder has been used to make a fragrant white wine, of modest but growing interest.

It was always considered a worthy table grape[26], but until 1822 was only used in blended table wines. In that year the first Vin Santo was made from it, which D'Agata says won a diploma of elegance at the Melbourne International Exhibition of 1825, a date preceding the foundation of Melbourne by nine years, and of the exhibition by 56 years.

Producer
Chalmers

Ondenc

World: 8 ha

A rapidly disappearing variety in France, having its moment in the sun when (falsely) thought to be partly resistant to phylloxera. It was also used to make Armagnac, and

---
26 D'Agata, *Wine Grapes of Italy*, p. 375.

even grown as a table grape. Its plantings have tumbled from 1589 hectares in 1958 to 8 hectares in 2012, and it has become commensurately obscure.

I have commented earlier (page 121) on the at times bewilderingly large number of synonyms (up to 50) for a given grape variety tracked by Robinson. These come about where the same variety has been grown over centuries in countries with different languages, and with none of the identification needs or skills of the twentieth and twenty-first centuries. Ondenc is not an important grape in Australia, and will become a curio before long. Its essential lack of aroma and flavour means it will not be swept up in the wave of enthusiasm for alternative varieties. But given we have a common language across Australia, and the grape has been here (at most) for 180 years, it becomes an object lesson as to how confusion can reign supreme in the identification of grape varieties.

Thus Kerridge and Antcliff say, 'It was probably among the many varieties called Piquepoule collected by James Busby in 1832 and the Victorian plantings may come from this source. The identity was lost, and the name Irvine's White commemorates the vigneron at Great Western who made the first substantial plantings.'[27] In Len Evans' *Australia and New Zealand Complete Book of Wine* (Paul Hamlyn, 1973), the research worker in history at the University of New South Wales, Jaki Ilbery, supplied the first 150 pages covering the history of grapes and wine in Australia. She recounts how Hans Irvine, who purchased what is now the Seppelt Great Western winery and vineyards, decided to make Champagne (sic) of a quality equal to the best from France. He made several trips to France, and brought back a skilled team of Champagne artisans headed by Charles Pierlot, who had learnt the trade in the cellars of Pommery. Pierlot was, of course, encouraged by the large underground drives (tunnels originally excavated by goldminers and extended by Irvine) that the founder of the winery, Joseph Best, had created. Ilbery continues, 'The variety he [Irvine] chose was White Pinot (since renamed Irvine's White; it is probably Folle Blanche).' Other authorities suggest he had imported the vines from France in the belief that they were Chardonnay (aka White Pinot).

Max Lake, in *Classic Wines of Australia* (Jacaranda Press, 1966), comments on the Hunter Valley Distillery (HVD) vineyards then owned by Penfolds. He writes, 'The H.V.D. soils are mostly sandy loam, and there are some 45 acres of Semillon planted. They are also fortunate in having quantities of White Pinot [Chardonnay!] and Blanquette, both of which enhance flavour greatly.' He then goes on to discuss various vintages of Penfolds Blanquette at some length, saying, 'Their early complexity of flavour develops into what can only be called White Burgundy after about five years.'

---

27 Kerridge and Antcliff, *Wine Grape Varieties*, p. 117.

If this were not enough, the variety was also planted in South Australia as Sercial. Kerridge and Antcliff discuss this etymology, saying the grape 'appears in the Rutherglen collection as Blanc Select, so was presumably imported at some time as Blanc Selection Carriere. The confusion could have arisen if Blanc Selection Carriere and the true Sercial, which is a different variety … had been imported from Portugal together.'

So we have had Ondenc called Piquepoule, Irvine's White, Folle Blanche, Blanquette (a synonym recorded by Robinson), Blanc Select, Sercial and (possibly) White Pinot. (Lake only mentions Chardonnay as a synonym for Aucerot.)

Pedro Ximenez

World: 9243 ha. Spain: 9036 ha. Australia: 3 ha, 26 growers/makers

While the viticulturally more robust and reliable Palomino has supplanted Pedro Ximenez in large parts of southern Spain, and in Jerez in particular, PX (as the grape is universally known) still accounted for over 9000 hectares in Spain in 2010 (Portugal had 197 hectares). It has various uses: first, in the black-coloured, unctuously rich and sweet fortified wine which, alongside Moscatel, parallels Australia's Tokay and Muscat; second, for sweetening various forms of Sherry; and finally, to make a bland and boring white table wine.

As recently as 30 years ago Australia had over 2500 hectares of Pedro Ximenez and Palomino (the varieties were linked for statistical purposes). Today plantings are disappearing year by year – 3 hectares is an estimate in the absence of official statistics. The decline has been due, in large part, to the steady decline in the overall fortified wine sector, and it is highly likely that the rate of decline will slow down significantly. The producers in Australia releasing wines labelled Pedro Ximenez are relatively few; much of the tonnage is used in Sherry-type blends. Stephen John was one of those to make a dry table wine with it, utilising the old dry-grown plantings in the Clare Valley.

Producers

Jones Winery (blend), The Settlement Wine Co., Tim Gramp, Turkey Flat

Petit Manseng

World: 1110 ha. Australia: 3 ha, 16 growers/makers

DNA analysis strongly suggests that this is a progeny of Savagnin. This variety is the vinous answer to shark's fin, rhinoceros horn and every other reputed aphrodisiac. Colette wrote of Jurancon (the French wine made from Petit Manseng), 'I was a girl when

I met this prince; aroused, imperious, treacherous, as all great seducers are – Jurancon.' Very late harvested, with or without the aid of botrytis, it makes an exotically spicy, fruity, sweet wine, balance provided by lingering acidity on the finish. Its small but thick-skinned berries result in loose bunches very resistant to botrytis bunch rot; harvest in November or even early December is not uncommon.

Producers
919 Wines, Chrismont, Gapsted, Marq, Symphonia, Topper's Mountain

Petit Meslier

World: 4 ha. Australia: 0.5 ha, 2 growers/makers

A once significant variety in the Aube region of Champagne which has all but disappeared owing to its sensitivity to downy mildew and botrytis, poor set being an additional nail in its coffin. The idiosyncratic Jim Irvine, however, incorporates it – coming from the only planting in Australia – in his sparkling wine.

Producer
Irvine

Picolit

World: 128 ha. Australia: 2 ha, 7 growers/makers

Robinson comments that Picolit is said to have been grown since Roman times, but there is no evidence of any botanical similarity between the grapes used by the Romans and modern varieties.[28] Its genetic history isn't known and, because of its very erratic yield, it almost became extinct – it was saved by a single producer in the first half of the twentieth century. It had risen to fame in the late seventeenth century, but its popularity hit its zenith in the late eighteenth/early nineteenth centuries, when it was bottled in Murano glass and became a major competitor to Hungarian Tokaji. Its extreme lusciousness came in part from botrytis, and in part from air-dried grapes. It was, however, very difficult to grow and make, and growers turned against it.[29] If the figures given by Robinson (97 hectares in 2000) and Anderson (128 hectares in 2010) are correct, it is undergoing a modest renaissance in Italy. D'Agata says that, along with

---

28 Robinson, Harding and Vouillamoz, *Wine Grapes*, p. 798.
29 D'Agata, *Wine Grapes of Italy*, p. 194.

Picolit

Nebbiolo, Piccolit is his favourite Italian grape, observing in passing that Luigi Veronello, Italy's greatest wine writer, called Picolit Italy's noblest wine.[30] D'Agata's endorsement may well assist its renaissance.

It is used to make a sweet, late-harvest style with floral aromas and the flavour of apricots and peaches. Producers whose wines (not necessarily Picolit) are sometimes seen in Australia are Ronchi di Cialla and Livio Felluga. The sweet fruit runs in a citrus, pear and apple spectrum, with crisp acidity.

Producers
di Lusso Estate, Turners Crossing

---

30 ibid., p. 394.

Pinot Blanc

Pinot Blanc

World: 14 972 ha. Australia: 3 ha, 10 growers/makers

Given the low profile of the variety in Australia, it is surprisingly widely planted around the world. Anderson records 25 countries with plantings, not far short of Pinot Noir, with 32 countries, and Chardonnay (the ultimate traveller), with 35 countries. It is open to conjecture how much of this is due to the fact that until the end of the nineteenth century, Pinot Blanc was frequently confused with Chardonnay. It is in fact one of the mutations of Pinot Noir, only officially recognised as such as recently as 1868.[31] It also seems there were several independent mutations, with observations of bunches of black, grey and white berries on the same Pinot Noir vine.[32] What is more, the French total of 1280 hectares is dwarfed by that of Italy (where it is known as Pinot Bianco, with 3086 hectares in 2010), Germany (where it is known as Weiß Burgunder or Weißer Burgunder, and covers 3941 hectares) and Austria (1914 hectares, also called Weiß Burgunder). Its French home is Alsace, with negligible amounts now grown in Burgundy.

---

31 Robinson, Harding and Vouillamoz, *Wine Grapes*, p. 821.
32 ibid., p. 806.

In Australia, the most distinguished producers are Hoddles Creek Estate and De Bortoli in the Yarra Valley. In this cool region, pear- and apple-flavoured fruit is accompanied by lemony acidity on the finish.

Producers
Amulet Vineyard, Clarence House, De Bortoli, Hoddles Creek Estate, jb Wines, Mosquito Hill

Prosecco

World: 18 437 ha. Australia: 10 ha, 22 growers/makers

It's curious how a given wine style can suddenly become popular in various parts of the world without cross fertilisation/communication/blog swapping. Rose suddenly found favour in the United Kingdom, the United States and elsewhere a decade ago. The same phenomenon has occurred with Prosecco, which was minding its own business, as it were, until 2009, when demand from around the world ignited for what is essentially a pleasant but unremarkable wine: with a light, gently floral bouquet and a fresh, crisp but flavour-neutral palate (unless sweetened by retention of residual sugar or by a heavy dosage).

Prosecco

LESSER WHITE VARIETALS 131

In a transparent move, the Italian Prosecco Consorzio sought to register Prosecco as a protected region in the EU, renaming the grape Glera. The consequence, pending various appeals underway (including one by Australia), is that wine made from what has always been called the Prosecco grape cannot be labelled with that word, Glera being the option offered by the Consorzio on the basis that it is an ancient version of Prosecco. Australian growers of Prosecco might seek to continue to market their wine in Australia under that name, but would not be able to export it.

Producers:
Boynton's Feathertop, Brown Brothers, Dal Zotto, Lana, Pizzini

Schonburger

World: 69 ha. Australia: 2 ha, 6 growers/makers

A very recent cross (1979), with Pinot Noir, Chasselas and Muscat Hamburg as its parents and grandparents.[33] Its chief virtue is its very early ripening habit, which has seen it planted with particular success in England. It is thus no surprise to find its Australian plantings in Tasmania (an estimated 2 hectares). The wine is moderately aromatic and quite soft in the mouth, thanks to its low natural acidity.

Producers
Barringwood Park, Bream Creek, Freycinet

Siegerrebe

World: 132 ha. Australia: <1 ha, 4 growers/makers

Another recent German crossing, with Gewurztraminer and a red table grape its parents. It is almost oppressively aromatic and flavoured, and can reach astonishing levels of ripeness. Palmara has produced wines that have all the expected characteristics of the variety.

---

33 ibid., p. 976.

Silvaner

World: 7389 ha. Australia: 3 ha, 8 growers/makers

Also widely known as Sylvaner, this ancient variety was a natural cross between Savagnin and Osterreichisch Weiss that occurred 500 years ago in Austria.[34] It was at one time the most widely planted variety in Germany, and in several surrounding countries. It ripens early, has high natural acidity, yields well, falling on the last hurdle by producing a wine that is in most circumstances devoid of meaningful flavour. The exception in Germany has been the Rheinhessen, and in particular the production of Auslese and Eiswines. The most fascinating aspect of it as far as Australia is concerned is the geographic spread provided by its eight growers/makers.

Producers
Ballandean Estate, Home Hill, Thick as Thieves

Taminga

Australia: 3 ha, 7 growers/makers

A variety bred by AJ Antcliff specifically for the warm climate of Australia, and which does have positive fruit flavour, especially when made in late harvest style by Trentham Estate. Its parents are Planta Pedralba and Sultana.

Producers
Hickinbotham of Dromana, Shedleys, Trentham Estate

Verdejo

World: 16 578 ha. Australia: <1 ha, 2 growers/makers

Robinson says that Verdejo most probably comes from Rueda, in Spain, where it was supposedly introduced by the Mozarabs before Moorish rule.[35] It is Spain's fifth most planted white wine variety, with 11 352 hectares in 2008. It is still most prominent in Rueda, but is also widely planted in Castille-la Mancha. Since the 1970s, when Marques de Riscal saw the promise of white wines in Rouada (rather than fortified wines), Verdejo has been a rising star, although often blended with Sauvignon Blanc.

---

34 ibid., p. 999.
35 ibid., p. 1117.

The only region outside Spain noted by Robinson is the US state of Virginia.[36]

Peter Lehmann made a 2014 Verdejo sourced from the Fichiger family vineyard in the Barossa. It is crisp and lively, with some pear and apple skin flavours on the fore-palate before bracing, lemony acidity comes through on the finish. Seems to have promise.

Verduzzo Friulano

Another of Italy's ancient varieties, first mentioned in 1409 primarily grown in Friuli[37], and used to make both dry and sweet wines. In either case, the wine is full-bodied, with considerable extract, which needs to be carefully managed. The plantings in Italy, also called Ramandolo, are in decline, with 1658 hectares in 2000 (Robinson) falling to 808 hectares in 2010 (Anderson). In one of those perverse plays, it is not genetically related to Verduzzo Trevigiano, an inferior variety also in decline.

It is appropriate that two of the Australian producers should be of Italian origin; Bianchet has been growing the variety since its foundation in 1976.

Producers
Bianchet, Billy Button, Carillion, Pepper Tree, Pizzini

Vermentino

World: 8873 ha. Australia: 93 ha, 80 growers/makers

Morphological and DNA research has established that Vermentino is identical to Favorita (Piedmont) and Pigato (Liguria), and is grown under its own name in Liguria, Sardinia, Tuscany and Corsica. This, however, does not establish where and how it originated, but because it is an important variety in both Corsica and Sardinia, it has often been said that it was introduced by Spain between the fourteenth and seventeenth centuries[38], although it has never been found in Spain. Other theories place it in the Middle East, or central Greece. Robinson suggests it is more widely planted in southern France than in Italy, with 3453 hectares compared with Italy's 3000 hectares. Anderson has similar figures for France, but far greater plantings in Italy, with 5046 hectares. What is not in dispute is that Vermentino is the most important white variety in Sardinia, granted its own DOCG in 1996 (the only variety so recognised). Part of the discrepancy in the planting figures

---

36   ibid., p. 1118.
37   ibid., p. 1125.
38   ibid., pp. 1127–29.

Vermentino

may well lie in the fact that Italy separately records Favorita (276 hectares) and Pigato (255 hectares).

It is one of the most widely propagated alternative varieties in Australia. It is a vibrant wine, with a full range of citrus flavours cropping up in different examples, and shows the same excellent acidity as it does in Italy and France.

Producers
Angove Family Winemakers, Beach Road, Billy Button, Boynton's Feathertop, Bremerton, Bress*, Chalmers, di Lusso Estate, Ducks in a Row, Flynns, Fowles*, Golden Grove Estate*, Landaire*, Marq*, Millbrook, Mitolo, Willem Kurt, Yalumba, Yelland & Papps*

Other White Varietals

The following varietals, available from Chalmers, have been grown in Australia, but have either disappeared or exist only as vines making no particular contribution to the wine they are directed to.

Arinto de Bucelas

World: 4446 ha. Australia: <1 ha, 1 grower/maker

This is an old Portuguese variety, its high quality and high acidity making it an important variety in the Vinho Verde region. There are, however, a number of varieties starting with 'Arinto', and while the full name isn't always used, care has to be taken.[39] There are tiny plantings in the Paso Robles region of California, and Australia's one producer (with 1950 vines, close to 1 hectare) is Dell'uva Wines, which recently increased its plantings to the present level in response to market demand.

Bianco d'Alessano

World: 419 ha. Australia: 4 ha, 1 grower/maker

It is grown through southern Italy and until recently often blended with other local varieties, including Verdeca. It has also been used to make Vermouth, but its fortunes have been somewhat restored through recent interest. Salena Estate is the sole Australian producer, and won three trophies at the Australian Alternative Varieties Show in 2010.

Bourboulenc

World: 583 ha. Australia: <1 ha, 2 growers/makers

Bourboulenc is an old variety from Provence, references to it dating back to 1515.[40] There are various hypotheses about its origin, none especially convincing; more DNA research will be necessary to settle the matter.

Best producers
Charles Melton, Yangarra Estate

---

39 ibid., pp. 32–33.
40 ibid., p. 129.

Canada Muscat

World: 1 ha. Australia: <1 ha, 2 growers/makers

This is a complex hybrid created in 1928 by Richard Wellington at New York State's Cornell University by crossing Muscat of Hamburg with Hubbard (not *Vitis vinifera*). Once planted in Ontario, Canada, it is now being grown by McWilliam's in the Riverina, and Patritti has made a blend of Canada Muscat and Muscat Blanc a Petits Grains.

Crouchen

World: 725 ha. Australia: 95 ha, 4 growers/makers

Robinson summarises it neatly by saying, 'Widely travelled neutral French variety from the western Pyrenees, that for long benefitted from naming confusion.'[41]

South Africa has the dubious distinction of having the lion's share of the world's plantings, with 629 hectares. The confusion there parallels that in Australia, which I will revert to in a moment. It arrived in the Cape in 1656, and was soon named Cape Riesling, Paarl Riesling and South African Riesling. True Riesling, which became known as Weisser Riesling or Rhine Riesling in South Africa, apparently arrived a few years later, in 1664. In the 1950s it was realised that there were two different varieties called Riesling in South Africa, but only one was true Riesling. Although the confusion was ended in the 1980s, the more widely planted Crouchen continued to be sold under the name Riesling until legislation in 2009 provided that Crouchen had to be labelled as such, and Riesling no longer needed to be described as Weisser or Rhine.

Exactly the same pattern occurred in Australia, although Crouchen was by no means the only variety to falsely travel under the name Riesling. Indeed, this was so until a persistent campaign by Clare Valley Riesling growers, led by Jeffrey Grosset, finally succeeded in precluding the use of the word 'Riesling' to denote a style (made from whatever variety the producer chose).

Clare Valley winemakers had a particular interest in restricting the name Riesling to the (true) variety, because Crouchen had for long been called Clare Riesling in that region. I disagree with Robinson's assertion that it (Crouchen) shares only one thing with Riesling – the ability to age. In fact, it is a variety that oxidises quickly if given half a chance before it is in bottle, and once bottled, quickly becomes flabby and coarse. The quicker it departs from the Australian viticultural landscape, the better.

---

41 ibid., p. 281.

Ehrenfelser

World: 114 ha. Australia: <1 ha, 1 grower/maker

Ehrenfelser was believed to be a Riesling cross bred at Geisenheim in 1929. However, DNA profiling shows that Silvaner is not one of the parents, so one side of the family remains unknown.[42] The objective of the cross was to produce a grape that would taste like Riesling, but ripen in a wider range of sites. It failed to achieve its aim; it is attractively fruity when first bottled, but develops quickly and loses its aroma and flavour. Small plantings are dotted around the world – in California, New York State, British Columbia and Tasmania, where Palmara has grown it since 1984 but usually blends it with Semillon and Sauvignon Blanc.

Flora

World: 8 ha. Australia: 3.7 ha, 1 grower/maker

This is a cross of Semillon and Gewurztraminer bred by the distinguished Californian research academic Harold P Olmo in 1938 at the University of California, Davis, and released in 1958. It has had limited success; it was bred with the hot Central Valley in California in mind, but did not retain enough acidity. Thus its limited plantings are now in cooler parts of California, where its delicately aromatic bouquet shows through. Brown Brothers has 3.69 hectares at its Mystic Park Vineyard, and use it in a blend with Orange Muscat to produce what is little more than off-dry dessert wine (fresh fruit or cake-like desserts are the best food match).

Inzolia | Ansonica

World: 6133 ha. Australia: <1 ha, 1 grower/maker

This wine travels under a number of names: Inzolia is its Sicilian name, Ansonica its Tuscan name.[43] D'Agata is adamant that its correct name is Ansonica, not Inzolia.[44] However, it is listed as Inzolia in Anderson's data, itself the primary data used by Robinson.

It is one of the most important and ancient white grapes of Sicily, and is part of numerous Sicilian DOCGs. Both there and in Tuscany its primary use has been as a blend ingredient.

---

42 ibid., p. 323.
43 ibid., p. 472.
44 D'Agata, *Wine Grapes of Italy*, p. 180.

It has been cultivated since the sixteenth century in both Tuscany and Sicily. DNA research has shown that it has genetic links with Grillo and other Sicilian varieties, including Moscato Giallo. This has put an end to earlier research suggesting that it was of Greek origin. Its plantings in Tuscany are scattered and small. The best wines have a nutty flavour but are often deficient in acid.

Its Australian producer is Dell'uva Wines, which also uses it as a blend to lift Vermentino. It has 650 vines, and intends to plant more.

Melon

World: 12 306 ha. Australia: <1 ha, 2 growers/makers

This is an ancient Burgundian variety, dating back to the thirteenth century. DNA analysis has established that Melon is a natural cross of Pinot Noir and Gouais Blanc. It makes wine that is typically crisp and relatively neutral in flavour, with some citrussy nuances. Tiny plantings are dotted in Washington State, California, Oregon and Australia, where it is grown by Crittenden Estate and Whinstone Estate.

Mondeuse Blanche

World: 6 ha. Australia: <1 ha, 5 growers/makers

This is one of Shiraz's parents, and famous for that reason if no other. Indeed, it has almost become extinct in its former fortress of Savoie in France, with a handful of makers sharing 5 hectares. Its other claim to fame is its genetic links with Viognier.

It is being trialled by Yangarra Estate as part of a program to evaluate as many Rhône varieties as possible.

Orange Muscat

World: 91 ha. Australia: 5 ha (estimate), 5 growers/makers

The correct name for the variety is Muscat Fleur d'Oranger. This highly aromatic variety with orange featuring on the bouquet has been recently identified by DNA as a cross between Chasselas and Muscat Blanc a Petits Grains, although it's not known where the crossing took place. It's grown in Italy, California, Washington State and British Columbia, everywhere in small quantities. Producers include Brown Brothers (the most important), Amulet Vineyard, Dindima, Monichino and Scion Vineyard.

Piquepoul Blanc

Palomino

World: 22 645 ha. Australia: 49 ha (2008), 3 growers/makers

Palomino Fino (to give the grape its full name) was originally grown exclusively around Sanlúcar de Barrameda, for the production of Sherry. After phylloxera, its ready availability and productivity led to widespread planting, first in Spain, and thereafter in Portugal, Cyprus, California and South Africa (270 hectares), but with Spain (18 836 hectares) and Portugal (3033 hectares) still by far the most important. At one stage Australia had 700 hectares planted for the production of premium dry sherries.[45] The plantings of 919 Wines (in the Riverland) and Chambers Rosewood (in Rutherglen) are certainly dedicated to Sherry, those of Kaesler (in the Barossa Valley) presumably the same. The area shown in 2008 will have declined since then.

---

45 Kerridge and Antcliff, *Wine Grape Varieties*, p. 121.

Parellada

World: 8847 ha. Australia: <1 ha, 1 grower/maker

Plantings of the variety date back to the fourteenth century in northeast Spain, and that country remains by far the most important producer, the plantings dedicated to the production of Cava. It can be made into table wine that is delicate, has fruity acidity and is best drunk young. Mansfield Wines is the sole Australian producer of record.

Piquepoul Blanc

World: 1492 ha. Australia: <1 ha, 1 grower/maker

France has a near-monopoly on the plantings, with 1455 hectares, and it is on the increase, unlike so many native varieties, which are under pressure from EU planting controls. Its high acidity makes it a blending partner for many varieties in the extreme south of France, but it is also one of the permitted varieties in Châteauneuf-du-Pape.

Australia's grower is Yangarra Estate, which is trialling it with a view to include it in their Rhône portfolio.

Chapter 8

The Classic Red Varietals
Cabernet Sauvignon

288 781 ha is grown in 40 countries, Myanmar and the United Kingdom having 1 ha each. Those with over 500 ha are: Algeria 1510 ha, Argentina 16 372 ha, Australia 25 333 ha, Austria 592 ha, Brazil 914 ha, Bulgaria 8436 ha, Canada 542 ha, Chile 40 728 ha, China 22 612 ha, Croatia 646 ha, France 54 434 ha, Greece 1550 ha, Hungary 2836 ha, Italy 13 724 ha, Mexico 756 ha, Moldova 7500 ha, Portugal 1671 ha, Romania 3718 ha, Russia 3593 ha, Slovakia 570 ha, South Africa 12 325 ha, Spain 23 237 ha, Ukraine 4869 ha, United States 34 788 ha, Uruguay 682 ha.

International History

The most noble red grape has had a relatively short reign, but there are no pretenders to the throne, only a consort in the form of Merlot: Cabernet is the world's most widely planted variety; Merlot is in second place, with 267 215 hectares. Even its ancestral tree was not traced until as recently as 1997, when DNA analysis at UC Davis showed its parents to be Cabernet Franc and Sauvignon Blanc. Its birth is believed to be due to a spontaneous crossing of the varieties interplanted in the vineyards, as was common in the late Middle Ages.

This discovery was almost accidental. A PhD student of Carole Meredith at UC Davis, John Bowers, noticed that the DNA profile of Cabernet Sauvignon was precisely what should be expected from a cross between Cabernet Franc and Sauvignon Blanc. It caused a surge in research work around the world, which has continued to gather pace. The research showed (controversially at the time) that a red grape could have a white grape parent. (Later studies have shown that one of Shiraz's parents is Mondeuse Blanche.)

It's not yet clear when this crossing occurred. The first mentions of Cabernet Sauvignon were between 1763 and 1784 (as Gros Cavernet Sauvignon), the first modern spelling in 1840.[1] (I shared in a bottle of 1825 Château Gruaud Larose in 1977, courtesy of Michael Broadbent MW, who could give *Doctor Who*'s Tardis a run for its money.)

How long before the first description did the vines come into being? This takes the focus back to Cabernet Franc and Sauvignon Blanc. Cabernet Franc turns out to be one of the most important and ancient varieties in Bordeaux. Remarkably, it has a parent–offspring relationship with two varieties in Spain's Basque country – Morenoa and Hondaribba Beltza – and possibly dates back to 1050.[2] Sauvignon Blanc appears to have been mentioned in 1534 in the Loire Valley, its parents Savagnin and an unknown partner.[3]

Finally, Cabernet Sauvignon first emerged from the shadows of Bordeaux in the late eighteenth century, with no prior references in literature. Moreover, it was only after the enforced replanting in the wake of phylloxera that it became the dominant variety in the Haut Medoc and Graves, replacing varieties including Malbec and Carmenere.

Notwithstanding this late start, it is the most widely planted noble variety in the world, with over 288 000 hectares planted in 2012, just keeping Merlot (267 215 hectares) at bay. It has spread prolifically throughout France, aided by its small berries, tough skins and loose bunch conformation, which make it resistant to rot, and also mean its colour is deep and extract high unless it is deliberately over-cropped or grown with a dense canopy. Languedoc-Roussillon boasts 18 700 hectares, Provence 3480 hectares and the Loire Valley 128 hectares.

It is widely grown in Eastern Europe with a total of 28 206 hectares. As much of this hectarage is old, and the quality of the grapes is known to be high – there are Australian and New World winemakers who have worked there – these states could become significant players in the world export game if and when they become politically and economically stable.

The cooler central and northern regions of Italy planted Cabernet Sauvignon with enthusiasm over the late 1980s and '90s (and ongoing). As at 2010, there were 13 724 hectares in bearing. Apart from some confusion between Cabernet Sauvignon and Cabernet Franc, the former has chiefly been employed in blends with indigenous varieties, often to great effect. The so-called super-Tuscans have married Sangiovese with either or both of Cabernet Sauvignon and Cabernet Franc – hence Solaia, Tignanello and

---

1 Jancis Robinson, Julia Harding and Jose Vouillamoz, *Wine Grapes*, Ecco/HarperCollins, 2012, p. 160.
2 ibid., p. 161.
3 ibid., p. 952.

so forth. In best Italian fashion, neighbour Brunello di Montalcino's black-letter law did not permit the use of Cabernet Sauvignon as a blend component, but many producers quietly used it – until a whistleblower caused a major contretemps in 2008.

Piedmont has been a little more cautious, although Angelo Gaja has grown and produced the 100 per cent Cabernet Sauvignon wine branded Darmagi (Italian for 'what a shame'), and there are some highly successful blends with Barbera.

While Spain (with 23 237 hectares in 2010) has not gone overboard with the variety, it has a relatively long history there, having been imported by the Marques de Riscal into Rioja in the middle of the nineteenth century, and by Vega Sicilia in 1864. There was then a long break before Miguel Torres Jnr and Jean Leon brought it into the Penedes region, and planted it in cool, high-altitude sites. Torres Mas La Plana Cabernet Sauvignon triumphed in the 1979 re-run of the famous 1976 Judgement of Paris, placing first above the might of Bordeaux, the Napa Valley et al. Both in the Penedes and elsewhere in Spain it is increasingly blended with Tempranillo.

There may well come a time when the blending with great indigenous varieties such as Tempranillo and Sangiovese in their homelands will be seen as no more than contamination, robbing the wines (and their regions) of typicity, their point of difference, their sense of place.

The New World faces no such dilemmas, and has (if somewhat belatedly) adopted Cabernet Sauvignon with enthusiasm, thereby helping underline (and underwrite) its position as the king of red grapes. One of the world's focal points is the Napa Valley, which has always hung its national and international reputation as the greatest region in the United States on the doorknob of Cabernet Sauvignon.

It was introduced in the latter part of the nineteenth century, and all the finest, most revered and long-lived wines made up to the onset of Prohibition were made from 100 per cent Cabernet Sauvignon. The entrance of the other Bordeaux varieties to make what Californians call Meritage blends was left until the 1970s and '80s. It is equally important in the Sonoma Valley, and has a strong presence elsewhere along the central and northern Californian coast.

Cabernet Sauvignon was one of the varieties planted when the modern era of viticulture in Washington State began in 1954. Merlot swept past it in the 1990s, but Cabernet Sauvignon has fought back, and is now clearly the preferred variety, with 4160 hectares in 2011.[4]

---

4   ibid., p. 167.

As Chile began to look to export markets, so did its meagre plantings of Cabernet Sauvignon increase, gathering pace throughout the 1980s, and accelerating even faster through the 1990s. It is Chile's leading red grape, with 40 728 hectares in 2010, a 250 per cent increase on the figure for 2002. Chile, like most of Australia, does not – nor ever did – have phylloxera, and the variety (planted on its own roots) thrives in the equable climate of Chile.

Across the Andes in Argentina, with 16 372 hectares in 2010, there is a much larger and older wine industry, and a significantly greater variation in site and climate (or terroir). On the downside, Argentina does have phylloxera; the main regions are subject to intermittent growing season rain and hail; and Cabernet Sauvignon is dwarfed by the plantings of Malbec. Argentina's economic and social problems since the 1920s are well documented, and when this resource-rich country will get itself into gear is anyone's guess. Growth in the export quarter of the wine industry will increasingly come from foreign-owned enterprises, and Cabernet Sauvignon will stand alongside Malbec.

South Africa (12 325 hectares in 2010) has grown Cabernet Sauvignon for a long time, but (particularly under the dead hand of the state-owned KWV co-operative winery) only had virus-ridden vines available, which reduced yield and (usually) produced attenuated flavour. However, in the late 1980s importations of new Italian clones gave rise to what the vine growers of the Cape enthusiastically called the minty clone. And indeed it is minty, which may well be a point of difference, but in time may also lead to the planting of less idiosyncratic clones.

Finally, and most recently, the Hawke's Bay region of New Zealand (249 hectares of the New Zealand total of 289 hectares) has gained significant recognition for its Cabernet Sauvignon and Cabernet blends. The Gimblett Gravels district is a very special piece of terroir and, with honourable exceptions such as Te Mata, is the epicentre of New Zealand's finest – and seriously good – Cabernets and Bordeaux blends. New Zealand's first prophet was the Italian-trained Romeo Bragato, 'lent' to New Zealand authorities by Australia, and who enthusiastically endorsed the prospects for Cabernet Sauvignon. The second was the legendary Tom McDonald, who made Cabernet Sauvignon in the Hawke's Bay region from 1926.

International Styles

BORDEAUX, FRANCE
France: 54 434 ha

As I have related, Cabernet Sauvignon may have been a relatively recent arrival in what is now regarded as its ancestral home, and from which it spread around the world.

Moreover, it has always been joined by varying percentages of Merlot, Cabernet Franc, Petit Verdot and the fast-disappearing Carmenere and Malbec.

It is on the left bank of the Gironde River in the Haut Medoc and Graves that it finds its greatest expression, and in all places it is accompanied by Merlot (the 'insurance' grape), and varying percentages of others which fulfill similar functions. Cabernet Sauvignon does not always ripen fully on the left bank (and barely exists on the right bank in St Emilion and Pomerol), but Merlot does, thus making its contribution essential in the cooler vintages. However, the new normal (since 1982) has seen warmer summers coming to the aid of Cabernet Sauvignon, making insurance of little moment.

Modern viticultural methods (notably better control of mildew and botrytis, reduction of the potential crop by shoot and bunch thinning, and a move to organic and, controversially, biodynamic management) and vastly improved winery technology (stainless steel fermentation, temperature control, sophisticated bunch- and berry-sorting tables/belts and, more recently and controversially, reverse osmosis, cross-flow filtration and pumps) have fundamentally changed the dynamics of making Bordeaux red wines based on Cabernet Sauvignon, and led to the belief that (for example) the 2000 vintage in Bordeaux is the greatest ever, followed – of course – by the greatest ever 2005, 2009 and 2010 vintages.

To accept that view, you have to discount the great pre-phylloxera vintages of 1864, 1865 and 1874, and great twentieth-century vintages such as 1928, 1929, 1945, 1949 and 1961. Then you have to decide whether you are comparing the best wines of each vintage or the worst.

What is clear is that the style of Bordeaux Cabernet-based wines is changing, that the problems of the wet years have been diminished, and that the average quality across the lesser chateaux and lesser years is distinctly higher.

I am not going to list the classed growth wineries of the Haut Medoc, simply because they are the subject of countless specialised books.

ITALY AND SPAIN

Italy: 13 724 ha. Spain: 23 237 ha

While some very distinguished wines are made with the aid of Cabernet Sauvignon (and other Bordeaux varieties) blended with indigenous varieties, it is not Cabernet Sauvignon which leads the way.

UNITED STATES
34 788 ha

Napa and Sonoma Valleys

I give this abbreviated list with a considerable degree of hesitation; new stars burst on the scene in the Napa Valley every day, while others fade. Most are built in heroic style, with black fruits, monumental tannins and copious amounts of oak, the saving grace being mid-range alcohol levels. They are continuing a journey – which began in 1974 – of ever so slowly moderating extract and, in particular, tannins. Oak use, too, has become more sophisticated (French rather than American) but still very much in the recipe. The concept of best producers has little relevance here, for this is a distillation of a much, much larger group. The wineries nominated make varietal Cabernet Sauvignon and/or Cabernet blends which are labelled Meritage.

Best producers

Araujo Estate, Beaulieu, Beringer Blass*, Cakebread, Caymus*, Chappellet, Chateau Montelana, Chateau St Jean*, Chimney Rock, Clark-Clauden, Colgin*, Corison, Cosentino Dalla Vale*, Cuvaison, Diamond Creek, Dominus Estate*, Duckhorn*, Dunn Vineyards*, Flora Springs, Forman Vineyard, Freemark Abbey, Frog's Leap, Grace Family*, Grgich Hills Cellar, Groth Vineyards, Hall, Harlan Estate, Jordan, Kenwood Cellars, Lamborn Family, Laurel Glen, Robert Mondavi, Newton Vineyards*, Opus One*, Joseph Phelps*, Ridge Vineyards, Saddleback Cellars, Screaming Eagle*, Selene, Shafer Vineyards, Silverado, Spottswoode*, Stag's Leap Wine Cellars*, Philip Togni*, Vlader Estate, Volker Estate

Washington State

Quilceda Creek may well be the exception which proves the rule, for its Cabernet Sauvignons are quite outstanding: ripe and fleshy but with great structure and complexity. At the other extreme come bony, lean wines notable for their austerity rather than their charm. But there are some occupants of the middle ground, even if most rely on the softening effects of Washington Merlot.

Best producers

Cadence, Columbia Crest, DeLille Cellars, Fidelitas, L'Ecole No. 41, Leonetti Cellar*, Long Shadows, Pepper Bridge Winery, Quilceda Creek*, Seven Hills Winery, The Hogue Cellars, Woodward Canyon*

ARGENTINA
16 372 ha

Argentina has as much diversity of climate and terroir as does Australia, with production spread over 15 provinces. The centre of viticulture is, however, Mendoza, and even though Malbec remains the most widely planted red grape, Mendoza produces some excellent Cabernet Sauvignon: supple and textured, with clear varietal character.

Best producers
Atamisque*, Bodega Catena Zapata, Bodega El Eskco*, Bodegas Fabre*, Bodega Norton, Caserena Winery*, Cavas del 23*, Decero*, Finca Flichman, Finca Sophenia*, Kaiken, La Anita, Pulenta Estate, Riglos, Ruca Malen, Rutini Wines, Terrazas de los Andes, Trapiche*

SOUTH AFRICA
12 325 ha

As with Chardonnay, South Africa had to contend with such a number of obstacles – sanctions, the KWV, and virus-infected vines – that it is surprising it is where it is today.

The KWV was stripped of its monopoly powers, sanctions are gone, and new clones of Cabernet Sauvignon have arrived (more of which in a moment), but the shadows remain. Moreover, there is one more obstacle that is a permanent feature: the compressed growing season, which comes about largely by virtue of its latitude, which is precisely the same as that of Sydney.

Thus Cabernet Sauvignon is picked in late February to mid-March, more often in stressed condition than not. When the effects of virus and extended post-fermentation maceration were added, traditional South African Cabernet Sauvignon had harsh, bitter, green tannins which numbed the mouth.

Nor did the first of the new clones solve much: the so-called minty Italian clone simply introduced a novel form (for South Africa) of lack of ripeness in the form of mint. But as in so many ways in this country, progress has been made, and far better structured wines are the result, with Vergelegen one of the early leaders. Its Bordeaux blend flagship is a wine of world class, vividly demonstrating the difference between ripe and unripe tannins. Its vineyards were smashed by bushfires in 2009, but 80 per cent were eventually brought back into production.

Best producers

Backsberg, Boekenhoutskloof*, Cederberg Private Cellar*, Conde, Constantia Clen, Delaire Graff*, Delheim*, De Trafford*, Diemersdal Estate*, Diemersfontein Vineyards, Eikendal*, Ernie Els, Flagstone, Glenelly Estate, Hartenberg, Jordan Wine Estate, Kaapzicht Wine Estate, Kanonkop*, Klein Constantia, Kleine Zalze Wines, Meerendal, Meerlust*, Mischa, Morgenhof, Mulderbosch*, Nederburg Wines*, Rustenberg*, Simonsig, Stark-Condé*, Stellenzicht, Thelema Mountain Vineyards*, Tokara, Vergelegen*, Villiera Wines, Waterford*

CHILE

40 728 ha

Chile has massive plantings of Cabernet Sauvignon. As with all Chilean vines, it is on its own roots: phylloxera has never come to the country. French and United States investment, however, has come, the former drawing some of the biggest names, including Château Lafite, Château Mouton-Rothschild, and Château Margaux winemaker Paul Pontallier.

Chilean Cabernet Sauvignon is usually soft, accommodating and with excellent colour – and cheap. But there are an increasing number of super-premium wines made in small quantities from old vines, and on trellised hillsides. Because of the gulf between the fighting varietal form of Cabernet Sauvignon and the top echelon, it should be assumed that I am referring to the best wines from each producer.

Best producers

Acquitania*, Almaviva*, Altair, Calcu*, Calina*, Canepa*, Canta Carolina*, Chateau Los Boldos*, Concha y Toro, Cono Sur, De Martino*, Echeverría, Errazuiz*, O Fournier, Gillmore, Haras de Pirque, Indomita, Los Vascios*, Miguel Torres*, Montes*, Montgras, Perez Cruz, Quebrada de Macul, San Pedro, Santa Alicia, Santa Rita, Valdivieso, Ventisquero*, Viña Carmen, Viñedo Chadwick

NEW ZEALAND

289 ha

Hawke's Bay

249 ha

For many years (starting in 1982) Te Mata was a voice crying in the wilderness, producing Cabernet Sauvignon Merlot blends incomparably better than all others. Two events changed perceptions forever: the 1998 vintage and the development of the Gimblett Gravels. The region would welcome more evidence of global warming: its best Cabernet Sauvignon and Cabernet blends are made in the warmest vintages. In these years the cassis and redcurrant fruit flavours are incontestably ripe, but retain freshness and elegance.

Best producers
Church Road Winery*, Craggy Range Vineyards*, Delegats, Mission Estate, Newton Forrest, Pask, Sacred Hill Wines*, Te Awa, Te Mata*, Trinity Hill*, Vidal Estate*, Villa Maria*

Waiheke Island
25 ha (estimate)

The unique climate serves to push rain away during the crucial late summer/early autumn months, and operates to produce some of New Zealand's finest Cabernets and Cabernet blends. The downside is their limited volume and hefty prices. The ultimate maritime climate, and near perfect temperatures, is seen to best advantage in the classically framed wines of Stonyridge.

Best producers
Destiny Bay, Fenton Estate, Goldie Wines, Kennedy Point, Man O' War, Miro Vineyard, Obsidian*, Peninsula Estate, Stonyridge Vineyard*, Te Motu Vineyard, Te Whau Vineyard

Australian History

Cabernet Sauvignon arrived in Sydney with the country's vinous 'first fleet', as part of the James Busby collection. It was then known (or spelt) as Carbenet Sauvignen, an infinitely preferable phonetic alternative to today's nauseating 'cab sav'. Like other varieties in the collection, it spread to all parts of the colony, but its hold remained tenuous throughout the nineteenth century, notwithstanding the endorsement it received from the experts of the day.

With the encouragement of industry leaders such as Thomas Hardy, Cabernet Sauvignon, Shiraz and Malbec were widely planted in the Clare Valley towards the end of the nineteenth century. It was also planted at the Kalimna Vineyard in the Barossa Valley (now owned by Penfolds) in 1886, which provided the 1953 Grange Cabernet Sauvignon, Show Bins 58 (1961) and Bin 54 (1963), the first vintage of Bin 707 (1964) and in 1996 Block 42 Cabernet Sauvignon (the first of periodic releases of Block 42). John Riddoch planted it in Coonawarra in 1893, the Chaffeys at McLaren Vale at the end of the century, Hans Irvine at Great Western and at Tahbilk in the Goulburn Valley.

Much earlier in the piece, George Wyndham had planted it at his Dalwood Vineyard in the Hunter Valley, alongside tiny plantings of Petit Verdot. A 1930 marriage of these two varieties would inspire Max Lake to plant Cabernet Sauvignon at Lake's Folly in 1963, simultaneously establishing the first boutique weekend commercial winery in Australia, and re-establishing the then still relatively unfashionable Cabernet Sauvignon in the Hunter Valley.

Why, then, did it not flourish? We know all the plantings recorded above survived (with the exception of the Dalwood vines) because they are here today, though in smaller amounts due to the passage of time. There were doubtless many other plantings which did not survive, and yet others which did survive well into the twentieth century before disappearing. The answers are (at least) three-fold: it has a lower yield than Shiraz; its tough canes make it less easy to prune; and (the freak 1945 Stonyfell Vintage Port notwithstanding) it is not suitable for fortified winemaking.

So when the statistical recording of Australian grape varieties began in 1956, Cabernet Sauvignon was not officially recorded; in 1966 the crush amounted to a derisory 621 tonnes compared with 12 410 tonnes of Shiraz and 32 000 tonnes of Grenache. It is highly likely that there was both under-reporting and over-reporting in this figure. On the one hand, the Australian Bureau of Statistics did not collect figures under a certain dollar value; on the other, varieties with invalid synonyms (for example, Cabernet Gros in the Barossa Valley) were included in the census.

Although all states shared in the rapid growth which followed, South Australia – led first by the Limestone Coast Zone regions of Coonawarra and Padthaway, thereafter by its other regions – was the first chief driver of that growth. Coonawarra, with its climatic similarity to Bordeaux, grew in reputation, as did Cabernet Sauvignon. Which was the chicken and which the egg does not really matter; the result was the recognition of Coonawarra as Australia's best Cabernet Sauvignon producer by the end of the 1960s.

Unfortunately, between 1970 and 1990 (the years approximate) the large corporate owners of most of Coonawarra were lured into a lowest-possible-cost viticultural regime; everything was done by machines, and for a while 'minimal pruning' made a poor situation worse. The vines were not pruned in winter, leaving the canopy to grow in a cascade down to the ground; it was thin-skirted, allowing airflow of sorts under the canopy.

Much of the following 25 years was spent repairing the damage, Wynns going further than all others. Labour shortages mean that machine pruning in winter (with hand pruning to clean up) and machine harvesting are near-universal practices. The one silver lining is the development of new machine harvesting and berry-sorting systems that do as good (if not better) a job as hand pruning.

The unsurmountable problem is that Coonawarra opened the way for the newer regions to assert their claims, Margaret River the most obvious (and important), but with many handmaidens.

The graph following shows an even more disturbing pattern of declining production since 2004. Fortune favouring the bold, I suggest that there will be no further decline, but much depends on the demand for low-priced Cabernet Sauvignon. Thus in New South Wales, the Big Rivers Zone (29 532 tonnes) produces 70 per cent of the state total (37 482 tonnes), in Victoria the Murray Darling and Swan Hill regions (22 500 tonnes) account for 76 per cent of the state total (29 400 tonnes), and in South Australia the Lower Murray (63 300 tonnes) provides just under 50 per cent of the state total (129 700 tonnes).

Australian Statistics
25 333 ha, 207 558 tonnes

Cabernet Sauvignon: tonnes crushed in Australia, 1976–2012

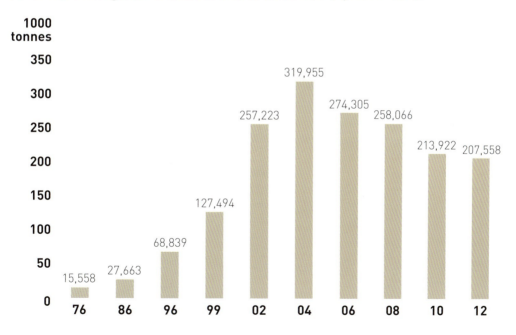

Australian Winemaking

The basics of making Cabernet Sauvignon are neither particularly complex nor especially varied, particularly when compared with those for (say) Pinot Noir. But there are real choices with equally real consequences, and hence points of difference in the techniques adopted.

For a start, Australian winemakers tend not to make wines by formula. At its most basic, this means that what is considered an appropriate approach in a warm region with older vines and relatively low yields will be markedly different from that used in a cool region with younger vines and (perhaps) a slightly higher yield. In the first situation, the aim will be to ensure that the wine does not end up over-extracted and excessively tannic. In the second the aim will be to maximise the available tannins and extract, yet handle the grapes and the must relatively gently (to avoid coarseness or roughness).

It may be unfair – or perhaps outdated – to suggest that Napa Valley's winemakers of Cabernet Sauvignon adopted Bordeaux's winemaking techniques without sufficiently (if at all) pausing to consider the difference in the respective climates and the consequent difference in anthocyanin and dry extract potential. Putting this into simple language, Californian Cabernet Sauvignon grapes have super-abundant levels of tannin, while those of Bordeaux (in all but the warmest, driest vintages) require particular attention to coax out all the potential tannins.

Although Australia may justly be accused of falling into the high-alcohol trap with its Shiraz and Grenache, it has not fallen for the tannin trap which so bedevilled Napa Cabernet Sauvignons. An American observed not so long ago, 'Those wines were made never to be drunk.'

What, then, are the Australian methods? What are they intended to achieve, and how have they changed? The use of whole bunches in, or return of stems to, the fermenting must is very rare, though a few do use these tricks. Temperatures are much lower than for Pinot Noir, and usually lower than for Shiraz. Whole berry fermentation is practised by some, and pre-fermentation cold soak is now widely used, especially by those who rely on indigenous yeasts. All of these practices (or abstentions) reflect the abundance of anthocyanins (coloured tannins) in the grape.

Treatment at the end of fermentation varies widely, in large part due to the winemaker's response to climate and its impact on the composition of the grapes. While allowing some time to pass after the end of the fermentation before pressing used to be standard practice – the main question turning on the length of maceration (anything from one to 30 or more days) – pressing part of the total must before dryness and running the wine more or less directly to barrel is an increasingly used option.

Pausing here, I should clarify a couple of points. First, most of the choices and refinements are relevant to limited-production, high-quality wines. The bigger the volume, and the lower the price point, the less relevant they become. But there is no hard and fast dividing line; some of the large-volume wines involve sophisticated technology, as you will see in a moment.

Next, the great joy of winemaking (and hence wine) is that every vintage presents a new opportunity, a new challenge, the unceasing quest being to make a better wine than any preceding it. So neither the technique nor the philosophy, the science nor the art, is frozen in time.

One of the technological advances of the past decade, applicable not just to Cabernet Sauvignon but particularly useful with it, has been the technique of micro-oxygenation. It was developed by a leading winemaker in Cahors, that region in France noted for its dense, inky, tannic reds made from Malbec. Frustrated by the length of time it took for these wines to even approach drinkability, and understanding that the softening (the polymerisation) of tannins was dependent on the gradual absorption of oxygen by the wine, he seized upon the idea of introducing minute amounts of oxygen to the wine while it remained in tank.

The patent was developed in conjunction with the large French company Pechiney, and launched onto the world wine markets in the early 1990s. It involved the release of a microscopic stream of oxygen bubbles from a ceramic pad placed in the bottom of a tank of predetermined dimensions. The stream never became visible on the surface of the wine, because all the oxygen had already been absorbed.

If oak chips or oak staves were used during fermentation, it was possible to produce a wine, in six months or less, which had only ever been stored in tank but which tasted like a wine which had been matured in small oak barrels for 12 to 18 months, and which has a much, much lower production cost.

There turned out to be an object lesson in all this. While some exercised restraint, others didn't, and increased the amount of oxygen, effectively oxidising the wine. Thus the technology did not catch on; after some years of frustration, Pechiney hit upon the idea of only selling the equipment as a package with practical lessons on its use provided by a consultant oenology firm in the country of sale.

Its uptake was immediate, and it is now used in many parts of the world, with wines of many types and prices. Simply called micro-ox, its practitioners are many, including the articulate and often controversial Californian winemaker Randall Grahm.

Coming back to the point where the wine is being taken to barrel (assuming it is so treated) the choice of oak type is, as ever, important. American oak is significantly cheaper than French, especially when supplied by businesses such as World Cooperage, and is still used in Australia for commercial Cabernet Sauvignon. However, with more expensive wines, French oak has replaced American, and experience shows that using a little bit of American oak along with French is like being a little bit pregnant (American oak flavour is very assertive).

Likewise, the malolactic fermentation of more expensive Cabernet Sauvignon will take place in barrel rather than in tank, despite the latter being far easier and less labour-intensive. Then, notwithstanding the crusade by American wine critic Robert Parker, after 12 to 18 months in barrel with a number of rackings along the way, the winemaker will determine whether the wine needs fining (to soften the tannins) and/or filtration. Overall, Australian winemakers are far more aligned with the famed French oenologist Professor Emile Peynaud, who says, 'I have never seen a red wine that was not improved by filtration', than with Robert Parker, who once famously wrote that he automatically down-pointed a wine if he learnt it had been filtered and/or fined. For good measure, cross-flow filtration is vastly improved (more gentle) than the systems used in Peynaud's days (pad/earth/cartridge).

Australian Regional Styles

SOUTH AUSTRALIA

Coonawarra
3452 ha, 11 995 tonnes

Climate: Moderate, MJT 19.9°C, E° Days 1379, SH 7.5, Rain 272 mm, Alt 60 m

The lion's share of the Cabernet Sauvignon grapes grown in Coonawarra go to make a 100 per cent varietal wine. The need to fill in the much-talked-about doughnut hole, the mid-palate, does not exist here. Coonawarra Cabernet Sauvignon is, by nature, a medium-bodied wine with a supple palate and particularly well-balanced tannins. The fruit flavours can vary substantially depending on vintage and maker: blackcurrant/cassis, redcurrant, blackberry and mulberry are most frequently encountered in young wines, which develop a distinctive array of earthy, savoury, spicy, black olive characters with age. Mintiness is noted (usually unfavourably) by some observers; it is difficult to explain given the relative absence of gum trees adjacent to vineyards.

The once lionised and famous 1963 Mildara Coonawarra Cabernet Sauvignon had only one true comparison: Heitz Martha's Vineyard in the Napa Valley. But Mildara only produced that wine once, Heitz repeating the style for decades.

However, super-cuvees of the kind pioneered by Wynns John Riddoch are becoming increasingly common. These do not rely so much on higher alcohol (as is the case with Shiraz) but on higher extract and more deliberately opulent use of oak. For the first ten years or so of their life these wines can seem over the top, and unlikely to open up and invite consumption in the foreseeable future, but then they transform themselves overnight as they pass their tenth birthday, becoming great wines.

The ultimate lifespan of these wines is still to be fully tested. Even with the vagaries of cork, Coonawarra Cabernet Sauvignon could live for 30 years or more if all went well. I see no reason why 50 years should not become possible, although outright and continuing improvement will cease well before that as the wine enters its plateau of peak development.

Cabernet Sauvignon has two major blend-mates in Australia: the Bordeaux group of Merlot, Cabernet Franc, Petit Verdot and Malbec, and Shiraz. I discuss the two blends and styles in the context of the Barossa Valley on page 159.

In the case of Coonawarra, 100 per cent Cabernet Sauvignon rules the majority roost; blends with Shiraz are as common as those with Merlot and friends.

Best producers
Balnaves*, Brand's Laira*, Hollick, Katnook Estate*, Leconfield, Lindemans*, Majella*, Parker Coonawarra Estate*, Penfolds*, Penley Estate, Petaluma*, Rymill, Wynns Coonawarra Estate*, Yalumba, Zema Estate

Padthaway
896 ha, 3810 tonnes

Climate: Warm, MJT 21°C, E° Days 1550, SH 7.8, Rain 210 mm, Alt 50 m

The region has suffered from endemic over-cropping over the years, simply to provide low-cost grapes. However, if properly pruned and trained, the vines can produce excellent Cabernet Sauvignon in a slightly softer mode than Coonawarra.

Producers
Henry's Drive, Morambro Creek Wines

McLaren Vale

1305 ha, 6013 tonnes

Climate: Warm, MJT 21.3°C, E° Days 1680, SH 8.4, Rain 230 mm, Alt 130 m

One of the discoveries of my early wine-buying life was 1961 Seaview Cabernet Sauvignon. Twenty-five years or so later a bottle of 1959 Seaview Cabernet Sauvignon brought to the Royal Sydney Wine Show for one of the judges' dinners (by one of the judges) validated my early enthusiasm for the wine, not to mention the overall suitability of the region for the variety. The key lies in the maritime climate, mimicking that of Bordeaux, albeit with more E° days.

It is an opulent style, with abundant ripe tannins rounding off the often plush palate, but the most distinctive mark of the region is the addition of a touch of bitter chocolate to the normal spectrum of Cabernet Sauvignon fruit flavours.

Best producers

Chalk Hill, Chapel Hill, Clarendon Hills, Coriole, d'Arenberg, DogRidge Wine Co., Geoff Merrill, Hardys*, Kangarilla Road, Kay Brothers Amery Vineyard, Mitolo, Oliver's Taranga Vineyards, Paxton, Penny's Hill, Primo Estate*, Reynella, Richard Hamilton*, RockBare, Serafino, Shaw Family, Shingleback*, Tintara*, Wirra Wirra*, Yangarra Estate*

Barossa Valley

1528 ha, 5203 tonnes

Climate: Warm, MJT 21.4°C, E° Days 1571, SH 8.6, Rain 199 mm, Alt 270 m

In cooler vintages Cabernet Sauvignon features rich and ripe fruit, which provide an ample base for the confident use of oak; the result is an easily accessed and enjoyed wine which will repay cellaring. The substantial gaps in the production of Penfolds Block 42 signify the vintages in which Peter Gago (and team) felt Block 42 could best be employed as a blend component.

Thus some of the greatest wines (notably the special show wines pioneered by Max Schubert) have used Barossa Valley Cabernet Sauvignon as part of a regional and varietal blend (with Shiraz).

It is at this point that I should come clean, as it were, and face up to two complications. First, the concept of regional styles does not readily accommodate itself to the regional blends which have been so important in the development of the Australian wine industry.

All the big companies put a great deal of effort into such blends, which were often the finest red wines they produced.

Second, blends of Cabernet Sauvignon and Shiraz have also been of particular importance. The maker who took this genre to the highest was Max Schubert, with 1962 Bin 60A, a blend of two-thirds Coonawarra Cabernet Sauvignon and one-third Barossa Shiraz, considered by many to be the greatest single Australian red wine ever made. I once wrote of it thus: 'You can lose yourself in the depths of this wine, with its magical complexity of aromas which almost defy description, and a palate gloriously silken in texture, with the flavours shining like a hologram.'

The Barossa Valley is far from a homoclime, becoming much cooler in the foothills of the Eden Valley (see next), so one has to be careful about generalisations, but the absence of many of the highly acclaimed Barossa Valley wineries highlights their dependence on Shiraz for their ratings. It is also notable how many Cabernet Shiraz blends there are, with Yalumba (see also Eden Valley) a master exponent, likewise regional blends, Penfolds Bin 389 unchallenged in this category. Whatever else, these are generous, fleshy and full-bodied wines.

Best producers
Dutschke, Elderton, Glen Eldon, Grant Burge, Hart of the Barossa, Hemera Estate, Hentley Farm*, Kalleske, Penfolds*, Rockford, Saltram, Turkey Flat, Yalumba*

Eden Valley
303 ha, 723 tonnes

> Climate: Moderate, MJT 20.2°C, E° Days 1460, SH 8.5, Rain 275 mm, Alt 420 m

The distinctly cooler climate of the Eden Valley invests its Cabernet Sauvignon with a somewhat tighter, more elegant style (which makes a great blend with its warmer neighbour). A handful of key makers keep the variety in the public eye, for the plantings are not particularly large. I have accorded Yalumba dual citizenship, reflecting its position on the border between the Eden Valley (where it is technically domiciled) and the Barossa Valley.

Best producers
Eden Hall, Flaxman Wines, Heathvale, Henschke*, Poonawatta*, Thorn-Clarke, Yalumba*

Clare Valley
1193 ha, 3476 tonnes

Climate: Warm, MJT 21.4°C, E° Days 1493, SH 8.9, Rain 248 mm, Alt 450 m

The region makes strong and bold, powerful and earthy Cabernet Sauvignon almost from the outset. It is perhaps for this reason that the juicy, jammy Malbec has been a traditional blend-mate with the region's National Treasure winery, Wendouree, joined by Leasingham for this particular wine. Wendouree's 100 per cent Cabernet Sauvignon is gloriously pure, intense and perfectly structured.

Best producers
Crabtree Watervale Wines, Erin Eyes, Greg Cooley, Grosset*, Kilikanoon*, Knappstein*, Leasingham, Mitchell*, Mount Horrocks, Pikes, Skillogalee, Taylors, Wendouree*

NEW SOUTH WALES

Hunter Valley
99 ha, 253 tonnes

Climate: Hot, MJT 23.6°C, E° Days 1823, SH 7.3, Rain 534 mm, Alt 110 m

It was (and is) appropriate that the (late) quirky, quixotic and tendentious Max Lake should have decided to plant Cabernet Sauvignon (and Cabernet alone initially) in a climate far too warm for it – hence Lake's Folly. And it is the ultimate compliment to the red volcanic soils on which the Cabernet Sauvignon is planted that it repaid his faith in the fashion it did. By 1994, Shiraz, Merlot and Petit Verdot had joined what is called 'Cabernets', and no other producer of Hunter Valley Cabernet comes close.

Mudgee
804 ha

Climate: Hot, MJT 23.3°C, E° Days 1663, SH 9, Rain 441 mm, Alt 480 m

The continental climate of Mudgee, and its cold nights, have proved an amenable host for Cabernet Sauvignon, notwithstanding the heat of the summer days. While richly structured and flavoured, the wines are supple and smooth. Nonetheless, Huntington Estate and Robert Stein are the only two producers able to make wines of notable quality.

Orange
300 ha

> **Low Altitude** Climate: Warm, MJT 22.9°C, E° Days 1571, SH 8.9, Rain 414 mm, Alt 670 m
> **High Altitude** Climate: Moderate, MJT 19.6°C, E° Days 1250, SH 8.7, Rain 524 mm, Alt 950 m

Orange and its immediate Central Ranges Zone surrounds are the most important producers of quality Cabernets and Cabernet blends in the greater zone. Neither Mudgee nor Cowra suits Cabernet as well as the higher altitudes of Orange. Here elegant, medium-bodied wines with clear varietal expression are regularly produced in one or other elevations. Orange spans 600 metres to 900 metres, its surrounds 450 metres and above. In the warmer vintages the highest vineyards do best; the converse is the case with cooler vintages, when the lower regions shine. Blends from varying altitudes can also work well.

Best producers
Belgravia*, Bloodwood*, Brangayne of Orange*, Carillion, Centennial Vineyards*, Cumulus, Gordon Hills Estate, Mayfield, Patina, Philip Shaw*, Printhie, Ross Hill*, Sons & Brothers, Tamburlaine

WESTERN AUSTRALIA

Margaret River
1120 ha

> **Yallingup** Climate: Moderate, MJT 20.5°C, E° Days 1655, SH 7.6, Rain 221 mm, Alt 100 m
> **Wallcliffe** Climate: Moderate, MJT 20°C, E° Days 1552, SH 7.4, Rain 261 mm, Alt 90 m
> **Karridale** Climate: Cool, MJT 18.8°C, E° Days 1497, SH 7.1, Rain 305 mm, Alt 50 m

Although the history of Margaret River stretches back little more than 40 years, the sheer number of first-class producers of Cabernet Sauvignon and Cabernet blends leaves only one conclusion: it is the foremost region in Australia for these wines. There are over 160 wineries in Margaret River, 71 with five stars, so it is possible to argue that I should single out yet more producers for special mention.

Its strongly maritime climate has been divided into six subregions by the eminent researcher and climatologist Dr John Gladstones. From north to south they are Yallingup, Carbunup, Wilyabrup, Treeton, Wallcliffe and Karridale. The style of Cabernet Sauvignon varies subtly in each, but the majority of the most highly regarded producers are grouped in the Carbunup and Wilyabrup subregions just to the north of the town of Cowaramup, and in another group just to the south of the Margaret River township.

The differences lie as much in texture, weight and mouthfeel as in flavour. Margaret River Cabernet is seldom green, the flavours running in the classic blackcurrant/cassis spectrum with a juicy mid-palate, then moderately firm tannins running through the notes of black olive and earth on the finish. The power of the fruit allows expansive use of new French oak if the winemaker is so inclined, adding cedar as the wines slowly move towards maturity 20-plus years down the track.

Where there is the full suite of Cabernet Sauvignon, Merlot, Malbec, Cabernet Franc and Petit Verdot (the components other than Cabernet in variable percentages), greater fragrance and a fuller range of black, blue and red fruits can be achieved.

Best producers
Amelia Park, Brookland Valley*, Burch Family Wines*, Cape Mentelle*, Clairault | Streicker, Cullen*, Deep Woods Estate*, Devil's Lair, Evans & Tate, Fire Gully, Flametree, Flowstone*, Flying Fish Cove*, Forester Estate*, Grace Farm, Happs, Hay Shed Hill*, Houghton, Juniper Estate, Larry Cherubino*, Leeuwin Estate, McHenry Hohnen*, Mandoon Estate, Moss Wood*, Pierro, Robert Oatley Vineyards, Thompson Estate, Umamu Estate, Vasse Felix*, Victory Point, Voyager Estate*, Warner Glen Estate, Watershed Wines*, Woodlands Estate*, Woody Nook, Xanadu*

Great Southern
512 ha

> **Frankland River** Climate: Moderate, MJT 20.7°C, E° Days 1574, SH 7.6, Rain 203 mm, Alt 230 m
> **Mount Barker** Climate: Moderate, MJT 20°C, E° Days 1548, SH 7.3, Rain 280 mm, Alt 220 m
> **Denmark** Climate: Cool, MJT 18.9°C, E° Days 1512, SH 6.7, Rain 332 mm, Alt 130 m

Just as the Great Southern shines with Riesling, so it does with Cabernet Sauvignon. In all except the Albany subregion, the climate is strongly continental, and this helps define a style that is largely consistent across the region. US wine writers would describe it as tightly focused, for its varietal fruit flavours are bright and clearly defined, its aromas intense. They run the full spectrum from blackcurrant through to blackberry, red fruit nuances also popping up here and there.

These fresh fruit characters are bound together by typically fine but persistent tannins, which support the innate elegance of the wines. French oak is used almost exclusively, and always sympathetically.

The Great Southern and Margaret River regions produce all but 700 tonnes of the state's total.

Best producers
Alkoomi, Burch Family Wines*, Castelli Estate*, Duckett's Mill, Duke's Vineyard*, Frankland Estate, Harewood Estate, Montgomery's Hill, Moombaki Wines, Plantagenet*, Poacher's Ridge Vineyard, Singlefile*, West Cape Howe*

VICTORIA

Bendigo
136 ha

Climate: Warm, MJT 21.8°C, E° Days 1581, SH 8.3, Rain 269 mm, Alt 220 m

The Cabernet Sauvignons made by then pharmacist Stuart Anderson at Balgownie between 1973 and 1995 (and also thereafter) still stand as landmark wines in the development of the weekend/boutique winery in Australia. They – and so many subsequent vintages – also proved the synergy between Bendigo and the variety. The wine is generous and full, with sturdy tannins, but retains its varietal character in an unashamedly Australian fashion.

Best producers
Balgownie Estate*, Harcourt Valley*, Laanecoorie, Mount Alexander, Pondalowie, Turners Crossing*

Goulburn Valley

250 ha

Climate: Warm, MJT 21.6°C, E° Days 1534, SH 8.2, Rain 285 mm, Alt 140 m

The Cabernets made in this region (and in particular the Nagambie Lakes subregion) are very long-lived and structurally durable. Tahbilk has repeatedly shown how long these wines will live: 30 years will not tire them.

Best producers
Dalfarras, McPherson, Tahbilk*

Heathcote

84 ha

Climate: Warm, MJT 21.6°C, E° Days 1534, SH 8.2, Rain 285 mm, Alt 140 m

This is the very heart of red wine country, and although the focus is more on Shiraz than Cabernet Sauvignon, some magnificently rich and bold Cabernets are made here.

Best producers
Domaine Asmara, Downing Estate*, Margaret Hill Vineyard, Merindoc Vintners, Paul Osicka*, Red Edge, Sanguine Estate*

Yarra Valley

332 ha

Lower Climate: Moderate, MJT 19.4°C, E° Days 1463, SH 7.4, Rain 437 mm, Alt 120 m
Upper Climate: Cool, MJT 18.4°C, E° Days 1253, SH 7.3, Rain 700 mm, Alt 200 m

Cabernet Sauvignon was one of the major red varieties planted in the Yarra Valley around the middle of the nineteenth century, the cuttings for Yeringberg having come (it is said) from Château Lafite. With the rebirth of the Valley from the mid-1960s onwards, it was once again one of the first varieties to be planted, albeit in company with lesser amounts of the other four Bordeaux varieties.

Mount Mary, Yeringberg, Seville Estate and Yarra Yering all chose prime, north-facing slopes which favoured the late-ripening Cabernet Sauvignon, and (blended with judicious amounts of Merlot, etc) produced outstanding wines in all but the worst vintages.

An outside view, as it were, came early in the piece from Brian Croser, ever the iconoclast. He observed that the Yarra Valley was best suited to Cabernet Sauvignon (rather than Pinot Noir) and could challenge Coonawarra and Margaret River for primacy. It was an interesting opinion, doubtless shared by Graeme Miller, whose Chateau Yarrinya Cabernet Sauvignon won the Jimmy Watson Trophy in 1978, Dr John Middleton (Mount Mary) and Dr Bailey Carrodus (Yarra Yering), but not by too many others.

The style is very much governed by site selection and the climatic conditions of each year: Cabernet Sauvignon shines in warmer vintages, but can struggle in cooler, wetter ones. To this day it remains unsuited to the red soils of the Upper Yarra Valley, with Seville Estate (at a lower altitude but on red soil) an exception. At its best it has pristine blackcurrant aroma and flavour, a supple, indeed silky, texture and a long finish supported by fine-grained tannins. There may be a touch of olive and mint in the background; in the lesser years those characters become more obvious.

As the Cabernet wines from Yeringberg that are more than 100 years old (which very occasionally appear) attest, these are wines which are deceptively long-lived; deceptively because tannins and extract are seldom, if ever, high.

Best producers
Coldstream Hills, De Bortoli, Dominique Portet*, Hillcrest Vineyard, Mount Mary*, Oakridge Estate*, Punch, Rochford*, St Huberts*, Seville Estate, Sutherland Estate, Tokar Estate, Yarra Yarra*, Yarra Yering*, Yering Station*, Yeringberg*

Chapter 9

The Classic Red Varietals
Merlot

267 215 ha of Merlot is grown in 33 countries, Peru and the United Kingdom with 2 ha each as the low scorers. Those with over 500 ha are: Algeria 1510 ha, Argentina 6282 ha, Australia 9286 ha, Austria 644 ha, Brazil 766 ha, Bulgaria 10 573 ha, Canada 1139 ha, Chile 10 041 ha, China 3560 ha, Croatia 780 ha, France 114 675 ha, Greece 1248 ha, Hungary 1907 ha, Italy 28 042 ha, Japan 817 ha, Moldova 8123 ha, New Zealand 1290 ha, Portugal 772 ha, Romania 10 988 ha, Russia 1588 ha, Slovenia 996 ha, South Africa 6497 ha, Spain 15 540 ha, Switzerland 1028 ha, Ukraine 2820 ha, United States 22 729 ha, Uruguay 875 ha.

International History

With over 267 000 hectares under vine, Merlot is the second most widely planted grape in the world, Airen (a Spanish white grape of little quality) having slipped from first place to third in 2010. Its principal place of residence in the eighteenth and nineteenth centuries was Bordeaux, and it was not until the last quarter of the twentieth century that it set out to conquer first France and then the rest of the world. In 1970 the area planted was five times as much as that of Cabernet Sauvignon. Up to and including 1990 it remained in front of Cabernet Sauvignon, albeit with a steadily eroding lead that it has since lost altogether in global plantings.

Given the importance of Merlot, the discovery of its parents through DNA analysis is of surprisingly recent origin. In 1999 one parent – father Cabernet Franc – was identified, the other remaining unknown. In 2009 it was revealed to be a variety no longer commercially cultivated, but with five vines surviving, four in the Charente region of France. One vine was found in front of each of four houses in four villages, and – no longer having an ampelographical name – it has been called Magdeleine Noir des Charentes, the mother of Merlot.[1]

Its birthplace was almost certainly Bordeaux (near Libourne, on the right bank of the Gironde), and by 1783 this was written: 'Merlau … makes a black and excellent wine.' The modern spelling, Merlot, was first used in 1824.[2]

In 1960 there were 17 000 hectares in France; by 1980 that figure had risen to 87 000 hectares, compared with 36 500 hectares of Cabernet Sauvignon. Merlot's march south then gathered pace. Over the next 30 years plantings rose dramatically, before easing back to the present level of 114 675 hectares.

While its throne is the right bank of the Gironde in the communes of Pomerol and St Emilion, it is endemic throughout the many communes of greater Bordeaux, with 69 297 hectares in bearing (twice as much as Cabernet Sauvignon). In all instances it is its earlier ripening habit than Cabernet Sauvignon (at least a week) and its consequent ability to deal with colder, wetter, clay-based soils which led vignerons to plant twice as much Merlot as Cabernet Sauvignon. The fact that it can yield three times as much as Cabernet no doubt fortified the choice.

It is precisely this fecundity which has caused vignerons to blink. Great Merlot produces sumptuously rich, velvety, beautifully balanced wine that will live for half a century or more if carefully cellared. Think Château Pétrus and say no more. The soft and very large underbelly of Merlot, whether from Bordeaux's Entre Deux Mers, Languedoc-Roussillon, Italy's Veneto or Australia's Riverland, has plum-fruit pastille flavour, minimal tannins, and is frequently given an extra layer of sweetness from residual sugar. It is an anodyne counterpart to Pinot Grigio, and familiarity with it breeds boredom at best, and contempt with prolonged exposure.

It is planted in 35 official regions of France, an impressive number until you find it is planted in 106 regions in Italy. There it is still flourishing, its plantings of 25 614 hectares in 2000 rising to 28 042 hectares in 2010. It has three faces: first a sweet and sour mix of stewed fruit and herbaceousness from overcropped vines in Veneto[3]; second, as a blend-mate with Sangiovese and other noble Italian varieties; and third, as a voluptuously rich wine from some of Tuscany's biggest names.

---

1   Jancis Robinson, Julia Harding and Jose Vouillamoz, *Wine Grapes*, Ecco/HarperCollins, 2012, pp. 629–30.
2   ibid., p. 629.
3   ibid., p. 631.

Prior to 1970, there were virtually no plantings in California (the first recorded wine was a 1969 Sterling Vineyards Merlot), and the growth of the plantings in the early 1970s was very modest, reaching a mere 800 hectares by 1985. Since then growth has been as dramatic as the subsequent boom in Australia (it is quite remarkable how Australia five or ten years later has followed in the footsteps of California), with plantings rising to 13 400 hectares by 1996. Just as phylloxera led to a major increase in the plantings of Cabernet Sauvignon in Bordeaux (and the near disappearance of Malbec and Carmenere), so the invasion of phylloxera Type B in the Napa Valley in the early 1990s led to a massive change in the varietal make-up of the region, with Merlot a major beneficiary. It reached a peak of 20 640 hectares in 2004, but has since fallen back to a still-impressive total of 18 924 hectares in 2010. These days it is the red wine equivalent of Chardonnay, the preferred choice of those simply seeking a glass of red.

Along with the other Bordeaux varieties, Merlot went to South America prior to the outbreak of phylloxera in Bordeaux. For Chile this meant (as it has in most of Australia) no phylloxera or grafting, and the establishment of what was thought to be Merlot, but 2600 hectares has turned out to be Carmenere, leaving the country with a total of 10 041 hectares. Chilean Merlot has become well known around the world.

Together with Chardonnay, it was the variety which powered the growth of the Washington State wine industry during the 1980s and 1990s: there are now 3334 hectares planted.

Canada's even quirkier (from a climatological viewpoint) Okanagan Valley (641 hectares in 2008) has also put some of its money on Merlot; like in Washington, part is used in Bordeaux/Meritage blends, part as a varietal wine. On the opposite side of the country, Ontario has found sufficient warm sites to plant 498 hectares (2008).

International Styles

BORDEAUX, FRANCE

France: 114 675 ha

Haut Medoc

In the Haut Medoc, it has long been called the insurance grape, providing cover for those vintages in which the Cabernet Sauvignon doesn't ripen fully. Such vintages are significantly less common in the twenty-first century than they were in the twentieth century, but this hasn't led to the replacement of Merlot by Cabernet. There are two reasons: first, the economic cost of deliberately reducing the size of the make for reasons other than quality (Merlot has a high yield); second, because the style of the Cabernet made could vary too much from year to year.

St Emilion and Pomerol

In my discussion of Merlot in the French context, I have deliberately bypassed the fact that all the Right Bank wines have a significant proportion of Cabernet Franc in their make-up: Château Cheval Blanc tops the poll with two-thirds Cabernet Franc and one-third Merlot (and 1 per cent Malbec). Only Château Pétrus has 95 per cent Merlot (with up to 5 per cent Cabernet Franc), which is an exceedingly hard varietal act to follow. The Cabernet Franc was planted only after the 1956 frosts decimated Bordeaux. There was a patch at Château Pétrus that was less perfectly suited to Merlot than the rest, and this is what was planted to Cabernet Franc. However, it was more than 20 years before it was included in the wine, and then it was included strictly on the basis of the individual year's quality.

Partly because of the blend issues, but in no small measure because there is little or no consensus on the flavour great Merlot should exhibit (there is more agreement on its texture), I duck the issue here, but return to it in the discussion of Australian winemaking of Merlot on page 174.

As with Cabernet Sauvignon, I shall not list the best producers: here, too, there are dozens of books and websites that, coupled with the official classification of St Emilion (true, there is no classification for Pomerol), provide the information.

UNITED STATES
22 729 ha

Napa and Sonoma Valleys, California

When Merlot first started to come on-stream in the 1980s, the approach was to extract every shred of tannin and then to add 25 per cent Cabernet Sauvignon to further fortify the wine. Duckhorn (which crushed 28 tonnes of Merlot in 1978) was the first to make a name for itself, but ten years down the track Dan Duckhorn was able to say, 'I really don't like Merlot on its own in most years; every now and then you get a vintage when it can perhaps account for 95 per cent of the finished wine, but in most years it needs more support – around 25 per cent.' He went on to describe his Three Palms Merlot as 'a big, brawny style, more power than fruit, and a touch of bitterness'.[4]

---

4   James Halliday, *Wine Atlas of California*, Angus & Robertson, 1993, p. 98.

By the 1990s there was a major change, encapsulated in the phrases 'Cabernet without the pain' and 'mellow Merlot'. The result has been the association of Merlot with cheap, soft, fruit-sweet wines, in much the same fashion as in Australia. The reputation of the variety is protected by what we know in Australia as Bordeaux blends, called Meritage in California.

Best producers
Barnett Vineyards*, Benziger Family, Beringer Blass*, Cafaro Cellars, Chappellet*, Chimney Rock, Duckhorn, Eagles Trace, Kenefick Ranch, Newton Vineyards, Niebaum Coppola, Pahlmeyer*, Robert Sinskey Vineyards, St Clement Vineyards, Shafer Vineyards*, Stag's Leap Wines Cellars*, Truchard Vineyards

Washington State
Merlot is singularly well adapted to the unusual climate and growing conditions of the Columbia Valley. Once the winter pruning is done, the vine seems to self-regulate thereafter, and to require a minimal amount of summer training to achieve good fruit exposure and a balanced canopy. Where California's Merlots are powerful and masculine, Washington's are fragrant, willowy and feminine.

Best producers
Columbia Valley: Andrew Will, Chinook Wines, Columbia Crest*, Hogue Cellars, Snoqualmie Vineyards; Walla Walla: L'Ecole No. 41*, Leonetti Cellar*, Long Shadows, Northstar, Pepper Bridge Winery

CANADA
1139 ha

Merlot is British Columbia's most planted variety (641 hectares) along both sides of the Okanagan Valley. Unlimited water from Lake Okanagan and a dry summer are its strengths, a short growing season its limitation. On the opposite side of the country is Ontario (498 hectares), which cannot ripen Cabernet Sauvignon, and doesn't always succeed with its light-bodied Merlots.

Best producers
Burrowing Owl, Cedar Creek, Gehringer Brothers, Mission Hill Winery, Sumac Ridge

CHILE
10 041 ha

While Merlot was one of the original Bordeaux imports, it was not until the 1990s that it really took off. In 1993 there were only 12 labels on the market; by 1998 there were 75, and today the total is over 100, coming from 10 041 hectares under vine. In sharp contrast to California's Merlots, Chile's are soft and supple, and often have herbal/olive characters.

Best producers
Caliterra, Canepa, Carmen*, Casa Lapostolle*, Concha Y Toro, Cono Sur*, Del Bosque, Leyda, Montes*, Puertas*, Santa Rita, Valdivieso, Villard

NEW ZEALAND
1290 ha, 10 756 tonnes

Counterintuitively in one sense, but understandably in another, plantings of Merlot have declined from 1487 hectares in 2004 to 1290 hectares in 2014. The development of Hawke's Bay, and warmer vintages, would suggest an increase, but the variety suffers the same malaise that affects other regions around the world: a hangover the morning after its surge leading up to the end of the twentieth century.

Hawke's Bay
1080 ha, 9043 tonnes

As with Cabernet Sauvignon, the 1998 vintage redefined what was possible in New Zealand, but common sense would tell you that Merlot should be an easier proposition in less beneficent vintages. That said, New Zealand's winemakers are as conscious these days as their counterparts elsewhere of the distinction between green tannins and ripe tannins – a distinction having nothing to do with yield. The other game changer has been the development of the Gimblett Gravels; ironically, however, this has been an even greater boon for Cabernet Sauvignon. In the final analysis, Hawke's Bay has a near-monopoly of New Zealand's Merlot, Gisborne (103 hectares) accounting for most of the balance.

Best producers
Craggy Range Vineyards*, Esk Valley, Kingsley Estate, Matua Valley*, Mills Reef, Mission Estate*, Ngatarawa, CJ Pask, Sacred Hill Wines, Saint Clair Estate*, Sileni Estate, Te Mata Estate* (blend), Trinity Hill, Vidal Estate (blend), Villa Maria

SOUTH AFRICA

6497 ha

South Africa has a very respectable 6497 hectares, which is strange given the grudging acceptance – at best – of the wine by South African wine judges and critics. Perhaps the answer lies in the difference between serious Merlot (made in small quantities) and the far cheaper, lighter and sweet Merlot made for casual consumers.

As with the wines of other countries, I include Merlot-dominant blends in this section.

Best producers
Amani, Bein*, Eagles Nest*, Elgin Vintners, Hillcrest Estate*, Jordan Wine Estate, Laibach, Nederburg Wines, Remhoogte, Rust en Vrede, Saxenburg, Shannon, Spier, Thelema Mountain Vineyards, Veenwouden, Vergelegen*, Vergenoegd, Yonder Hill

Australian History

In 1980, 68 tonnes of Merlot were crushed in Australia; to the extent that if the grapes were grown in Victoria, they were as likely as not to in fact have been Cabernet Franc. The variety thereafter disappeared from statistical sight until 1989, when it reappeared with 2419 tonnes from 274 hectares in bearing (another 109 hectares was still to come on-stream). Its growth over the next seven years was, on one view, impressive, rising to 9227 tonnes from 1246 hectares in 1996. Thereafter it took off like a space rocket, dwarfing the growth of all other varieties, to reach 104 423 tonnes from 10 100 hectares in 2002.

A decade later, in 2012, the plantings had fallen to 9286 hectares, 214 hectares having been removed that year, albeit offset by new plantings of 69 hectares; production of 117 383 tonnes had basically stalled.

Australian Statistics

9286 ha, 117 383 tonnes, 1282 growers/makers

Merlot: tonnes crushed in Australia, 1996–2012

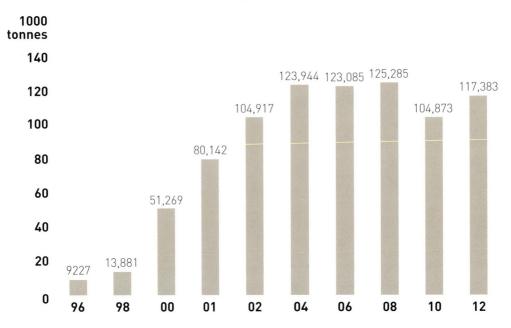

Australian Winemaking

Plantings are recorded in 78 zones, regions, subregions and 'other' districts. Of the total, 4182 hectares are in the hot irrigation regions spread along the Murrumbidgee and Murray rivers; with the best will in the world, these locations cannot be described as suitable for wines other than cheap, soft reds for bulk exports, bag-in-box, and sub-$10 bottles. Because the yield per hectare of each of these regions is at least double that of the other two categories covered in the next two paragraphs, their contribution to the total crush is closer to 80 per cent than 40 per cent. This is reinforced by the fact that Merlot's average production (2012) was 13 tonnes per hectare, by some distance the highest of the Classic Red Varieties, with only the low-quality and fast-disappearing Ruby Cabernet (15 tonnes per hectare) and the fast-increasing (and far superior) Petit Verdot (17 tonnes per hectare) more productive.

The next group of regions are warm, basically unsuited to Merlot, producing wines generally high in alcohol and lacking varietal expression. In all they account for 972 hectares, many with only token plantings. They produce wines that have plummy fruit, negligible tannins, and often a little residual sugar (±5 grams per litre). They are the red wine equivalent of commercial Pinot Gris and/or low-priced Sauvignon Blanc.

The area of the third group is roughly 75 per cent of that of the irrigation regions, here 3394 hectares. Because Merlot – even good Merlot – has a number of varietal expressions (floral, plum, red berry, blackcurrant, black olive, herbaceous, earthy) driven by different terroirs, I have adopted an inclusive approach in coming to the 4134 hectares.

The decisions for the winemaker are how ripe Merlot should be before it is picked; whether or not it should be given pre- or post-fermentation maceration to boost its body and tannins; and how much new oak (French) it should be given. American oak, new or used, is no longer considered suitable. While these are real choices, with significant consequences, the rest of the winemaking is largely standard practice.

I should add that much Merlot is blended with Cabernet Sauvignon, whether at the top of the quality tree or the bottom. If the former, the most important region for the variety, Margaret River, will most likely include lesser amounts of some or all of the other Bordeaux varieties (Cabernet Franc, Malbec and Petit Verdot) in the blend.

The fall from grace of Merlot in Australia is matched in other countries, but there has been increasing disquiet from winemakers about the quality of the clones available here. Peter Bissell, winemaker at Balnaves of Coonawarra, returned after doing a vintage in Pomerol a decade ago with wines from the vintage he had just made there, and compared those with Balnaves' current vintage. He had expected to see a significant difference, but it wasn't there initially.[5]

Nonetheless, Yalumba (in its extensive nursery propagation of numerous clones and varieties) and Pepper Tree have variously focused on three new clones: 8R, Q45 and 141. Having seen Yalumba's clonal trials in Wrattonbully, Pepper Tree planted 4 hectares of 8R, and made its first vintage in 2012. In blind tastings of that vintage, it was clearly a better wine than Pepper Tree's wines from its vineyards in Wrattonbully and Coonawarra. The colour is deeper, the fruit spectrum darker, purer and more focused, the structure significantly better, with good tannin/acid interplay providing excellent length. These clones may yet redeem the reputation of the variety.[6]

---

5   Peter Bissell, personal communication.
6   Jim Chatto, personal communication.

Australian Regional Styles

SOUTH AUSTRALIA

Adelaide Hills
176 ha, 686 tonnes

Climate: Cool, MJT 18.9°C, E° Days 1359, SH 8.4, Rain 352 mm, Alt 500 m

Arguably, the best is still to come, but the climate (or choice of site climate) seems tailor-made for the variety, producing wines of exemplary varietal character, weight and structure.

Best producers
Bird in Hand*, Mike Press, The Lane Vineyard*

Barossa and Eden Valleys
Barossa Valley: 377 ha, 1967 tonnes. Eden Valley: 78 ha, 213 tonnes

Barossa Valley Climate: Warm, MJT 21.4°C, E° Days 1571, SH 8.6, Rain 199 mm, Alt 270 m
Eden Valley Climate: Moderate, MJT 20.2°C, E° Days 1460, SH 8.5, Rain 275 mm, Alt 420 m

These regions are grouped first because the Barossa Zone encompasses both regions, but can be used whether the wine is a blend from the regions, or is 100 per cent from one or the other. The second reason is that the warm Barossa Valley is by far the largest grower, but the much smaller Eden Valley has a climate better suited to the variety.

But there are hidden questions: what do those who pay more than $20 to $25 a bottle expect from the wine? Simply more depth, but still with plummy fruit (that of the Barossa Valley)? Or do they want some savoury black olive nuances to run alongside blackcurrant (and some plum) fruit flavours backed by moderate tannins? This is more likely to come from the Eden Valley. In either case, how much oak is too much?

These questions are also relevant to my discussion of new clones in eminently suited regions such as Coonawarra and Wrattonbully (see page 175). Given all these questions, the list of producers does not attempt to delve further into the nebulous quest of 'Best'. They are makers who have gained more recognition from time to time than their compatriots.

Best producers
Burge Family, Craneford, David Franz, Dutschke, Haan, Hemera Estate, Irvine, Robert Johnson Vineyards, Rohrlach

Coonawarra
371 ha, 1459 tonnes

Climate: Moderate, MJT 19.9°C, E° Days 1379, SH 7.5, Rain 272 mm, Alt 60 m

This is an ideal place for growing Merlot if ever there was one. The wines have all the sweet berry fruit one could wish for, yet retain a silky elegance which is wholly admirable. As elsewhere, much is pressed into service as part of a Bordeaux blend, but some of the best parcels escape. That there isn't more grown and/or branded Coonawarra has much to do with public perception (and wine show judges) that high-quality Merlots are few and far between. For example, no Treasury Wine Estates Coonawarra Merlot is made, despite the size of its vineyards (all varieties) in Coonawarra, leaving the field open for Margaret River, the one region that really does perform, to have a clear run.

Best producers
Katnook Estate, Leconfield, Majella, Parker Coonawarra Estate*

Wrattonbully
299 ha, 2220 tonnes

Climate: Moderate, MJT 20.4°C, E° Days 1473, SH 7.6, Rain 227 mm, Alt 60 m

The region (unnamed) had been in production since 1973, 32 years before the Wrattonbully name was finally agreed on and registered. The reasons are ancient history, made more irrelevant by the dramatic increase in plantings during the 1990s. The climate is poised between those of Coonawarra and Padthaway, warmer than the former and cooler than the latter, variations within the region due to the Naracoorte Range that bisects it. It shares the same terra rossa soil as that made famous in Coonawarra, and good-quality underground water is still freely available and used in most vineyards. A large custom-crush winery was constructed in 1998, servicing the needs of the major grape (and bulk wine) buyers from the region. Yalumba's Smith & Hooper Vineyard is of long standing, and particularly noted for its Merlot, as are two much smaller high-profile businesses, Tapanappa (a partnership with Brian Croser at its head) and Terre à Terre (that of the husband and wife team of Xavier Bizot of the Bollinger family and Lucy Croser, daughter of Brian Croser).

Best producers
Smith & Hooper, Tapanappa, Terre à Terre

McLaren Vale
249 ha, 1820 tonnes

> Climate: Warm, MJT 21.3°C, E° Days 1680, SH 8.4, Rain 230 mm, Alt 130 m

Here the climate borders on being that little bit too easy, the wines becoming that little bit too big and generous for the purists. For most consumers this generosity is all to the good. So what if the borderline between Merlot and other full-bodied varieties is blurred? Voluptuous, plummy/dark berry fruit with touches of bitter chocolate is an enticing proposition. As in the case of the Barossa Valley and Eden Valley, I am simply giving a list of best producers without discrimination between them.

Best producers
Clarendon Hills, Fox Creek, Penny's Hill, Pirramimma, Yangarra Estate

VICTORIA

Yarra Valley
118 ha

> **Lower** Climate: Moderate, MJT 19.4°C, E° Days 1463, SH 7.4, Rain 437 mm, Alt 120 m
> **Upper** Climate: Cool, MJT 18.4°C, E° Days 1253, SH 7.3, Rain 700 mm, Alt 200 m

The variety had a history of constant problems with fruit set and hence very irregular cropping from one year to the next. That vignerons persevered with it was a tribute to the quality of the wine which is made when there are grapes to pick. These problems have diminished with greater vine maturity, and warmer growing seasons. Most of the production is dedicated to Bordeaux blends, but some varietal wines are made, with little to choose between them.

Best producers
Elmswood Estate, Hillcrest Vineyard, Mandala, Morgan Vineyards, Oakridge Estate, Punt Road, Seville Hill, TarraWarra Estate, Wedgetail Estate

WESTERN AUSTRALIA

Margaret River
416 ha

> Climate: Moderate, MJT 20°C, E° Days 1552, SH 7.4, Rain 261 mm, Alt 90 m

The variety is ideally suited to the region, and much is dedicated to Bordeaux blends. Fruit set is consistent, yields to the point where fruit thinning is necessary to protect quality. The style is as close to perfect as one could wish, a gentle mix of small red berry fruit and more savoury/olivaceous notes, the tannins fine and soft.

Best producers
Cape Naturaliste, Fermoy Estate, Gallows Wine Co, Island Brook, Laurance*, Moss Wood*, Oceans Estate, The Alchemists*

Manjimup and Pemberton
Manjimup: 33 ha. Pemberton: 47 ha

> **Manjimup** Climate: Moderate, MJT 20.6°C, E° Days 1591, SH 7.3, Rain 269 mm, Alt 260 m
> **Pemberton** Climate: Moderate, MJT 19.2°C, E° Days 1468, SH 7, Rain 326 mm, Alt 170 m

Although these two areas (they are Siamese twins, still joined) were originally conceived for Pinot Noir and Chardonnay, many producers now believe the Bordeaux varieties – and in particular Merlot – are better suited. Site selection and site climate will always come up, with examples to suit either side of the argument; perhaps we will know more in 20 years' time.

Best producers
Castelli Estate, Hillbrook, Truffle Hill, Woodgate Wines

OTHER REGIONS

The following producers have produced meritorious Merlots in recent years:

Albany: Parish Lane; Central Victoria Zone: Brave Goose*; Denmark: Yilgarnia; Geelong: Bellarine Estate; Granite Belt: Sirromet; Heathcote: Granite Hills*; Mount Barker: Poacher's Ridge Vineyard*; Orange: Cargo Road, Cumulus*; Pyrenees: Mount Avoca*; Tasmania: Stefano Lubiana; Upper Goulburn: Mount Cathedral Vineyards, Sedona Estate.

Chapter 10

The Classic Red Varietals
Pinot Noir

98 744 ha of Pinot Noir is grown in 32 countries, Peru and Thailand with 1 ha each. Those with plantings in excess of 500 ha are: Algeria 1510 ha, Argentina 1802 ha, Australia 4978 ha, Austria 646 ha, Canada 640 ha, Chile 2884 ha, Czech Republic 688 ha, France 29 738 ha, Hungary 1091 ha, Italy 5046 ha, Moldova 6521 ha, New Zealand 5509 ha, Romania 1089 ha, Russia 533 ha, South Africa 962 ha, Spain 1044 ha, Switzerland 4402 ha, Ukraine 767 ha, United States 16 776 ha.

International History

Until DNA analysis began in 1993, with four Australian-based researchers, MR Thomas, S Matsumoro, P Cam and NS Scott (the last a next-door neighbour of mine in the 1970s in Sydney) making the breakthrough, and much of the subsequent DNA profiling by Jose Vouillamoz et al., it had always been assumed that Pinot Noir, Pinot Gris, Pinot Blanc and Pinot Meunier were distinct varieties within the Pinot family, but DNA has established that all have the same genetic fingerprint. They are mutations that have evolved over 1000 or so years, hence the use of Pinot simpliciter in this discussion of the history of what are four mutations.

As I have outlined in the introduction to this book, Pinot is one of a group of four varieties that have played a major role in the evolution of the 1368 grape varieties known to be – or to have recently been – in commercial production in 2011. It is thus one of the most ancient surviving varieties, its complete parentage still unknown. (For extended discussion, see Robinson.[1])

---

1   Jancis Robinson, Julia Harding and Jose Vouillamoz, *Wine Grapes*, Ecco/HarperCollins, 2012, pp. 221, 805–15.

Its ancient origins are reflected in two ways: there are more than 1000 registered clones or biotypes of Pinot, and it is probable that Pinot had been propagated throughout Western Europe for centuries before its present name was given.[2] Robinson's Pinot Pedigree diagram[3] includes three key varieties among the 156 Western European varieties: Savagnin, Gouais Blanc and Pinot.

The surprises come thick and fast. Pinot is a probable grandparent of Teroldego, Marzemino, Lagrein and Dureza; since Dureza is a parent of Shiraz, Pinot is its likely great-grandparent. Moreover, if as Robinson suggests, Pinot is a parent of Savagnin, it is a grandparent of Chenin Blanc and Sauvignon Blanc, and – most dramatically – a great-grandparent of Cabernet Sauvignon. (If, as is possible, Savagnin is the parent, Pinot the offspring, the family still exists, with siblings coming into the frame.)

And so to the problem of connecting the dots of ancient or vague references to the variety we now know as Pinot Noir. What is clear is that Morillon (itself spelt in four different ways), Noirien and (less commonly) Auvernat were all synonyms of Pinot Noir. Moreillion (so spelt) was used in 1283, Noirien appearing alongside Morrillon in the mid-thirteenth century. The earliest uses of the name Pinot were in 1375[4], and again in 1394, both times spelt Pinoz (denoting the plural).

Its battle for supremacy with Gamay in Burgundy dates back to the adoption of the name Pinot Noir in the fourteenth century. In 1395 Phillip the Bold issued a decree ordering the uprooting of 'the bastard Gamay', a decree honoured more in the breach than the observance in the southern parts of Burgundy.

Pinot Noir's arrival – and that of Chardonnay and Pinot Meunier – in Champagne predated the development of Champagne (the wine) as we know it today, which followed the doubtless apocryphal cry of Dom Pérignon, 'Come quickly, Brothers, there are stars in the wine.'

It began to be grown in small amounts in the Loire Valley, Alsace, Germany and throughout most of both Eastern and Western Europe, which simply served to demonstrate how hard to please the variety is. The first reliable mention of Pinot Noir in Germany was in 1470 at Hattenheim in the Rheingau. However, Berhard Huber in Baden, Germany, is one of those whose wines suggest we may be seeing a full-blown return of the Medieval Warm Period.

---

2 ibid., p. 810.
3 ibid., pp. 806–07.
4 ibid., p. 809.

Its extreme sensitivity to place is paralleled by the importance of clonal selection, a process given special importance in the last 30 years of the twentieth century and extending to the present time.

In the mid-1970s Burgundy – like Bordeaux – was going through a difficult economic period, with the market flooded and prices at all-time lows. Increasing the yield and hence reducing the cost per tonne seemed the answer. Whether the slump was to prove short- or long-lived (it was in fact short), the fallacy of the 'solution' quickly became apparent: producing greater amounts of weak and watery Burgundy only worsened the situation.

Clones 113, 114 and 115, identified by Professor Raymond Bernard at the University of Dijon, were soon replaced in favour by the lower-yielding, smaller-berried clones 776, 777 and 828 (114 had proved the best of the initial three). While conventional wisdom pointed to a mix of these 'new' clones, many of the most famous estates preferred the 'clonal massif' field selection of their own vines.

Finally, as Burgundy continued to prosper mightily through the 1980s and 1990s, the replanting of entire blocks (rather than simply replacing missing or dead vines one by one) became a familiar sight – a large slice of the Domaine de la Romanée-Conti's La Tache remained fallow during 2000 and 2001. In the case of DRC (as it is known for short), the replanted material all came from cuttings originally emanating from Romanée-Conti itself.

Both the inherent allure of great Pinot Noir and the reputation (and fortune) to be gained by successfully growing and making it led both the Old World outside of France and the New World to plant it. The early efforts in California and Australia were equally disastrous: areas far too warm were selected, with the consequence that in the 1970s Californian Pinot Noir grapes sold for less per tonne than Thompson's Seedless.

It quickly became apparent that a climate as cool as that of Burgundy was the first requirement, and that the replication of the limestone soil was of less importance. Patterns are emerging in the twenty-first century, but there is still much to be learnt, and (particularly outside Burgundy) better wines to be made as greater vine age is matched by growing experience.

International Styles
BURGUNDY, FRANCE
France: 29 738 ha

Give or take a century or two, the region we now know as Burgundy was pinpointed as a great wine-producing area by the end of the first millennium. For the next 600 years, the monasteries and monks painstakingly discovered, defined and refined the precise parameters for the growing of the greatest, great, very good, good and unsuitable plots of Pinot Noir (and Chardonnay). The distances involved were as often measured in metres as in kilometres. The classification into Grand Crus, Premier Crus and Commune wines was formalised in 1861, but not given full legal status until 1936 and 1937, as part of the formal Appellation Contrôlée System of France.

While Burgundy remains by far the most eloquent and convincing demonstration of the importance of terroir, the consequences of the multitude of winemaking choices, and the skill with which those choices are realised, can all but obliterate the influence of terroir. This was the principal accusation raised against the wines made by the disciples of Guy Accad towards the end of the 1980s, and the reason for some having modified or abandoned his techniques. These involved the addition of very high levels of SO_2 to delay the onset of fermentation for two weeks or more. The issue in Burgundy was the accusation that his extreme forms of extraction of colour, flavour and tannins subverted the sense of place.

While the SO_2 approach has been abandoned, 'pre-fermentation cold soak', chilling the must below 10°C, is a widespread – though not universal – practice in the New World, and either happens with cold grapes in cold cellars in the Old World, or is deliberately achieved by chilling the must.

All of this adds up to the undeniable truth that Pinot Noir is the most translucent, the most transparent, the most hauntingly ethereal and fragile of all wines. Even blockbusters such as those made by Leroy are so described within the context of Burgundy, and are positively delicate when compared with (say) a blood and thunder high-alcohol Californian Pinot Noir (up to 17 per cent alc/vol) or Barossa Valley Shiraz.

There was a time when, unburdened with too much knowledge, I was prepared to describe the fragrant peacock's tail of Chambolle Musigny (and Musigny in particular), the velvety, deep richness of Chambertin and the subtle differences of the other Grand Crus of that commune; the racy power of the Grand Crus of Vosne Romanée; and how much the chunky power of Pommard or Corton (in the Côte de Beaune) could lead you to think (in blind tastings) the wine(s) came from the Côte de Nuits.

Older and wiser, I expect to find the nuances of terroir most clearly expressed when tasting from barrel to barrel in the cellar of a fine producer in Burgundy, or in Australia, and to search for – and hope to find – similar differences when I know the identity of the maker. What I am saying, therefore, is that the philosophy and techniques of the maker can be every bit as important as the terroir.

There are, of course, characteristics which all great Pinot Noirs share. The importance of the aroma transcends all else: the Burgundians say, get the bouquet right and the palate will take care of itself. The Bordelaise take the opposite point of view: if the palate is correct, the bouquet will follow.

The greater the Burgundy, the more entrancing the bouquet will be. (Pausing here for a moment: fine Pinot Noir of any provenance deserves a purpose-designed Burgundy crystal glass of the type provided by Riedel; mercifully, the once-common ISO XL5 tasting glass commits murder of Pinot Noir and has been banished.) It – the bouquet – will be intensely aromatic, with myriad fruity, flowery, spicy, savoury, foresty scents, perhaps even the forest floor.

Like a Catherine wheel, the aromatic sparkles will constantly change and then return. It is extremely easy to lose yourself in the bouquet of a great Burgundy, the minutes passing by all but unnoticed. Not infrequently, I have hesitated to take the first sip, lest the magic of the bouquet be lost or tarnished.

Barnyard and other similar notes were once tolerated, welcomed even, but today are often regarded with extreme suspicion as indicators of bacterial activity, and – in particular – the presence of brettanomyces.

Once in the mouth, it is the length of flavour, the finish and the aftertaste which, more than anything else, define the quality of Burgundy. I describe the flavour profile as silky and linear, but this is in no way intended to suggest that the wine is simple. The tannins are – or should be – finer, softer and less obvious than in the other great red varieties.

The flavours change dramatically as the wine ages, giving rise to the most vexed and often argued question about Burgundy: when does it reach its peak? The answer depends on the value you place on the primary fruit – violets, strawberry, raspberry, cherry, red plum, black plum – and how much on the more complex, savoury, spicy, foresty, tobacco characters which reveal themselves as the wine ages.

The greater the wine's quality, the more gradual this change will be. And great or not so great, there will be no precise moment when the wine will pass from youth to maturity, reach its peak, or start to decline. Ideally, a fine Burgundy will always retain significant primary fruit at its core, with a web of secondary characters surrounding that core.

From this point on, as one looks at the relatively few other parts of the world in which Pinot Noir flourishes, the same themes occur repeatedly, and I shall by and large take them for granted. Nor, incidentally, is there any particular magic in the order in which they are discussed.

Best producers

The following is an abbreviated list, chosen partly because all are imported into Australia (often in minuscule quantities) and partly because they are personal favourites.

Armand Rousseau*, Benjamin Leroux, Bouchard Père et Fils*, Chandon de Briailles, Comte de Vogue*, Domaine de Bellene, Domaine de la Romanée-Conti*, Domaine de l'Arlot, Domaine de Montille*, Domaine Dujac*, Georges Roumier, Henri Gouges, J Confuron-Coteditot, Jean Grivot*, Jean-Jacques Confuron, Marquis d'Angerville, Mongeard-Mugneret*, Jacques-Frederic Mugnier*, Simon Bize et Fils*, Tollot-Beaut et Fils

NEW ZEALAND

5509 ha, 36 499 tonnes

A minnow in overall world production terms, New Zealand has unlimited potential for the production of world-class Pinot Noir. Although relatively small in total land mass, it stretches from 34°S to 47°S, over 1600 kilometres. Too warm in the north, and too cold in the far south, it nonetheless provides six regions which have already produced outstanding Pinots (Martinborough/Wairarapa, Marlborough, Nelson, Waipara, Canterbury and Central Otago) with a seventh (Hawke's Bay) seeking to demonstrate that its cooler sites, inland and higher, can do likewise.

All the pioneer producers were small, producing tiny quantities of Pinots with great character and individuality. Then Montana joined the fray with stupefying speed and commitment; in the space of a few short years, it came from a zero base to challenge Louis Jadot of France and Kendall-Jackson of California as the largest maker of Pinot Noir in the world.

The styles of the individual makers, and those of the regions in which they are situated, vary from moderately to unashamedly powerful; luscious Pinot Noir varietal fruit is the rule, not the exception, reaching its highest expression with several of the Martinborough makers, and again in Central Otago. While many will remain small producers through choice or necessity, they have established a strong and loyal market in Australia, and unchallenged reputations in the United Kingdom and the United States.

Wairarapa

500 ha, 2279 tonnes

This was the first region (known by its subregion Martinborough) to demonstrate New Zealand's capacity to make world-class Pinot Noir; earlier attempts around Auckland had been a dismal failure. But at the southern end of the North Island, top-quality Pinots are grown on the particular geology of gravelly terraces tightly clustered around the town of Martinborough. The style varies from the sophisticated restraint of Martinborough Vineyards to the awesome power, depth and longevity of Ata Rangi. More recently, the Larry McKenna–inspired (and co-owned) Escarpment has convincingly stretched the borders of the traditional Martinborough region with emphatic Pinot Noir.

Best producers
Ata Rangi*, Craggy Range Vineyards*, Dry River Wines*, Escarpment*, Martinborough Vineyards, Palliser Estate*, Te Kairanga, Voss Estate

Nelson

241 ha, 1416 tonnes

A small region with unusually varied topography and soil (by New Zealand's standards), producing a wide range of varietals, wines of great structure and finesse, Pinot Noir included, led by Neudorf.

Best producers
Greenhough Vineyards, Neudorf Vineyards*, Te Mania, Woollaston*

Marlborough

2492 ha, 18 940 tonnes

Pinot Noir was grown in Marlborough for upwards of 30 years, with large yields from the Bachtebel clone specifically directed to sparkling wine. Almost overnight, it seemed, small and large wineries alike recognised the potential of the region if appropriate clones were planted and yields held under control. Montana, the pioneer of broadacre viticulture in Marlborough, set about developing specialised fermentation tanks for large-scale production of Pinot Noir, but also planted vines on terraces and hillsides (as well as the flat shingle floors of the Marlborough valleys), and has reinvented itself. (The hillside Clayvin Vineyard, purchased from the Eaton family by Fromm, produces outstanding grapes, and Mike Eaton started again with TerraVin.) The Marlborough style is one of silky restraint and spicy finesse, the rule being proved by the exception of the awesome power of Fromm Winery.

Best producers
Ara, Auntsfield Estate, Churton, Clos Henri*, Dog Point Vineyard*, Foxes Island, Fromm Winery*, Giesen Estate, Greywacke*, Hans Herzog, Jackson Estate, Julicher, Lawson's Dry Hills*, Montana, Nautilus Estate, Saint Clair Estate, Seresin Estate, Spy Valley*, TerraVin*, Tongue in Groove, Vavasour Wines, Villa Maria*, Wither Hills Estate

Canterbury
72 ha, 135 tonnes

While Martinborough was the first region to gain recognition, the 1982 St Helena Pinot Noir made by Danny Schuster was the first wine to set the heart throbbing, exquisitely perfumed and lingering. It is no more, but Bell Hill and Pyramid Valley are kindred spirits.

Best producers
Bell Hill*, Pyramid Valley*, Mud House/Waipara Hills, Waipara Springs

Waipara
344 ha, 1833 tonnes

Adjacent to the Canterbury region; the wines have considerable complexity and undeniable character, those of Pegasus Bay taking no prisoners, Muddy Water's purchase of Greystone providing synergy.

Best producers
Greystone/Muddy Water*, Pegasus Bay*

Central Otago
1484 ha, 7989 tonnes

The range of site climate, geology and topography of this southernmost region in the world is the key to understanding the spectacular richness and intensity the Pinot Noirs from here can attain. The growing season is short in terms of days, but each day has significantly more sunshine hours than more northerly regions; the nights are cool, but the days hot, the often rocky soil absorbing heat for re-radiation in the evening. Indeed, if there be a complaint, it can be that some of the wines (though never the superb Felton Road) are too dense.

Bob Campbell MW, New Zealand's Len Evans, came up with a great description in the early days: tadpole wines, signifying a great volume of flavour when the wine enters the mouth, but tailing away on the finish. It is the reverse of the description traditionally given to Chambolle Musigny: expanding like a peacock's tail on the finish and aftertaste. However, the best producers are no longer required to live under this stigma.

Best producers
Akarua*, Bannockburn Heights, Carrick*, Chard Farm*, Cloudy Bay Vineyards*, Dry Gully, Felton Road*, Gibbston Valley, Lowburn Ferry*, Misha's Vineyard, Mt Difficulty Wines, Peregrine, Pisa Range*, Quartz Reef*, Rippon Vineyard*, Rockburn Wines, Terra Sancta, Wooing Tree

UNITED STATES
16 776 ha

Oregon
Due in no small measure to the early success of David Lett at Eyrie Vineyard, the establishment of Domaine Drouhin by Robert Drouhin and daughter Veronique, and the International Pinot Noir Celebration held every year at McMinnville, Oregon has achieved international recognition as a top-flight Pinot Noir producer.

As befits any area given to making great Pinot Noir (one may argue), the vagaries of the weather during the growing season and at harvest play a major role in determining the success or otherwise of the vintage; it is so in Burgundy, and it is certainly so in Oregon, with rainfall in late summer and autumn one of the threats. But when things go right, Oregon produces beautiful Pinots, full of expression and in strikingly diverse modes.

Best producers
The list is in part the result of repeated trips to Oregon over a 25-year period; by no means are all the wines brought into this country.

Adelsheim*, Amelie Robert Estate, Anam Cara Cellars, Argyle Winery*, Beaux Frères, Benton Lane, Bergstrom*, Bethel Heights, Broadley Vineyards*, Chehalem*, Cristom*, Dobbes Family Estate*, Drouhin Estate*, Domaine Serene*, Et Fille*, Eyrie Vineyards*, Ken Wright Cellars*, Lange Estate, Lemelson, Ponzi Vineyards*, Rex Hill*, Scott Paul Wines*, Shea Wine Cellars, Soter Vineyard*, Stoller Family Estate, Willakenzie Estate

Sonoma County, California

The principal AVAs providing notable Pinot Noirs are Carneros, Russian River Valley, Sonoma Coast, Sonoma Mountain and Sonoma Valley.

It is, I suppose, arguable that the most these AVAs have in common is their (relative) proximity. Carneros's climate is shaped by the incessant wind which arrives around midday and blows until sundown across the bare, gently undulating hills. It is this wind which causes the stomata of the vine's leaves to close down, thus slowing the ripening process even though the temperature might suggest otherwise. One producer – Saintsbury – has towered above all others in Carneros, constantly refining and expanding the range of its Pinots.

The feel of the serpentine Russian River, its pine-clad ridge tops, and its fogs sucked inland from the cold ocean, is altogether different. Its wines, too, have a slightly wilder cast, a touch of the 'sauvage', making them exciting without compromising their elegance. Then there is the even wilder quality of the ridge tops of the Sonoma coast developed by Jesse Jackson, Helen Turley and other luminaries.

Best producers
Clos du Bois, Dehlinger, Domaine Chandon, Merry Edwards*, Flowers Vineyards, Gary Farrell*, Hanzell*, Hartford, Iron Horse Vineyards, Kistler Vineyards, La Crema, Rochioli, Saintsbury*, Siduri, Torres Estate, Walter Hansel, Williams Selyem*

South Central Coast | Edna Valley | Arroyo Grande | Santa Barbara

The South Central Coast is, technically speaking, my own creation (in my 1993 *Wine Atlas of California*), and, for good measure, I have split San Luis Obispo County in half, recognising only Edna Valley and Arroyo Grande for the purposes of Pinot Noir (and Chardonnay). These two, plus the Santa Barbara, Santa Maria and Santa Ynez valleys, are strongly maritime influenced, courtesy of the upwelling of cold water from the depths of the ocean which begins in May and reaches its peak in August. Pinot Noirs of outstanding varietal character and quality are made with seeming ease – an illusion, no doubt, but a tribute to the terroir nonetheless. Jim Clendenen of Au Bon Climat deserves to be recognised as a national vinous treasure.

Best producers
Au Bon Climat*, Babcock Vineyards, Bonnacorse*, Byron Wines, Cambridge*, Edna Valley Vineyard, Fiddlehead, Gainey Vineyard*, Lane Tanner*, Sanford Winery, Santa Barbara Winery, Talley Vineyards, The Hitching Post*

Rest of California

In their different ways, these two wineries are epitomes of the agonies and ecstasies of growing and making Pinot Noir. Josh Jensen of Calera, in particular, has scaled mountains, literal and figurative, which would have caused a less fanatical vigneron to simply give up. From my viewpoint, this makes his hard-won success – and his sense of the absurd – all the more enjoyable.

Producers
Monterey County: Chalone Vineyard; San Benito: Calera

CANADA

British Columbia and Ontario
British Columbia: 384 ha. Ontario: 256 ha

Pinot Noir is planted up and down the length of the Okanagan Valley in British Columbia; Blue Mountain is said to make a good wine, but I have not tasted it. Reasonably extensive exposure to the wines of the other producers suggests this is the wrong region. Were it not for the joint venture between Jean Claude Boisset (of Burgundy) and Vincorp in Ontario, at one time with the most amazingly designed winery in the world on the drawing board, I would be tempted to say the same for Ontario, although its climate is very much cooler than that of the Okanagan Valley. Opinions are sharply divided on the ability of Ontario to satisfactorily ripen Pinot Noir, given the ultra-compressed (albeit powerful) growing season.

REST OF FRANCE AND EUROPE

Varying amounts of Pinot Noir are planted in Alsace, the Loire Valley (France), the warmer regions of Germany and through Eastern Europe. (It is of course planted widely in Champagne, but only a hatful is used to make table wine, most notably by Bollinger.) For the record, as it were, more Pinot Noir is grown in Champagne (with 12 900 hectares in 2010) than in greater Burgundy (10 691 hectares), and only 6579 hectares in the Côte d'Or. Continuing climate warming is seeing some impressive Pinots from Austria (Gerhard Markowitsch), Germany (notably Bernard Huber) and Alsace, so far exceptions that prove the rule.

SOUTH AFRICA
962 ha

The two contradictions underlying South Africa's Pinot Noir are, first, its latitude, which is equal to that of Sydney, and second, the cooling effect of the Southern Ocean. I suppose I should add that, despite the magnificence of the mountains overlooking the Cape District, any form of cultivation is physically impossible, the result being the absence of high-elevation vineyards. The exception proving the rule is Thelema, and even it does not produce Pinot Noir; instead it works hardest with Cabernet Sauvignon and Merlot, and creates some of South Africa's best red wines.

There are, as ever, site climates that complicate the situation. The long-term leaders of the pack (Hamilton Russell and Bouchard Finlayson) are established within a few kilometres of the Southern Ocean at Walker Bay, well to the south of the main viticultural area of Stellenbosch. Finding the right site to produce Pinot Noir with fragrance and elegance has been frustratingly slow.

Best producers
Bouchard Finlayson*, Cabriere, Cape Chamonix*, Creation Wines*, Glen Carlou Vineyards, Hamilton Russell Vineyards*, Meerlust, Newton Johnson, Paul Cluver, Shannon

Australian History

Pinot Noir arrived in Australia with the James Busby collection in 1831, and some vines were quickly taken to the Hunter Valley. When John Riddoch began the development of Coonawarra in the 1890s, doubtless encouraged by the limestone soil and by the climate, Pinot Noir was planted alongside Shiraz and Cabernet Sauvignon. As if sounding a warning note, it failed to produce wine of quality, and was soon abandoned. More recent attempts have been equally unsuccessful: the Coonawarra climate is simply that little bit too warm. Its southern neighbour, Mount Gambier, huddled up against the Victorian border near Henty, clearly has the right climate.

It was successfully grown in southern Victoria, especially in Geelong and the Yarra Valley, but was wiped out in the 1880s by phylloxera in Geelong and (later) by the switch to dairying in the Yarra Valley. A small amount planted in the Hunter Valley was used by Maurice O'Shea in various of his red wines, never named as such, partly because it was always blended with Shiraz, and partly because the wines were given elliptical names. Lindemans, too, had Pinot Noir, and released a 1959 Bin 1600 which was labelled as such. After O'Shea's death in 1956, McWilliam's also released the occasional varietal Pinot Noir, but it was left to Murray Tyrrell to score an amazing first place in the Gault Millau Wine

Olympics of 1979 with his 1976 Vat 6, featured on the cover of *Time Life* magazine along with the greatest wines of France. The energised Mount Pleasant is very serious about recreating wines in the O'Shea mould, and Tyrrell's is making conventional thinking about global warming stand on its head with recent vintages of Vat 6.

Pinot Noir reappeared in the Yarra Valley in the early 1970s, the first wines being made in 1976. When I tasted the first Pinots from Mount Mary and Seville Estate, I had an epiphany; somehow or other, I realised at that moment, that someday, someway, I would end up growing and making Pinot Noir in the Yarra Valley. (The realisation of that dream in fact came far earlier than I had ever anticipated.) Today, Pinot Noir is the most widely planted red variety in the Yarra Valley, with the major part being used to make table wine, the remainder for sparkling wine. By virtue of its wine show successes, if not the sheer number of producers, the Yarra Valley is entitled to be regarded as the premier region in mainland Australia.

The other regions around Melbourne – which I call the dress circle – followed suit through the 1970s. Macedon, the Mornington Peninsula, Geelong and (last) South Gippsland are now home to outstanding producers of Pinot Noir.

The Adelaide Hills is South Australia's only region for Pinot Noir, and seems likely to remain so. Even here site selection is all-important; many parts of the Hills are too warm.

The Pemberton/Manjimup regions of Western Australia, together with Albany in the Great Southern, caused hopes to rise early in the piece, but have infrequently delivered on those hopes. Wignalls in Albany has made good Pinots from time to time. Just when you are at the point of writing off the link between the Great Southern and the variety, up comes the Porongurup subregion and its master winemaker, Rob Diletti of Castle Rock. Pascal Marchand, a live-wire French-Canadian long since welcomed into the bosom of Burgundy, has teamed with the Burch Family and its Mount Barrow Vineyard in Mount Barker to make impressive, durable Pinot Noir (and Chardonnay) under the Marchand & Burch label.

Tasmania was fast out of the blocks – Moorilla Estate was established in 1958 – but took a considerable time to get its head round the variety.

By the mid-1990s the variety was being grown with great success in all parts of Tasmania: in the north with the Pipers Brook and Tamar Valley districts; on the East Coast on either side of Bicheno; and in the south across a spread of very different areas on the Lower and Upper Derwent, the Coal River/Richmond district, and to the extreme south of the Huon Valley.

Two contract winemaking businesses – Hood Wines/Frogmore Creek and Julian Alcorso's Winemaking Tasmania – provided the means for the upwards of 30 small vignerons to have their wines skilfully made. But the critical mass was still to emerge.

It has now done so through Pipers Brook Vineyard (with 194 hectares of vineyards); Tamar Ridge (acquired by Brown Brothers in 2010 for $32.5 million), which has retained 120 hectares after selling the 83-hectare White Hills Vineyard to Treasury Wine Estates in 2013; the Bay of Fires/House of Arras business owned by Hardys; Jansz Tasmania's ownership by the Hill Smith Family Vineyards; the growth of Frogmore Creek's own brand (18 000 cases as at 2014); and Heemskerk, owned by Treasury Wine Estates.

The acquisition of the Tolpuddle Vineyard by Shaw + Smith, the establishment of the Dawson & James partnership (and its eponymous brand) and Jim and Daisy Chatto's vineyard in the Huon Valley will exercise a disproportionate (compared to their size) influence on the making of the finest Chardonnays and Pinot Noirs in the years ahead.

I finish this overview with a question I am unable to answer: how is it that significantly more Pinot Noir was crushed in 2004, 2008 and 2010 than in 2012 – particularly given the quality of 2012?

Australian Statistics

4978 ha, 34 574 tonnes, 987 growers/makers

Pinot Noir: tonnes crushed in Australia, 1976–2012

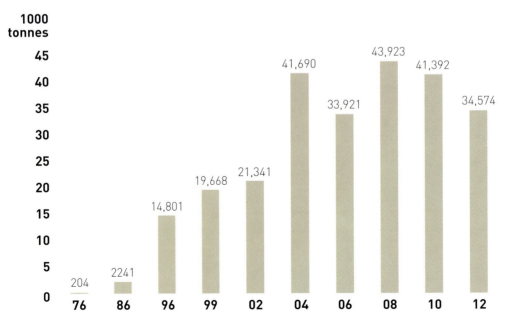

Australian Winemaking

Anyone who has become familiar with Burgundy (France) will know two things: first, that there are 101 winemaking methods used by Burgundian winemakers; second, that new methods (or, perhaps, the adaptation of old ones) keep the art in a constant state of flux.

As Australian winemakers have become more experienced in dealing with this most capricious of all grape varieties, they have watched the methods and trends of winemaking in Burgundy and other parts of the world.

In the wake of the comet-like appearance of Lebanese-born oenologist Guy Accad, what is variously called cold-soak or pre-fermentation maceration has become widely used around the Pinot world. This involves chilling the must (the freshly crushed grape berries, skins and juice) to delay the onset of fermentation. Accad recommended the addition of large amounts of SO_2 (±200 parts per million) with the three objectives: further delaying fermentation, binding the colour, and making way for the use of cultured yeasts to initiate fermentation.

Australian winemakers have tended to rely mainly on chilling the must to 10°C or below, partially or totally eliminating the use of SO_2. This allows the choice of using cultured yeast or relying on natural/indigenous/wild yeast (the terms are interchangeable) once the must is warmed up to 15°C or more and fermentation is initiated.

Pinot Noir has been the template for other red varieties (especially Shiraz) to follow with the incorporation of a varying percentage of whole bunches in the ferment; the use of open fermenters with either manual or hydraulic punch-down (or plunging) of the cap (the skins which rise to the surface); and significantly higher fermentation temperature peaks (up to 35°C). Less common is to ferment whole bunches only, relying on foot-stamping (pigeage) or, latterly, hydraulic rams.

Towards the end of fermentation there is a major choice: either delay pressing the must (post-fermentation maceration) with the aim of extracting more tannins and (arguably) more stable colour; or press before dryness and take the wine straight to barrel for the completion of primary fermentation and (sooner or later) malolactic fermentation. A recent innovation, as yet sparingly used in Australia, is to flash-heat the must to 45°C/50°C at the end of fermentation, the aim being to increase colour density.

The choice of oak type; the degree of toast; the percentage of new and used oak barrels; the length of time the wine spends in oak; the use (or not) of lees contact; the decision whether to fine and/or filter; and the temperature and humidity of the barrel-storage facility are all of crucial importance to a wine type which is as capricious and temperamental in the winery as it is in the vineyard.

There are no hard and fast rules determining these choices, but the wine in the bottle will quickly tell you if any of the decisions were wrong.

Australian Regional Styles

Just as in Burgundy, it is very difficult to separate regional/terroir influence from the impact of the hand and mind of the winemaker. Moreover, many of the regions have substantial subregions, and these in turn often have radically varying site climates. Thus Tasmania has so far wisely declined to even seek to divide itself into zones: for example, north, south and east. Each of these zones would (sooner or later) then have multiple regions. Vintage variation then plays further havoc with attempts to generalise.

It is with more than the usual degree of trepidation that I attempt the following summaries, recognising that (at best) the exception will prove the rule.

VICTORIA

Yarra Valley
706 ha

Lower Climate: Moderate, MJT 19.4°C, E° Days 1463, SH 7.4, Rain 437 mm, Alt 120 m
Upper Climate: Cool, MJT 18.4°C, E° Days 1253, SH 7.3, Rain 700 mm, Alt 200 m

The best wines from the best vintages have exceptional aroma, finesse, intensity and length. By and large they are made in light- to medium-bodied style, without resorting to over-extraction or excess oak influence. With five years of bottle age they can acquire distinctly Burgundian characteristics, and can fool even the most (but not all) one-eyed Francophiles in blind tastings. However, once past 15 years of age, most quietly fade away, with only the most committed vino-necrophiliac happy to cellar them longer. Vintage variation is significant: thus between 2005 and 2014 inclusive, only 2006, 2010, 2012 and 2013 are very good years.

Best producers

Coldstream Hills*, De Bortoli, Gembrook, Helen's Hill*, Hoddles Creek Estate*, Innocent Bystander*, Mac Forbes*, Mandala, Mayer*, Mount Mary*, Oakridge Estate*, PHI, Pimpernel, Punch*, Rochford*, Serrat*, Seville Estate*, TarraWarra Estate*, Toolangi, Yarra Yering*, Yering Station*, Yeringberg

Mornington Peninsula
325 ha

> **Mornington** Climate: Cool, MJT 18.9°C, E° Days 1428, SH 7.1, Rain 380 mm, Alt 60 m
> **Red Hill South** Climate: Cool, MJT 17.5°C, E° Days 1240, SH 6.8, Rain 400+ mm, Alt 180 m

Overall, the wines are similar to those of the Yarra Valley, perhaps slightly less structured: the climate is a little cooler and wetter, and the harvest dates a week to ten days later on average. The two outstanding exceptions are Paringa Estate and Yabby Lake, which produce wines of amazing richness and complexity. Then there are another dozen or so making silky wines relying on elegance to handsomely make their point. There is no question that the Mornington Peninsula will come into its own if continued climate warming becomes a problem.

Best producers
Allies, Crittenden Estate, Dexter, Eldridge Estate of Red Hill, Foxeys Hangout, Garagiste, Handpicked, Hurley Vineyard*, Kooyong, Main Ridge Estate*, Montalto*, Moorooduc Estate*, Ocean Eight Vineyard*, Paradigm Hill, Paringa Estate*, Port Phillip Estate*, Portsea Estate, Scorpo Wines, Stonier*, Ten Minutes by Tractor*, Tuck's Ridge, Yabby Lake*

Geelong
108 ha

> Climate: Cool, MJT 18.5°C, E° Days 1377, SH 7.2, Rain 319 mm, Alt 70 m

More wind, less rainfall and tougher soils were the background for Gary Farr to fashion the powerful, brooding wines of Bannockburn and Farr, the close-planted Serre Vineyard of Bannockburn the most imperious and worth ageing/cellaring. Increasing vine age – and experience – mean these two are simply the leaders of a pack that is steadily growing in number.

Best producers
Austin's, Bannockburn*, Brown Magpie*, Clyde Park*, Farr | Farr Rising*, Lethbridge, Provenance, Scotchmans Hill

Macedon Ranges
30 ha

> Climate: Cool, MJT 18.2°C, E° Days 1149, SH 7.8, Rain 428 mm, Alt 500 m

The windiest and coolest of the five regions circling Melbourne, with many of the vineyards better suited to the production of sparkling, rather than table, wine. It is difficult to achieve full ripe flavour in Pinot in many vintages, but Bindi and Curly Flat showed that it could be done with appropriate site selection.

Best producers
Bindi*, Curly Flat*, Granite Hills, Kyneton Ridge, Lane's End*, Shadowfax*, Silent Way

Gippsland
84 ha

> **West** Climate: Moderate, MJT 19.3°C, E° Days 1400, SH 7.2, Rain 518 mm, Alt 140 m
> **East** Climate: Cool, MJT 18.7°C, E° Days 1360, SH 7.3, Rain 353 mm, Alt 40 m
> **South** Climate: Cool, MJT 17.9°C, E° Days 1288, SH 6.6, Rain 446 mm, Alt 80 m

Phillip Jones of Bass Phillip (in South Gippsland) towers above the other makers in the region, if not Australia. Perhaps more than with any other Australian Pinot maker, the mark of the terroir (and the ultra-high density plantings) shows through. Jones himself certainly believes it to be the case, and I am not going to suggest otherwise. The region is a far-flung and diverse one, with a handful of wineries producing Pinots from rustic to sophisticated, and from lighter- to fuller-bodied.

Best producers
Bass Phillip*, Bass River, Bellvale, Caledonia Australis, Narkoojee, Tambo Estate

Ballarat
20 ha

> Climate: Cool, MJT 18.6°C, E° Days 1191, SH 7.8, Rain 348 mm, Alt 380 m

Ballarat was the birthplace of Yellowglen, established in 1971 by Melbourne food and wine identity Ian Home. The initial plantings were of Cabernet Sauvignon and Shiraz, but it soon became clear that the climate was too cool to satisfactorily ripen those varieties. Indeed, between 1975 and 1979 further plantings of Chardonnay and Pinot

Noir proved that even these varieties could not ripen sufficiently to make table wine, but were ideally suited to sparkling wine. Home recruited Dominique Landragin from Seppelt in the Grampians to become part owner and winemaker of Yellowglen. The first wines were released in 1982, using the traditional method, and Yellowglen became a cult producer across the length and breadth of the country. In 1984 Mildara became the owner, although Ian Home stayed on for a while (and returned much later as a brand ambassador during ownership of TWE). Overnight, Yellowglen had no option but to abandon its birthplace, with its microscopic plantings, in favour of the larger areas needed to make ever-increasing volumes of the various Yellowglen labels.

In 1983 Eastern Peake was established, followed the next year by Tomboy Hill. The learning curve for these two wineries was long and painful, but the Latta family at Eastern Peake established 5.6 hectares of Pinot Noir and Chardonnay, and Ian Watson at Tomboy Hill managed to supplement his plantings of 3.6 hectares with micro-quantities of grapes grown by other farmers in the region in their (metaphorical) backyards. The turning point came in 2002, and although some vintages are more satisfactory than others, Tomboy Hill led the way by producing some stunning cool-climate Pinots, and Eastern Peake has now thrown down the challenge. Even in the cool, wet vintage of 2011, Tomboy Hill picked Pinot Noir in May, and made a thoroughly meritorious wine from it. Watch this space.

The plantings in the region are still way short of the area required for recognition as a Geographical Indication.

Best producers
Eastern Peake*, Tomboy Hill*

Henty
72 ha

Climate: Cool, MJT 17.4°C, E° Days 1213, SH 6.8, Rain 345 mm, Alt 70 m

This is Australia's coolest region, as classified by Dr John Gladstones, which in one line explains why it took Seppelt decades to coax the vines to reliably bear economic crops, and why to this day Pinot Noir and Riesling are the standout varieties, Chardonnay next in line. All three varieties are intense and elegant, acidity a given. By way of a note, Mount Gambier is very nearly as cool, and it too is a Pinot Noir haven, sure to become better known in the near future.

SOUTH AUSTRALIA

Adelaide Hills

446 ha, 2496 tonnes

> Climate: Cool, MJT 18.9°C, E° Days 1359, SH 8.4, Rain 352 mm, Alt 500 m

Slope, aspect and location provide an infinitely complex mosaic, and it is hardly surprising that South Australia's only – and relatively small – regional producer of high-quality Pinot Noir should provide wines ranging from taut and racy to rather ponderous, with minimal varietal character.

Best producers

Ashton Hills*, Barratt, BK Wines, CRFT, Grosset*, Michael Hall, Mount Lofty Ranges Vineyard, Murdoch Hill*, Nepenthe, Ochota Barrels, Pike & Joyce, Riposte*, Warwick Billings

TASMANIA

515 ha, 2241 tonnes

> South Coast Tasmania
> **Lower Derwent** Climate: Cool, MJT 18.2°C, E° Days 1268, SH 7.3, Rain 280 mm, Alt 80 m
> **Huon Valley** Climate: Cool, MJT 16.8°C, E° Days 1115, SH 6.5, Rain 458 mm, Alt 40 m
> Northern Tasmania
> **Tamar Valley** Climate: Cool, MJT 18.1°C, E° Days 1307, SH 7.5, Rain 321 mm, Alt 50 m
> **Pipers Brook** Climate: Cool, MJT 17.6°C, E° Days 1208, SH 7.5, Rain 477 mm, Alt 120 m
> East Coast Tasmania
> Climate: Cool, MJT 17.4°C, E° Days 1233, SH 7.2, Rain 388 mm, Alt 50 m

It is difficult to know where to start (or finish) with a state bursting with so much potential and, for that matter, achievement. Certainly overall it is vintage dependent, but so are all Pinot Noir regions worthy of the name; spring frost is the major threat. The Pipers River, Tamar Valley, Derwent, Huon Valley, Richmond/Coal River and East Coast all have ever-increasing numbers of producers making ever-greater Pinots.

There are significant differences in style linked to the different districts' mesoclimates – the Coal Valley, Upper Derwent, East Coast, Tamar Valley, Richmond and Huon Valley all have different voices. Tasmania has far more producers than any mainland region, albeit most with small volumes that sell out quickly.

Best producers
Barringwood Park, Bay of Fires*, Bream Creek, Chatto*, Clemens Hill, Dalrymple Vineyards, Dawson & James*, Devil's Corner, Freycinet*, Frogmore Creek, Ghost Rock, Heemskerk, Home Hill*, Holm Oak, Moorilla Estate, Moores Hill Estate, Pooley Wines, Stargazer Wines, Stefano Lubiana, Stoney Rise*, Tamar Ridge, Tolpuddle*, Velo

WESTERN AUSTRALIA

Great Southern

Denmark Climate: Cool, MJT 18.9°C, E° Days 1512, SH 6.7, Rain 332 mm, Alt 130 m

The peculiarities of the Great Southern region, and its subregions to one side, make tracking the development of Pinot Noirs in the context of their varying climates not easy.

Denmark is the coolest of the subregions, and has the largest number of producers making fine-quality Pinot.

There are no climate statistics available for Porongurup, but it is a subregion with particular promise. Castle Rock is the best-performing winery, with winemaker Rob Diletti working his magic as contract maker for others both within and beyond the borders of Porongurup.

Best producers
Denmark: Robert Oatley Vineyards, Rockcliffe, Singlefile, The Lake House; Porongurup: Abbey Creek, Castle Rock, Evans & Tate

Mount Barker

Climate: Moderate, MJT 20°C, E° Days 1548, SH 7.3, Rain 280 mm, Alt 220 m

Until recently, it seemed that the climate of Mount Barker was too warm to produce good Pinot Noir, but the skills of Larry Cherubino and Pascal Marchand (a Burgundian winemaker of Canadian descent) have shown it can be done.

Best producers
Larry Cherubino, Marchand & Burch Wines

Chapter 11

The Classic Red Varietals
Shiraz | Syrah

184 834 ha of Shiraz is grown in 27 countries, Peru the smallest with 2 ha. Those countries with over 500 ha are: Algeria 1510 ha, Argentina 12 810 ha, Australia 42 012 ha, Chile 6027 ha, France 67 382 ha, Greece 641 ha, Italy 6739 ha, Portugal 3501 ha, South Africa 10 136 ha, Spain 20 000 ha, Turkey 1367 ha, United States 9197 ha.

International History

DNA research between 1998 and 2006 has unearthed many branches of the family tree of Shiraz (as I will usually call the variety), and conclusively ended the Syrian, Persian, Greek, Sicilian and Albanian hypothesis for the origin of the variety.[1] But the missing branches of the tree – due to the disappearance/extinction of some varieties that must have been partners in natural crosses – leave gaps in the sequence which give rise to multiple possible pedigrees.

What is certain is that Shiraz was the offspring of a natural cross between Dureza and Mondeuse Blanche.[2] More precisely, it first appeared in a vineyard in the Isere district of the Rhône-Alpes region, which had both of those varieties planted. At the risk of digressing, extension of the family tree suggests that Pinot was probably the great-grandparent of Shiraz, and that (for once) Gouais Blanche played no role in any of the crosses.

---

1   Jancis Robinson, Julia Harding and Jose Vouillamoz, *Wine Grapes*, Ecco/HarperCollins, 2012, p. 1026.
2   ibid., p. 1028.

Other varieties that come up in the near-family are Mondeuse Noire and Viognier on the French side, Teroldego, Marzemino, Lagrein and Refosco del Pedunculo Rosso[3] on the Italian side.

Until Shiraz was taken to Australia in 1832, the northern Rhône was the only region in which the variety was grown. Here it was the exclusive red grape in Hermitage, Côte Rôtie, Cornas, St Joseph and Crozes Hermitage.

Its limited distribution did not impair its reputation. The great English connoisseur Professor George Saintsbury, writing at the end of the nineteenth century, declared, '1864 Hermitage is the manliest wine I have ever drunk.' For decades prior to this, Hermitage had been taken to Bordeaux for blending with the greatest wines of that region when the vintage conditions in Bordeaux had been less than kind. Rather than keep the fact secret, the labels of wines such as Château Margaux proudly proclaimed 'Hermitagée', and the wines so treated sold for higher prices than their unblended counterparts. Contrary to public myth, Australia did not invent the Cabernet Shiraz blend.

Wherever in the world it is grown, Shiraz will over-crop if given encouragement. While its bunches are relatively loosely formed, the usually large berries have thin skins, making them targets for downy mildew and rot, and – even if protected from these scourges – producing dilute wine if over-cropped and/or imperfectly ripened.

The growers of the northern Rhône thus prize what they regard as a separate clone, which they call Petite Syrah (as opposed to Grosse Syrah) and which has smaller berries. It is not clear whether this gave rise to the entirely incorrect Californian use of the name of Petite Sirah for what is (or was thought to be) Durif.

It has only been in the wake of the Australian success with the variety and, more particularly, the massive surge in Australian exports through the late 1980s to 2002, that the plantings have proliferated in the south of France, Italy and across the New World. (Small amounts have been successfully grown on the upper reaches of the Rhône River in the region of Valais.)

---

3 ibid., p. 1026.

International Styles

FRANCE
67 382 ha

Hermitage, Northern Rhône Valley
132 ha

The terraced hillside soaring near-vertically above the town of Tain l'Hermitage, and that of the Hermitage appellation, is the size of the biggest wine Château in the Medoc. Moreover, there is little or no possibility of expansion of the south-facing wall of granite which is home to the various plots (or climats) of vines with their surprisingly varied surface soils. Only Hermitage and Crozes Hermitage are situated on the right (east) bank of the Rhône River; all the other regions are on the opposite bank.

Syrah is the only red grape used in Hermitage (i.e. no Viognier), but there are significant differences in the style of the wines. Some producers blend wines from multiple sites; others, often because of force of circumstance, produce only single-vineyard wines.

For many, Jaboulet's La Chapelle (returning to form after a dull period) and Chave's Hermitage are epitomes of the style. When young, the wine is deeply coloured and redolent of dark cherries; the late Gerard Jaboulet used to say that if spice was an obvious component, it simply meant the grapes were not perfectly ripened. The texture of the wine in the mouth is at once complex yet smooth, the red berry flavours rippling along the length of the palate, and with ripe, soft tannins. The only Guigal wine is Ex-Voto, the most recent arrival in its luxury series.

As the wine ages over 20 to 30 years, the secondary flavours become much more savoury, with soft leather, sweet earth and faintly spicy characters emerging.

Best producers
Chapoutier*, Jean-Louis Chave*, Yann Chave*, Emmanuel Darnaud, Delas*, E Guigal*, Paul Jaboulet Aîné*, Tardieu-Laurent, Marc Sorrel

Crozes Hermitage, Northern Rhône Valley
1250 ha (in cultivation)

Together with Hermitage, Crozes Hermitage is situated on the eastern side of the River Rhône. Like Hermitage, its red wine is usually 100 per cent Syrah, but there the similarities between the two regions come to an abrupt end. Crozes is situated on flat lands beneath the hill of Hermitage, with clay-limestone alluvial soils, unlike the schist of the hill. The fact that the appellation was not recognised until 1937 is further evidence of its limitations. It comes as no surprise, then, to find that the wines, while fruitier in their youth, are lighter-bodied than those of Hermitage, and are shorter-lived. For all that, Jaboulet's Domaine de Thalabert and the wines of Alain Graillot show just what can be achieved, and offer great value for money.

Best producers
Albert Belle, Les Chanets, Chapoutier*, Yann Chave, du Colombier, Combier*, Alain Graillot*, Michel Ogier, Etienne Pochon, Paul Jaboulet Aîné, Marc Sorrel

Côte Rôtie, Northern Rhône Valley
200 ha (in cultivation)

Considering its distinguished vinous history dating back to Roman times, it is incredible to think that in the early 1970s Côte Rôtie was so little regarded that only 70 hectares of vines were in production, smaller again than the diminutive Hermitage appellation. Part of the reason, no doubt, lay in the difficulty and expense of cultivating the near-vertical hillsides, the steepest in France.

Then Marcel Guigal came onto the scene, and everything changed. The brilliance of the single-vineyard wines La Mouline and La Landonne (followed much later by La Turque) caught the attention (and the wallets) of the world, with Robert Parker the Messiah. By the mid-1990s plantings were 200 hectares, still small enough to ensure that demand far exceeded supply, and impervious to prices reaching stratospheric levels.

Physically, Côte Rôtie is divided into two parts: Côte Blonde, where Viognier is routinely incorporated into the Syrah up to the legal limit of 20 per cent, produces aromatic, willowy wines; and Côte Brune, usually 100 per cent Syrah, gives wines of awesome power and complexity.

Côte Rôtie (typically a blend of both Côtes unless a single-vineyard wine) bursts out of the glass, the intense aromas offering an exotic mix of blackberry/black cherry, licorice/anise and spice, all with an undertone of wild game. It can be very difficult to decide (particularly in a blind tasting) whether that undertone is simply Côte Rôtie typicity, or evidence of bacterial activity associated with brettanomyces.

Best producers
Pierre Barge, Clusel-Roche, Yves Cuilleron, E Guigal, Joseph Jamet*, Patrick Jasmin*, Michel Ogier, Rene Rostaing*, Vidal-Fleury

St Joseph, Northern Rhône Valley
980 ha (in cultivation)

St Joseph is situated on the eastern (or left) bank of the River Rhône, between Côte Rôtie to the north and Hermitage to the south. It is second only to Crozes Hermitage in size, and stretches all the way north to Condrieu and south to Tournon. Its declared boundaries have grown from 90 hectares (1956) to 7000 hectares (1969), then shrank to 3004 hectares (1994), and are decidedly schizophrenic: its best vineyard sites are on old granite hillside terraces near the town of Tournon, and opposite the hill of Hermitage. The soil is perfect, but because the terraces face east (opposite Hermitage) they lose the afternoon sun up to two hours before Hermitage. Thus even the most distinguished sites (and there are many less distinguished) produce wines which are lighter-bodied – at best – than Hermitage. At their best, the wines are wonderfully expressive, almost flowery, with vivacious fruit flavours, and are best drunk young (say up to five years old). At their least, the wines are curiously overpriced.

Best producers
Chapoutier*, Yves Cuilleron*, Pierre Gaillard, Jean-Louis Grippat, E Guigal*, Alain Paret, Raymond Trollat, Francois Villard

Cornas, Northern Rhône Valley
100 ha (in cultivation)

Cornas, the southernmost appellation of the Northern Rhône, fell into even greater disuse than Côte Rôtie in the twentieth century, its terraces in terminal decay, and only Clape producing wine with any audience. The revival followed that of Côte Rôtie, with consulting oenologist Jean-Luc Colombo leading the charge. This still undervalued and misunderstood appellation can produce wine with a depth of colour, flavour and longevity every bit as impressive as that of Hermitage. One limitation is the small size of the numerous producers: Clape and Jean-Luc Colombo, each with 5.7 hectares, are medium-sized; Jean Lionnet, with 10 hectares, is one of the largest (although not the best).

Best producers
Thierry Alleman*, August & Pierre-Marie Clape*, Jean-Luc Colombo, Corbis, Yves Cuilleron*, Du Coulet*, Durand, Paul Jaboulet Aîné, Vincent Paris, Taridieu-Laurent

Southern Rhône Valley

Headed by Châteauneuf-du-Pape, the southern Rhône Valley produces many robustly enjoyable, at times very great, wines made from various cocktail blends which are discussed in the chapter on Grenache.

Rest of Southern France

The labelling of Syrah grown and made in the Midi (and exported to the United States as Shiraz) tells much the same story as Chardonnay from the same region for an English supermarket chain being (according to the front label) 'Made in the Australian fashion'. Total French plantings of Shiraz rose from 1602 hectares in 1958 to 68 587 hectares in 2009, with Languedoc-Roussillon accounting for 43 163 hectares. Its growth in Languedoc-Roussillon was part pull, part push as the EU subsidised the removal of unwanted varieties and the planting of better types, Shiraz to the fore.

While some varietal Syrah is made, most is still blended either with the traditional choice of Grenache, Mourvedre, Cinsaut et al., or (increasingly) with Cabernet Sauvignon. The wines do not aspire to greatness, but have what might be termed a sunny disposition reflecting the climate, and, like Vin Pays d'Oc, can deliver exceptional value for those who know where to look. This large area can produce wines that seriously challenge Australia's Shiraz at similar (low) price points.

SPAIN

20 000 ha

The sunny, but varied, terroirs of Spain, especially its central regions of Castille-La Mancha but spread to all points of the compass, offer all sorts of opportunities for Shiraz. Between 2004 and 2008 plantings rose from 3000 hectares to 16 500 hectares. Much of the wine is used as a blend with native varieties, its richness and succulent mid-palate reminiscent more of Australia's Barossa Valley than of France, north or south.

ITALY

6739 ha

It is ironic that Shiraz should have been planted in Italy as early as 1899 (as a response to phylloxera), but as at 2000, plantings were only 5357 hectares, reflecting Italy's continuing obsession with Cabernet Sauvignon and Merlot. Most has been planted in Sicily (with Planeta and Cottonera to the fore), but the much-travelled Paolo di Marchi of Isole e Olena produces admirable wines.

NORTH AMERICA
United States: 9197 ha. Canada: 274 ha

As I say on page 215, Australia's stellar success with Shiraz has led to a game of attempted catch-up by New World wine countries, but it is a constantly moving target. California has a more than usual array of climates when contrasted with the near-monocrus of Washington State, South Africa, Chile et al., so its best producers make very different styles.

Whichever they may be, the varietal character of the grape comes through, often without the green, vegetal characters that mark other red varieties grown at the cooler end of climatic viability.

The spread north to Oregon is an impressive testament to Shiraz's ability to adapt to any terroir.

Best producers
Clear Lake: Steele Wines; Edina Valley: Qupe; Lake County: Oak Cliff Cellars*; Mendocino: Hidden Cellars; Napa Valley: Araujo Estate, Arrowood, Joseph Phelps*, Neyers, Swanson; Oregon: Rustic Prayer Rock Vineyard; Russian River: Dehlinger; Santa Cruz Mountains: Kathryn Kennedy

SOUTH AFRICA
10 136 ha

Stung by Australia's export success in premium markets, South Africa has made a determined, and successful, effort with Shiraz. In 1990 it accounted for well under 1 per cent of the total vineyard area; now it is 10 per cent. The quality of the wines, and the number of producers making top-quality wines, has increased commensurately. The most tangible proof of South Africa's success came with the 2014 Six Nations Wine Challenge (held in Sydney, involving Australia, New Zealand, South Africa, Chile, Argentina and the United States), in which the Shiraz class was won by South Africa.

Best producers
Boekenhoutskloof, Cederberg Private Cellar*, Eagles Nest, Fable Mountain Vineyards*, Fairview, Klein Constantia, La Motte, Lievland, Mooiplaas, Mount Sutherland*, Muratie, Rust en Vrede*, Stark-Condé Wines, Stellenzicht*, Strandveld, The Foundry, Vergelegen*

NEW ZEALAND

433 ha, 2178 tonnes

Hawke's Bay: 332 ha, 1811 tonnes. Marlborough: 11 ha, 60 tonnes. Martinborough/Wairarapa: 9 ha, 30 tonnes

Hawke's Bay has joined the international pack of baying hounds, with spectacular results for its spicy, medium-bodied wines. It will remain the epicentre, but first-class results are coming (in smaller numbers) from other regions in the North Island (and Fromm in Marlborough).

Best producers
Hawke's Bay: Alpha Domus*, Bilancia*, Craggy Range Vineyards*, Kingsley Estate, Mills Reef, Palliser Estate, Te Mata*, Trinity Hill*, Vidal Estate*, Villa Maria*; *Marlborough:* Fromm La Strada; *Martinborough:* Dry River Wines, Kusuda*; *Waiheke Island:* Goldie Wines*, Passage Rock*

Australian History

Shiraz, called Scyras by James Busby, was one of the 453 varieties he collected that survived the journey to Australia in 1832, and was first planted near Sydney and in the Hunter Valley. From here it soon spread to all corners of the Australian viticultural canvas, until recently with the exception of Tasmania. It flourished wherever it was planted, and only went out of production when viticulture ceased in the region concerned.

In 1840 Sir William Macarthur (explorer and the father of the Australian wool industry, but a man of many parts) described it as 'an excellent grape … a very hardy plant [which] produces very well, and seems to be liable to no accident or disease'.

While Australia has never suffered Prohibition, and phylloxera was restricted to certain parts of Victoria when it made its appearance in the 1870s, the viticultural map shrank dramatically in the early years of the twentieth century as the country became ever more preoccupied with making fortified wine, which accounted for over 90 per cent of all wine production.

Shiraz survived this shift because it was as well suited to the making of tawny and vintage Port styles as it was for table wine. It had the added advantage of growing well and cropping better than Cabernet Sauvignon, and thrived in warmer climates. In 1956 – the first year in which varietal planting statistics for Australia became available – 12 410 tonnes were crushed. Cabernet Sauvignon and Merlot were not recorded, with a crush of less than 100 tonnes; Malbec provided 107 tonnes, and Pinot Noir 142 tonnes. The only other two red grapes were Mourvedre (then usually called Mataro) with 3800 tonnes, and Grenache, at the top of the totem pole with 21 200 tonnes. Australia was a Rhône Ranger 40 years before anyone recognised the fact.

Shiraz retained its status as a table wine variety in the Hunter Valley, with the legendary Maurice O'Shea crafting wonderful wines from the vines planted in the 1880s on the Old Paddock of Mount Pleasant, and vines he planted on the red soil around the winery. He also purchased selected parcels of newly fermented Hermitage (as the grape and the wine were then known in the Hunter Valley, at Great Western and in Coonawarra) from Tyrrell's, Tulloch and Elliot (who sold most of their wine in bulk to Sydney wine merchants such as Douglas Lamb and Caldwells).

Sometimes he would blend these parcels, but as often as not he would keep them separate, and, after maturation, bottle and label them with cryptic names: Mountain A, Mountain C, Mountain D, Henry I, II and III, KY, BL, KS, HT, Richard, Charles, and Philip. He normally added the variety and tacked on descriptions such as Light Bodied Red or Full Bodied Red.

I have been lucky enough to taste dozens of wines made by Maurice O'Shea between 1939 and his death in 1956. Even when 40, 50 and 60 years old, these wines retained extraordinary finesse and flavour complexity, and rank among the all-time greats.

The late Colin Preece worked similar magic at Seppelt Great Western from 1932 over a slightly longer time frame (he retired in 1963), using a much wider blending palette, blending other varietals, other regions and even multi-vintages in many of his wines. The oldest I have tasted was a 1925 DH18 Hermitage, but for overseas judges the Sparkling Burgundies (made from Shiraz) from 1944 onwards were the most remarkable.

When John Riddoch began the development of Coonawarra in 1893, he planted Shiraz, Cabernet Sauvignon and Pinot Noir. Within ten years Pinot Noir had vanished from the scene and Cabernet Sauvignon largely so. For much of the first 60 years of the twentieth century there was only one winery in operation in Coonawarra, initially known as Chateau Comaum, and then (from 1952) as Wynns Coonawarra Estate. Even in the darkest decades, when most of the Shiraz and Trebbiano was distilled to make Brandy, it was the former variety which held sway.

The other strongholds for Shiraz were first and foremost the Barossa Valley, with support from McLaren Vale and the Clare Valley. McLaren Vale (via the Emu Wine Company and others) specialised in the export of Shiraz with formidable levels of alcohol and extract to the United Kingdom. The wine, described as ferruginous, was prone to be prescribed by English doctors as a tonic for the weak or sickly, a century before the French Paradox exploded on the United States wine market. (This was a CBS *60 Minutes* program which claimed some cardiovascular protection offered by wine in the context of the Mediterranean diet.)

McLaren Vale also produced some astonishingly long-lived vintage Ports, including Hardys 1927, 1936 and 1946. In the Clare and Barossa valleys most was similarly used for Port, but in 1951 Max Schubert began experimenting with the development of what became Penfolds Grange Hermitage. (Ultimately 'Hermitage' was dropped as exports grew and access to the Common Market became important.)

His model was based on what he had observed in Bordeaux in the 1950 vintage, and his early trials with Cabernet Sauvignon (in 1953) left no doubt that this variety would have been ideally suited to recreating what he had both observed and tasted. The problem was that only a tiny quantity of Cabernet was available, so he really had little choice but to use Shiraz, of which there was a plentiful supply from dry-grown vineyards that, even back then, were approaching 100 years of age.

Today the Barossa Valley has a unique heritage of ancient Shiraz vines planted on their own roots because phylloxera never gained a foothold in South Australia. In recognition of this, and with Robert Hill-Smith of Yalumba its champion, a charter recognising the age and importance of these vines has been agreed. Barossa Old Vine: equal or greater than 35 years; Barossa Survivor Vine: 70 years; Barossa Centurion: 100 years; Barossa Ancestor Vine: 125 years.

Australian Statistics

42 012 ha, 362 217 tonnes, 2017 growers/makers

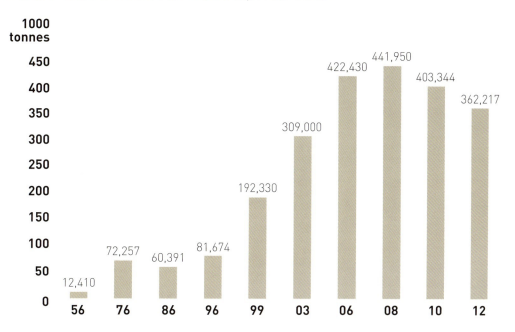

Australian Winemaking

Max Schubert fundamentally changed the way Australian winemakers approached the making of Shiraz. Not all the techniques he developed are used in the making of all Shiraz, particularly with lower-priced wines, but there is some resonance wherever you look.

Culling the fairly sparse writings of British journalists and authors about Australian red wines in the 1950s and '60s (even into the '70s) gives a common message: baked red wines, more brown than red in colour, and with relatively little varietal character.

By using juice run-off from and returned to open fermentation vats, Schubert was able to regulate the temperature of the ferment. By incorporating some cooler-grown, higher-acid grapes, he went a long way towards achieving the desired (natural) pH and acidity to give the wine freshness and vibrant, deep colour.

More significant still was his adoption of 100 per cent new American oak barrels, and pressing the wine before the end of fermentation, taking it immediately to those barrels to complete its primary and malolactic fermentation.

Just how revolutionary these techniques were is best judged by the reaction of other winemakers, judges and professionals to those wines. Among the many oft-quoted derisory barbs directed at Schubert (which he meticulously memorised and threw back at his critics after Grange was recognised as a great classic wine) were 'A concoction of wild fruits and sundry berries with crushed ants predominating' and 'Schubert, I congratulate you. A very good dry Port, which no one in their right mind will buy – let alone drink.'

Not only did Schubert have to bear the scorn of his peers, but the Board of Penfolds prohibited his continued use of new oak just prior to the 1957 vintage, with the intention of ending the Grange experiment. With the connivance of Jeffrey Penfold Hyland, he continued to make the wine, but the supply of oak was drastically reduced.

His moment of vindication, indeed triumph, came at the 1962 Royal Sydney Wine Show, when the much-reviled 1955 Grange swept all before it. More than fifty years later, well-cellared bottles of this wine are still superb; the 1952 and '53 are, in fact, even better, but are as rare as hen's teeth.

The inimitable and irrepressible Wolf Blass was the first winemaker outside the Penfolds stable to fully grasp the significance of the completion of fermentation in barrel, and the allied use of new American oak. But not every maker of top-end Shiraz has followed suit with barrel fermentation, and the use of French oak – particularly in cooler regions – is on the increase. (Incidentally, if both French and American oak are used, the American component is nearly certain to dominate, even if it is significantly less than 50 per cent.)

The ultra-premium Shiraz wines may be given post-fermentation maceration in tank in whole or in part; in the latter event the two components (barrel-fermented and extended-maceration) will be blended. Since the new millennium, an increasing number of small producers in cool regions have enthusiastically adopted the use of whole bunches (partial or even total) in the fermentation.

At the other extreme (of low-priced, commodity Shiraz), the French-developed technique of micro-oxygenation was adopted in Australia after a very slow start, and is used in many low- and mid-priced red wines. It bubbles a near-invisible stream of oxygen through the wine: the oxygen is completely absorbed before the stream reaches the surface, and softens the tannins in a similar fashion to the softening which would take place in (say) 18 months in bottle.

The oak influence (where required) is provided by oak chips or staves placed in the tank, and the wine does not require any barrel ageing. Traditionalists are, needless to say, very uncomfortable with this level of technology, but if it delivers a wine for $10 a bottle which would otherwise cost $20, it is difficult to mount a logical attack on the process.

Australian Regional Styles

Australia is growing Shiraz in every one of its official regions (GIs) from Queensland in the north to Tasmania in the south, from the Hunter Valley in the east to Great Southern in the west. Its style ranges from delicate, spicy and perfumed to rich, voluptuous, full-bodied and (often) with elevated alcohol. Its vines range from 175 years old to one or two years old, and every year across that range – so to talk of 'Australian Shiraz' as if it were one thing is at best meaningless, at worst misleading. It also means that the rest of the world is playing follow the leader, with no hope of ever catching up.

SOUTH AUSTRALIA

Barossa Valley
6513 ha, 23 934 tonnes, total all varieties 11 345 ha

Climate: Warm, MJT 21.4°C, E° Days 1571, SH 8.6, Rain 199 mm, Alt 270 m

This became its principal home almost from day one, and it has the largest area under vine today. Plantings began earlier in the Hunter Valley, but only two small plantings (at Tyrrell's and Mount Pleasant) date back to the nineteenth century. By contrast, there are several plantings in the Barossa Valley dating back to the 1860s, and a stream running through to 1900 (and subsequently, of course).

They have survived thanks to the ultra-conservative and equally stubborn nature of the German settlers who planted the vines and passed their care down through the generations. Bush-pruned (in other words, without a trellis) and dry-grown, the yield was low. The typical farmer worked from dawn to dusk six days a week – they were regular churchgoers on Sunday – and reckoned they had had a good year if they didn't owe the bank any more at the end of the year than at the beginning.

It was not until the 1980s that the true cost of growing these grapes, and, more importantly, their intrinsic value, began to be recognised. Schemes such as the Penfolds Grange Growers Club began to pay many times the otherwise prevailing rate per tonne, providing an income which ensured that the 'tender loving care' the ancient vines needed was unstintingly provided, protecting these living treasures for future generations.

These ancient, gnarled and twisted vines look substantial from a distance, but up close you can see that much of the trunk has rotted or disappeared, and that the live veins immediately inside the bark supplying moisture and nutrition are only a tiny fraction of the apparent mass. If clipped by a tractor wheel or plough, the impact may be terminal. So-called plough disease is a prime cause of disappearance of very old vines, and some growers are reluctant to interplant new vines and thus complicate or compromise the harvest process in the years ahead.

These vines are so much older than any European counterparts because there is no phylloxera in South Australia, and they are planted on their own roots. Grafted vines in Europe are regarded as reaching the limit of their useful life when 40 to 60 years old. One of the prime reasons is the incidence of viruses which seem part and parcel of the grafting process; another is the fact that some rootstocks, while increasing yield, also exhaust the vine.

Century-old vines do not automatically produce black-coloured, densely packed and tannic Shiraz. That is in the hands of the winemaker. But the grapes do provide wine of intense flavour and length which also has finesse and (if picked at the right time and handled correctly) great balance.

The flavours run in a cherry, plum, licorice, blackberry and mint spectrum, but seldom, if ever, display the spice found in wines made in cooler regions. The tannin level is usually up to the winemaker: in other words, they are naturally present in abundance (particularly in warmer vintages) and it all depends how much extract is desired.

Following, as it were, in the footsteps of Max Schubert, traditional makers use American oak, which imparts vanillan aroma and flavour to the wine, and marries well with the luscious dark fruit. However, French oak is increasingly used: Penfolds RWT Barossa Shiraz is an illustrious example. Regardless of the choice of oak, these wines live for decades before starting to dry out and gain the earthy/leathery character of old Shiraz.

Penfolds Grange and St Henri have always had a wandering geographic make-up, but the heart of each was fed by the Barossa Valley. For the purposes of this book, the 100 per cent single-vineyard Magill Estate is (notionally) moved from suburban Adelaide to the Barossa Valley. Likewise, the Cabernet Sauvignon component of St Henri is ignored.

The most controversial aspect of Barossa – and for that matter Australian Shiraz as a whole – is the ghetto blasters so beloved of the American band conducted by Robert Parker. Inky black, oozing extract, and routinely topping 15 to 16 per cent alcohol, these are strange wines. The fact that they are made in small quantities from century-old vines, and are stirred but never fined or filtered, adds to their allure. One glass is interesting; any more is satiating.

Best producers

Charles Melton*, Dutschke, Elderton, Glaetzer, Grant Burge*, Hare's Chase*, Hemera Estate*, Hentley Farm*, Hewitson, Kaesler*, Kalleske*, Langmeil, Laughing Jack, Maverick, Ochota Barrels, Orlando, Penfolds*, Peter Lehmann*, Rockford*, St Hallet*, Spinifex*, Thorn-Clarke, Torbreck*, Trevor Jones, Turkey Flat*, Westlake, Wolf Blass*, Yalumba*

McLaren Vale

3866 ha, 18 059 tonnes, total all varieties 7422 ha

Climate: Warm, MJT 21.3°C, E° Days 1680, SH 8.4, Rain 230 mm, Alt 130 m

McLaren Vale and the Barossa Valley are the two leviathan growers and makers of Shiraz, and in each case this variety accounts for more than half of the region's plantings. Many Shirazs of very high quality come from McLaren Vale, and do so with the imprint of the districts of their birth. Two that stand out are Clarendon and Blewitt Springs, the latter with cooler grower season temperatures.

At this point, discussion of the appropriate level of alcohol for McLaren Vale Shiraz becomes inevitable. You can't make great wine by numbers, so to arbitrarily dismiss any wine with an alcohol level above 14.5 per cent is wrong. If a given wine has balance, it shouldn't matter whether the alcohol is 13 per cent or 15 per cent. Put another way, the finish should not be hot, and this is often the Achilles heel of an otherwise generous, velvety Shiraz. The problem of specifying 14.5 per cent as a desirable maximum is that there are wines with lower alcohol that may seem to have a hot finish and, conversely, there are those with higher alcohol that can be supple, smooth and balanced.

Shiraz bunches picked at 15° baumé (or higher) will usually have a significant proportion of shrivelled, even raisined, berries. Before this stage is reached, the natural bloom of the grapes will have disappeared, and some dimpling of the skins will have occurred. Brian Croser has weighed into the debate, describing this as 'dead fruit', and asserts that the dead fruit character flows into the wine.

The contrary argument is that one of the peculiarities of Shiraz is that it is more prone to shrivel/desiccation than other varieties at the same baumé. Picking earlier just for the sake of doing so will leave the wine with inadequate flavour or lack of balance. Continuing the debate, those in the Croser camp will say this is a viticultural problem, not a winemaking issue. Either the site (in aspect and/or soil) is not appropriate, or the canopy management needs to change.

There are winemakers who deliberately seek even higher levels of alcohol, a few using the Italian Amarone method of picking, then partially drying the grapes.

When conventionally grown and harvested, the wines have an effortless opulence which is the envy of most of those countries that have recently become converts to the variety. Moreover, McLaren Vale Shiraz usually has a component of dark, even bitter, chocolate that works in conjunction with ripe tannins to provide a savoury balance to the luscious plum and blackberry fruits of the mid-palate. The result is a wine style very different from that of cool-climate Shiraz, but every bit as good. Finally, there is the perhaps endangered species of 'Vintage Port' made by Hardys and Reynella over many decades.

Best producers
Angove Family Winemakers, Battle of Bosworth, Bekkers*, BK Wines, Cape Barren, Chalk Hill*, Chapel Hill*, Clarendon Hills*, Coriole, d'Arenberg*, Dowie Doole, Fox Creek*, Gemtree*, Geoff Merrill*, Hardys*, Haselgrove*, Hewitson, Hugh Hamilton, Kangarilla Road, Kay Brothers Amery Vineyards, Lloyd Brothers, Maxwell Wines, Mitolo, Oliver's Taranga Vineyards, Patritti, Paxton*, Primo Estate, Reynella*, Richard Hamilton*, Rosemount Estate*, SC Pannell*, Serafino*, Shingleback*, Shirvington, The Old Faithful Estate*, Tintara, WayWood Wines, Wirra Wirra*, Woodstock, Yangarra Estate*

Clare Valley
1865 ha, 5896 tonnes, total all varieties 5339 ha

Climate: Warm, MJT 21.4°C, E° Days 1493, SH 8.9, Rain 248 mm, Alt 450 m

This region introduces an inner core of steel which may or may not be immediately apparent, but which gives the wines enough structure to age for decades. The fruit spectrum also shifts slightly more towards blackberry and black cherry fruit, which melds with that more masculine structure. There is no greater example in the Clare Valley (or anywhere else in Australia, for that matter) than the Shiraz or Shiraz blends of Wendouree, wines of awesome balance, concentration, power and longevity.

Best producers
Annie's Lane*, Atlas, Erin Eyes, Jeanneret, Jim Barry Wines*, Kilikanoon*, Kirrihill, Knappstein, Leasingham, Mitchell, Mount Horrocks, Neagles Rock, O'Leary Walker*, Pikes, Skillogalee*, Taylors, Wendouree*

Eden Valley

710 ha, 1420 tonnes, total all varieties 2264 ha

Climate: Moderate, MJT 20.2°C, E° Days 1460, SH 8.5, Rain 275 mm, Alt 420 m

Home of the iconic Henschke Hill of Grace, which exemplifies all that is good about the region. The Shiraz is exceptionally graceful, combining intensity with finesse, the tannins finer than those of the other regions north of Adelaide (and McLaren Vale). It seems nigh on impossible to over-extract or over-make Shiraz from the Eden Valley; the only downside is that in the cooler vintages it may be a struggle to attain full ripeness.

Best producers
Brockenchack*, CRFT, Dandelion, Eden Hall*, Eperosa*, Gibson, Grant Burge, Head, Henschke*, Heirloom Vineyards, Poonawatta*, Sons of Eden*, Torbreck*, Two Hands, Yalumba*

Langhorne Creek

2162 ha, 17 514 tonnes, total all varieties 5883 ha

Climate: Moderate, MJT 19.9°C, E° Days 1529, SH 8, Rain 206 mm, Alt 20 m

For long the poaching preserve of the big companies which knew the value of the wine in blends (notably Wolf Blass), and today the most important single resource for Orlando Jacob's Creek Shiraz Cabernet. A small but increasing number of quality producers are now resident in the area, joining the centenarian, Bleasdale. It is an intensely maritime region, with Lake Alexandrina on one side and the Southern Ocean on the other; the flavours are of red fruits, sometimes raspberry, and the texture invariably supple.

Best producers
Angus Plains, Bleasdale*, Bremerton*, Brothers in Arms, Heartland, Johns Blend*, Lake Breeze Wines

Coonawarra

1146 ha, 6818 tonnes, total all varieties 5603 ha

Climate: Moderate, MJT 19.9°C, E° Days 1379, SH 7.5, Rain 272 mm, Alt 60 m

Although it is now accepted as a first-class region for Cabernet Sauvignon in Australia, for most of the twentieth century its survival depended on its production of Shiraz. Modern winemaking methods – partial barrel fermentation, new French oak and American oak, and so forth – have added an extra dimension to what was the traditional style. Similarly, the special treatment given to the surviving vineyard blocks planted 100 years ago adds another layer.

The Woodley wines of the 1930s, '40s and '50s – all of which I have been privileged to taste – were supremely elegant wines relatively low in alcohol and extract, yet (self-evidently) of great longevity. Then there is the fabled, once-only, 1955 Wynns Michael Hermitage, matured in ex-whisky barrels, which gave an exquisite wine; I have never tasted a poor bottle. All subsequent attempts in the 1950s to reproduce the wine failed; the new generation Wynns Michael Hermitage, initiated in 1990, is a very good wine, but is made in a radically different style. Lindemans Limestone Ridge Shiraz Cabernet (the Shiraz is by far the dominant partner) is more traditional.

The flavour of Coonawarra Shiraz is centred on red and black cherry, with plum and spice components less obvious, the spice absent altogether in some years (when mint may take its place). The texture is typically supple, the tannins soft and ripe. A confounding factor has been the emergence of the super-cuvees, based on specially selected grapes (usually from old or older vines with reduced crops) which provide higher extract and sustain 100 per cent new oak. Brand's Stentifords Reserve (from 100-year-old vines), the new Michael Hermitage, and Punters Corner Spartacus Reserve are prime examples.

Best producers
Balnaves*, Brand's Laira*, Bundalong, Katnook Estate, Lindemans*, Majella*, Penfolds*, Parker Coonawarra Estate*, Rymill, Wynns Coonawarra Estate*, Zema Estate

Padthaway
1222 ha, 8153 tonnes, total all varieties 4052 ha

Climate: Warm, MJT 21°C, E° Days 1550, SH 7.8, Rain 210 mm, Alt 50 m

The region was originally identified by Karl Seppelt as suitable for the production of mid-quality table wines, and has been dogged by that perception ever since. It was correctly believed that generous yields of good (not great) grapes could be grown at a low cost. In fact the large companies – headed by Seppelt (which called the region Keppoch in the early years, not helping its profile), Hardys and Orlando – were surprised by the quality of the grapes.

Others with large wineries in Coonawarra, notably Wynns, Lindemans and Mildara, also joined the queue as the export boom fed demand. In 1998 Hardys built the $18 million

Stonehaven winery, the only facility in the region. But ten years later, as exports stalled, Hardys' owner, Constellation Wines, mothballed the winery after failing to find a buyer. It was ultimately acquired by a low-profile group offering contract winemaking services for the Limestone Coast Zone.

Best producers
Henry's Drive, Landaire, Morambro Creek Wines, Orlando

Wrattonbully
681 ha, 5767 tonnes, total all varieties 2679 ha

Climate: Moderate, MJT 20.4°C, E° Days 1473, SH 7.6, Rain 227 mm, Alt 60 m

The climate is poised between those of Coonawarra and Padthaway, the former cooler than the latter, although there is variation across the region. This is due to the Naracoorte Ranges, and the undulating slopes of between 75 metres and 100 metres. The vineyards are almost exclusively planted on the terra rossa soils made famous by Coonawarra. This is red wine country first and foremost, much of the production being purchased by South Australia's major wine companies, and typically initially processed at a large contract crush facility that was built in 1998 to handle the production of the region. Smith & Hooper of Wrattonbully is in fact an arm of Yalumba; Tapanappa is a business partnership headed by Brian Croser; Terre à Terre is owned by Xavier Bizot (from the Bollinger family) and wife Lucy Croser. Tapanappa's signature wine is a Cabernet Shiraz Merlot blend, and that of Terre à Terre a striking wood-fermented Sauvignon Blanc (its plantings also include 1 hectare of Shiraz).

Best producers
Smith & Hooper, Tapanappa, Terre à Terre

NEW SOUTH WALES

Hunter Valley
1024 ha, total all varieties 3380 ha

Climate: Hot, MJT 23.6°C, E° Days 1823, SH 7.3, Rain 534 mm, Alt 110 m

Shiraz was planted here before it was planted in any other region in Australia, and over the ensuing 185 years it has proved itself the foremost red variety, ignoring the outrageous barbs of fortune flung at it by the thoroughly capricious climate: hot, humid and prone to rain only when it is not wanted. In other words, during vintage. But on the small patches of red volcanic soil, and even on red brown clays, Shiraz can produce superb wine with a chameleon-like ability to transform itself with long bottle age.

The weight and style can vary markedly between makers, from the majestic power of the Brokenwood Graveyard Shiraz to the supple texture of the McWilliams Mount Pleasant Old Paddock and Old Hill Shiraz, produced from vineyards planted in the 1920s and 1880s respectively. The wines made by Maurice O'Shea at Mount Pleasant between the 1920s and his death in 1956 are justifiably revered.

The winemakers of the region are a tightly knit, highly skilled group with a knowledge horizon extending over all Australian regions, and equally to the Rhône Valley. They are making wines with alcohol levels of 12.5 per cent to 13.5 per cent, the palate structure positive but fine in extract, the tannins verging on silky. They are at the opposite end of the wine universe to Shiraz from the Barossa Valley.

Best producers
Briar Ridge, Brokenwood*, Capercaillie, Chateau Pato, De Iuliis*, First Creek, Glenguin Estate, Gundog Estate, Keith Tulloch, Leogate, Margan Family, Meerea Park*, Mount Pleasant*, Mount View Estate, Pepper Tree*, Tallavera Grove, Tempus Two, Thomas Wines*, Tinklers Vineyard, Tulloch, Tyrrell's*

Mudgee
1110 ha, total all varieties 3323 ha

Climate: Hot, MJT 23.3°C, E° Days 1663, SH 9, Rain 441 mm, Alt 480 m

The variety has been the red wine backbone of the region for over a century. The radically different continental climate (compared to the sultry coastal climate of the Hunter Valley) and cold nights produce Shiraz with black cherry, plum, prune and dark chocolate fruit supported by ample – if not buxom – tannins. The wines age particularly well, but there is a curious dearth of top-quality winemakers, given the large area of Shiraz.

Best producers
Huntington Estate*, Logan, Robert Oatley Vineyards, Robert Stein*

Orange

439 ha, total all varieties 1531 ha

> **Low Altitude** Climate: Warm, MJT 22.9°C, E° Days 1571, SH 8.9, Rain 414 mm, Alt 670 m
> **High Altitude** Climate: Moderate, MJT 19.6°C, E° Days 1250, SH 8.7, Rain 524 mm, Alt 950 m

This region has a much cooler climate than Mudgee (both regions are in the Central Ranges Zone), shaped by the higher altitude of the vineyards. Here Shiraz has a freshness and brightness contributed by its high natural acidity, sitting alongside vivid spice and red cherry fruit flavours.

Best producers
Bloodwood*, Highland Heritage Estate, Logan, Philip Shaw*, Printhie, Ross Hill, Tallavera Grove | Carillion

Canberra District

122 ha, total all varieties 360 ha

> Climate: Moderate, MJT 20.7°C, E° Days 1383, SH 8.5, Rain 398 mm, Alt 650 m

A strongly continental climate, with hot summer days and cold nights, compresses the growing season and can lead to problems with spring frosts. The rewards are abundant, with a number of wineries doing particularly well with Shiraz, none more so than Clonakilla. Co-fermented with a varying percentage of Viognier (as is the practice in the Northern Rhône), Clonakilla Shiraz has gained icon status with its elegant, spicy flavour and particularly long, sustained finish. Here natural acidity plays an important role in giving the wines a long life; 5 to 7 per cent Viognier is also part of the winning formula. Clonakilla has also released a 100 per cent estate Shiraz of excellent quality. This may be a small region, but (outside of the Hunter) it is an exciting region in which to make Shiraz – French oak (rather than American) is sensitively used by all the best makers. The cross-border incursions from the Hunter Valley speak for themselves, as do incursions by Canberra District makers into Hilltops.

Best producers
Audrey Wilkinson, Clonakilla*, Collector Wines*, Eden Road*, Even Keel, Four Winds, Gallagher, Lark Hill, Mount Majura, Ravensworth

Hilltops
162 ha, total all varieties 475 ha

Climate: Warm, MJT 22.1°C, E° Days 1492, SH 8.9, Rain 364 mm, Alt 540 m

While the climate is unequivocally continental, with substantial diurnal temperature variation during the growing season, the altitude at which most of the vineyards are established ensures a long and even ripening period. Heavy snowfalls in winter are quite common, but pose no threat to viticulture; spring frosts, however, do, and necessitate careful site selection along ridge tops and upper, well air-drained slopes. While substantial rain occurs in the growing season, most falls in spring; the dry summer and autumn provide excellent ripening conditions, but make irrigation essential.

Hilltops was not gazetted (formally recognised) until February 1998, but had had significant vineyards between 1860 and 1940; planting was disrupted by World War II, and thereafter by labour shortages, and the last vines were removed in 1960. Only nine years were to elapse before Peter Robertson began to plant Barwang. When McWilliam's purchased his 400-hectare property in 1989, only 13 hectares were under vine; this has since increased to over 100 hectares. Grover Estate (46 hectares) was established the same year, followed by Chalkers Crossing (27 hectares) in 2000. In 2004 a 73-hectare vineyard, previously simply selling grapes, was purchased by Jason and Alicia Brown. Jason, who has a fine wine and accounting background, and Moppity Vineyards, having been content to initially sell the grapes, began having wine made, and have enjoyed spectacular success, with a combination of high quality and (relatively) low prices. Clonakilla and Eden Road buy Hilltops grapes and make exceptional wine.

Best producers
Barwang, Chalkers Crossing*, Clonakilla*, Grove Estate, Moppity Vineyards*

VICTORIA

Heathcote
732 ha, total all varieties 1222 ha

Climate: Warm, MJT 21.6°C, E° Days 1534, SH 8.2, Rain 285 mm, Alt 140 m

After a leisurely start, Heathcote has established a deserved reputation as a producer of first-class Shiraz, its terroir immediately obvious to those on the ground, or those able to fly over it in a light plane or helicopter.

The prized soil is decomposed Cambrian-era igneous intrusion rock, known as greenstone, created 500 million years ago and forming the then higher spine of the Mount Camel Range. Progressive weathering caused it to move down the side of the range, covering sedimentary layers which now form the subsoil. Its pattern is sinuous and constantly changing: a distance of 50 metres can mark a radical change in soil type. It has the all-important combination of being well drained and having good moisture retention.

Site variations due to altitude and aspect to one side, the climate is similar to that of Bendigo, but a fraction cooler in terms of total growing season warmth in the south around Heathcote, and warmer in the northern end past Colbinabbin. Warm to hot summer days are ideal for full-bodied red wines.

This region is exceptionally well suited to Shiraz, which dominates the plantings. The wines are mouth-filling and mouth-coating, densely coloured and richly flavoured, their texture akin to a great tapestry, helping to highlight their multifaceted taste. The fruit flavours may range over blackberry, black and red cherry, plum, licorice, leather and spice, with the tannins supple and ripe.

A considerable number of the best producers are not resident, buying grapes and making the wines at their home base.

Best producers
Bress*, Buckshot Vineyard, Bull Lane, Chalmers*, Condie Estate*, Domaine Asmara, Dominique Portet*, Downing Estate, Flynns*, Graillot*, Greenstone Vineyard*, Hanging Rock*, Jasper Hill*, Journey, Margaret Hill Vineyard, Noble Red, Occam's Razor, Paul Osicka*, Red Edge*, Rochford, Sanguine Estate*, She-Oak Hill, Syrahmi*, Tyrrell's, Yarran*

Bendigo
415 ha, total all varieties 750 ha

Climate: Warm, MJT 21.8°C, E° Days 1581, SH 8.3, Rain 269 mm, Alt 220 m

This region formerly incorporated Heathcote as an unofficial subregion, but the divorce has not left Bendigo destitute. The Shiraz style is similar to that of Heathcote: generous, complex and mouth-filling. Balgownie Estate throws down the challenge with its Limited Release Old Vine Shiraz, made from the best of 12 rows of the 1969 vines, the 2008 and 2002 vintages still full of velvety black fruits offset by savoury tannins when released in 2013. While Passing Clouds' home base is now in the Macedon Ranges, it still buys grapes from vineyards it supported (and vice versa) while in the region, and the wines are seriously good.

Best producers
Balgownie Estate*, Blackjack Vineyards, Bress, Glenwillow, Harcourt Valley*, Munari, Passing Clouds*, Pondalowie*, Turners Crossing

Goulburn Valley
492 ha, total all varieties 1593 ha

Climate: Warm, MJT 21.6°C, E° Days 1534, SH 8.2, Rain 285 mm, Alt 140 m

Shiraz grown in this region tends more to the savoury, earthy end of the spectrum than that of Heathcote or Bendigo. At Tahbilk (which is in the Nagambie Lakes subregion) there is a 0.5-hectare block of Shiraz planted in 1860, and is believed to be the oldest in the world with no interplanting or replanting of younger vines. Most remarkably, it is surrounded by vineyards with active phylloxera; its immunity comes from the red sandy soil (devoid of clay) on which it is planted, through which phylloxera cannot pass.

The aim is to reflect the terroir and the extreme age of the vines, and in particular not lavish new oak on it, as Guigal, the famous Rhône Valley producer, might do. It is so well balanced, and so elegant, that it is able to communicate its message without assistance, and is one of the great treasures of the wine world, the 1860 Vines Shiraz. Production is fewer than 200 dozen bottles, with severe winter frost in 2007 having reduced the number of vines still further (after earlier deaths). Another special wine is the Tahbilk Eric Stevens Purbrick Shiraz, from vines with an average age of over 40 years. It is in a similar style, with savoury, sweet leather and briar flavours around a core of blackberry and blackcurrant fruit.

Best producers
Mitchelton, Tahbilk*

Grampians
323 ha, total all varieties 501 ha

Climate: Moderate, MJT 19.8°C, E° Days 1377, SH 8.2, Rain 261 mm, Alt 270 m

Until recently known as Great Western (Great Western is now a subregion of the Grampians region), this region is home to three outstanding makers of Shiraz – Best's, Mount Langi Ghiran and Seppelt – and others of real merit. Best's and Seppelt both have the advantage of a core of old vines, whereas Mount Langi Ghiran has a special vineyard site and site climate. While Best's and Seppelt have small cuvées of special Shiraz (respectively Thomson Family and Grampians, a 90-year-old block adjacent to the winery), there are common threads running through the output of the region: a supple, silky feel; a strong spicy accent to the cherry and mint fruit; and tannins which are almost invariably fine. While the alcohol levels are modest, and the wines typically only medium-bodied, they have impeccable balance. Moreover, as the wines of Seppelt and Best's demonstrate, they can live for 30 to 60 years without breaking up and decaying. The great wines made by the late Colin Preece between 1925 and 1962 are still living proof of his mastery.

This is also the source of one of Australia's unique icon wines, Seppelt Show Sparkling Shiraz, copied by other makers in other regions with the same or other varieties, but not coming close to the quality or style of the Seppelt wine. It is made (only in the best vintages) in exactly the same way as Champagne, except that it is kept on lees for ten years prior to disgorgement and sale. It will continue to improve in bottle for many years thereafter.

Best producers
AT Richardson, Best's*, Grampians Estate, Mount Langi Ghiran*, Seppelt*, The Story Wines

Pyrenees
393 ha, total all varieties 864 ha

Climate: Warm, MJT 21.3°C, E° Days 1440, SH 8.2, Rain 254 mm, Alt 330 m

Partly because this is one of the more distant regions from Melbourne, it tends not to receive the attention it deserves – this despite the awesome quality and consistency of its foremost producer, Dalwhinnie.

The inland location (and to a certain degree the altitude of 220–375 metres) gives rise to low midsummer relative humidity and substantial diurnal temperature ranges in spring and early summer. Late summer daytime temperatures are moderate, lowering the overall heat summation. The major limitations on viticulture are low growing season rainfall and the absence of underground water. This is true, also, of the new areas on the southern side of the Pyrenees Ranges, which are significantly cooler, but where the requirement of water (and the danger of spring frosts) is still substantial.

While Dalwhinnie is unchallenged, there are other high-quality winemakers supporting the case that the richly textured Shirazs of the region deserve more recognition.

Best producers
Ben Haines, DogRock*, Dalwhinnie*, M Chapoutier*, Mount Avoca*, Pyren Vineyard, Quartz Hill, Summerfield*, Ten Men, Warrenmang

Glenrowan and Rutherglen

Glenrowan: 84 ha, total all varieties 200 ha. Rutherglen: 372 ha, total all varieties 696 ha

Rutherglen Climate: Hot, MJT 23.7°C, E° Days 1591, SH 9, Rain 196 mm, Alt 170 m
Glenrowan Climate: Hot, MJT 23.4°C, E° Days 1647, SH 8.9, Rain 309 mm, Alt 220 m

Small quantities of inky, rich, boldly structured Shiraz are made in these regions. Booth's Taminick Cellars was the primary source (in the early days) for Wynns Ovens Valley Burgundy (sic), the last vintage of which was made in 1992, by which time its connection with the Ovens Valley did not satisfy labelling laws.

The standout producer for Glenrowan is Baileys of Glenrowan, where long-serving winemaker Paul Dahlenburg makes Shiraz that commands attention with its ability to marry power, concentration and elegance. Others have come and gone in this small region.

The power goes to Rutherglen with its much larger resources – and some thoughtful winemaking creating Shiraz with more elegance than the traditional blockbuster style.

Best producers
All Saints Estate*, Baileys of Glenrowan*, Campbells, Cofield, Jones Winery, Morris Wines, Pfeiffer*, St Leonards, Taminick Cellars, Warrabilla

Sunbury

44 ha, total all varieties 128 ha

Climate: Moderate, MJT 19.3°C, E° Days 1410, SH 7.6, Rain 420 mm, Alt 220 m

One of the historic homes of Shiraz in Australia, courtesy of the nineteenth-century wineries of Craiglee and Goona Warra. Craiglee's 1872 Hermitage is the second-oldest Australian wine I have tasted (on several occasions). Today Craiglee produces splendidly spicy, fine, medium-bodied Shiraz which is the epitome of elegance for the variety in Australia.

Best producers
Arundel Farm, Craiglee*, Galli Estate, Goona Warra, The Hairy Arm, Witchmount Estate

Macedon Ranges
30 ha, total all varieties 218 ha

> Climate: Cool, MJT 18.2°C, E° Days 1149, SH 7.8, Rain 428 mm, Alt 500 m

Granite Hills was one of the first truly cool-climate producers of Shiraz the second time around – in other words, post-1970. The vines are now over 40 years old, and the quality of the wine, always good, has blossomed. A combination of black cherry, plum, spice and feathery tannins puts it in the same extreme quality league as Craiglee. It is ironic that this pioneer of the region should be the only one to plant Shiraz – even Bindi Wine Growers and Hanging Rock source their Shiraz from Heathcote.

Best producers
Granite Hills*, Metcalfe Valley, Rowanston on the Track*

Mornington Peninsula
42 ha, total all varieties 732 ha

> **Mornington** Climate: Cool, MJT 18.9°C, E° Days 1428, SH 7.1, Rain 380 mm, Alt 60 m
> **Red Hill South** Climate: Cool, MJT 17.5°C, E° Days 1240, SH 6.8, Rain 400+ mm, Alt 180 m

While Chardonnay and Pinot Noir are in no way threatened by Shiraz, recent vintages have increased the footprint of Shiraz beyond that of the two pioneers, Merricks Estate and Paringa Estate (the latter the Crown Prince). Of the newcomers, the (relatively) warm location of Yabby Lake (and the skills of winemaker Tom Carson) has left no doubt that anyone wishing to step outside Chardonnay and Pinot Noir doesn't have to default to Pinot Gris.

Best producers
Merricks Estate, Paradigm Hill, Paringa Estate*, Port Phillip Estate, Yabby Lake*

Yarra Valley
244 ha, total all varieties 2408 ha

> **Lower** Climate: Moderate, MJT 19.4°C, E° Days 1463, SH 7.4, Rain 437 mm, Alt 120 m
> **Upper** Climate: Cool, MJT 18.4°C, E° Days 1253, SH 7.3, Rain 700 mm, Alt 200 m

Careful site selection by some of the doyens of the rebirth of the Yarra Valley provides beautiful Shiraz, its spice components proclaiming the cool climate, but with plush red cherry, plum and licorice fruit, and soft tannins flooding the mouth with sweet flavour. There is every reason to believe these wines will be exceptionally long-lived, as anyone who has tasted 1980 Yeringberg or Yarra Yering No. 2 recently will attest. So far, the best wines come from the Lower Yarra, little or none from the Upper.

Best producers
De Bortoli, Seville Estate, Yarra Yering*, Yering Station, Yeringberg*

Geelong
108 ha, total all varieties 506 ha

Climate: Cool, MJT 18.5°C, E° Days 1377, SH 7.2, Rain 319 mm, Alt 70 m

On the other side of Melbourne from the Yarra Valley, Geelong produces Shiraz with many of the same characteristics, albeit even more concentrated in the hands of Bannockburn's Gary Farr.

Best producers
Austin's*, Bannockburn*, Barrgowan*, Bellbrae, Brown Magpie, Clyde Park, del Rios of Mt Anakie, Farr | Farr Rising*, Lethbridge*, Oakdene, Paradise IV*, Provenance*, Scotchmans Hill*, Terindah Estate*

WESTERN AUSTRALIA

Great Southern
636 ha, total all varieties 2752 ha

Frankland River Climate: Moderate, MJT 20.7°C, E° Days 1574, SH 7.6, Rain 203 mm, Alt 230 m
Mount Barker Climate: Moderate, MJT 20°C, E° Days 1548, SH 7.3, Rain 280 mm, Alt 220 m
Denmark Climate: Cool, MJT 18.9°C, E° Days 1512, SH 6.7, Rain 332 mm, Alt 130 m

Shiraz excels in most parts of this far-flung region, with its cool, largely continental climate. The wines show intense varietal character, with spice and licorice running through the bright red berry and plum fruit. Finesse, rather than power, gives Shiraz its intensity; alcohol and tannin levels are always restrained.

Best producers
Burch Family, Byron & Harold, Castelli Estate, Duke's Vineyard*, Forest Hill Vineyard*, Houghton*, Larry Cherubino*, Mandoon Estate, Robert Oatley Vineyards, Rockcliffe, The Lake House*, West Cape Howe*, Xabregas

Margaret River
700 ha, total all varieties 4771 ha

> **Yallingup** Climate: Moderate, MJT 20.5°C, E° Days 1655, SH 7.6, Rain 221 mm, Alt 100 m
> **Wallcliffe** Climate: Moderate, MJT 20°C, E° Days 1552, SH 7.4, Rain 261 mm, Alt 90 m
> **Karridale** Climate: Cool, MJT 18.8°C, E° Days 1497, SH 7.1, Rain 305 mm, Alt 50 m

A relatively recent arrival (in any force) in the region, coming well after the Cabernet family, but growing day by day. Site selection is important, as is keeping the yields down, if wines with good structure are to be made. Once again, the style is relatively fine and unquestionably reflects the cool climate.

Best producers
Burch Family Wines, Cape Grace, Cape Mentelle*, Clairault | Streicker*, Credaro Family Estate, Evans & Tate*, Flying Fish Cove, Juniper Estate*, Leeuwin Estate*, Sandalford, Voyager Estate*, Watershed Wines*

Peel, Perth Hills and Swan District
235 ha, total all varieties 1353 ha

> **Peel (Inland)** Climate: Hot, MJT 24.4°C, E° Days 1707, SH 9.1, Rain 152 mm, Alt 320 m
> **Peel (Coastal)** Climate: Hot, MJT 23.2°C, E° Days 1841, SH 9.2, Rain 179 mm, Alt 30 m
> **Perth Hills** Climate: Hot, MJT 23.1°C, E° Days 1727, SH 9.2, Rain 224 mm, Alt 5260 m

While Perth Hills is marginally cooler than Peel, the Swan District is unambiguously hot. Shiraz, as ever, shows its capacity to adapt to each and every climate in which it is grown, and some most attractive wines can be made.

Best producers
Peel: Peel Estate; Perth Hills: Millbrook; Swan District: Faber Vineyard, Lamont's, Mandoon Estate, Paul Conti Wines, Upper Reach

Chapter 12

The Classic Red Varietals
Grenache | Garnacha Tinta

184 735 ha grown in 22 countries, Brazil and Peru with 1 ha each. Those with over 500 ha are: Algeria 6040 ha, Australia 1779 ha, France 90 991 ha, Italy 6372 ha, Spain 70 140 ha, Tunisia 2020 ha, United States 2666 ha.

International History

Once the world's most planted grape variety, Grenache is claimed both by Spain and Italy via the island of Sardinia. It is not yet possible to categorically say one of the two claims is correct, because no DNA parent–offspring relationship has yet been established for the variety.[1] What is not disputed is that mutations over the centuries have led to Grenache Rouge, Gris and Blanc – which in itself points to Spain. Whichever be the truth, it was in cultivation by the start of the fourteenth century, gradually spreading outwards from the Province of Aragon across northern Spain and southern France. And it is in fact France that has the largest planting.

Interestingly, it was not planted in La Rioja (where it is known as Garnacha Tinta) until phylloxera arrived in 1901, when its generous yield and soft, juicy fruit flavours must have been very handy in helping plug the hiatus in production. It is in third place in the dark-skinned (red) plantings in Spain, after Tempranillo (207 677 hectares) and Bobal (80 120 hectares).

Its spread across the entire south of France, and into the key area of the southern Rhône Valley, set the scene for its subsequent expansion into the New World.

---

1 Jancis Robinson, Julia Harding and Jose Vouillamoz, *Wine Grapes*, Ecco/HarperCollins, 2012, p. 397.

In Old World and New World alike it has a Jekyll and Hyde personality. If pruned severely and dry-grown in a very warm to hot climate, it can produce deeply coloured, deeply flavoured yet soft wine of great character. If allowed to grow as it wishes with the aid of irrigation, its excessive yield produces pale, insipid, faintly jammy wine already halfway to Rose – which is one of its legitimate manifestations.

It was embraced with fervour in only two of the New World areas, California and South Australia – in fact in the warmest, driest wine regions of those states. That said, it is grown in at least 22 countries.

International Styles

FRANCE
90 991 ha

Châteauneuf-du-Pape
The absolute magnificence of Château Rayas, made from 100 per cent old-vine Grenache, is, and I suspect always will be, the ultimate achievement and expression of the variety. I have tasted a bottle of 1934 in recent times, still full of perfumed life. And before the wine was canonised by Robert Parker, I was able to secure various vintages from the 1970s and '80s at what now seem ridiculously low prices. The wine has exotic aromas and flavours, and is sweetly spicy, with wafts of forest berries, tobacco, licorice and who knows how many other characters, changing both as you drink this bottle and as you drink the next.

While I have linked Grenache to Châteauneuf-du-Pape, this appellation permits the use of 18 varieties (increased from 13). I have taken this step because Grenache is the cornerstone for all the wines: Syrah, Mourvedre and Cinsaut are its most important blend-mates.

Overall, Châteauneuf-du-Pape is a minefield in much the same way as Côtes du Rhône. An intimate knowledge – or a mine detector – is needed to steer you away from the innumerable mundane wines to the good producers, of which there are plenty. Good Châteauneuf may not be in the Olympian class of Château Rayas, but it is a wonderfully satisfying wine.

Best producers
Château de Beaucastel*, Château de la Charbonniere, Château La Nerthe*, Château Mont-Redon, Château Rayas/Clos Pignan*, Delas*, De Marcoux, Domaine Bosquet des Papes, Domaine du Pegau, Domaine du Vieux Telegraphe*, Domaine la Barroche, E Guigal*, Les Cailloux, Roger Sabon, Tardieu Laurent*, Vieux Donjon

Côtes du Rhône

This vast appellation has a viticultural history stretching over 1000 years, and encompasses 56 400 hectares of vineyards. Grenache is the dominant variety (with a legal minimum of 40 per cent), supplemented in varying proportions by Syrah and Mourvedre, with smaller amounts of Carignan and Cinsaut.

Winemaking methods vary considerably, with carbonic maceration used more commonly where the wine is made in a nouveau style for early consumption. Wine quality is, if anything, more variable than that of Châteauneuf-du-Pape, but there are many bargains to be had.

With a production of around 1 million hectolitres, it is inevitable that co-operatives play a large part in the production of the wine, and negociants an equal part in the blending and/or selling of it. The most important negociant is the ubiquitous Guigal, whose Côtes du Rhône has been one of the great bargains of the international wine world, year in, year out, for almost 40 years. It has, incidentally, a higher percentage of Syrah than most, which explains why I still have the 1976 and 1978 in my cellar (and numerous more recent vintages).

The hallmark of all Côtes du Rhône, even one as concentrated and rich as Domaine Gramenon, is its sheer drinkability. While the fruit is there in abundance, the tannins are invariably soft. The wine moves imperceptibly from youth to maturity, and the choice of young or old may well vary with the spur of the moment.

It is a wine which Australians instinctively understand and, for this reason if no other, the overwhelming majority of the Côtes du Rhône wines brought into this country are from the top echelon of producers.

Best producers
Château de Fonsalette*, Château Mont-Redon*, Coudelet de Beaucastel, Domaine de l'Ameillaud, Domaine de la Réméjeanne, Domaine Gramenon*, E Guigal*, Grand Veneur*, La Vielle Ferme

Australian History

Uniquely for Australia, Grenache has established itself as important in only one state, South Australia. But since the new millennium, vignerons in the most unexpected places have ignored the apparent demise of the variety and planted vines. Unexpected, because conventional thinking is that Grenache performs best in warm to hot climates, which Heathcote (26 hectares), Margaret River (11 hectares) and the Yarra Valley (0.5 hectares) do not have.

Within South Australia, it is similarly limited to a few regions, but with a gulf dividing them. The most important (in terms of quality) is McLaren Vale, although the vignerons of the Barossa and Clare valleys may well take umbrage at this distinction between the three major dry-grown bushvine regions.

The dramatic fall in production shown by the chart is explained by two unrelated factors: first, the significant decline in production of fortified wine, and second, the Vine Pull Scheme of 1987, which most affected Grenache. I expect that plantings will now stabilise; it is now planted in 47 regions, admittedly in small amounts, but this is nonetheless impressive.

Australian Statistics

1779 ha, 14 919 tonnes

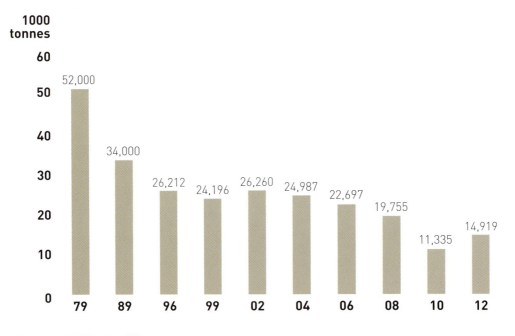

Grenache: tonnes crushed in Australia, 1979–2012

Australian Winemaking

In 1960, 80 per cent of Australian wine was fortified; this had been the case for most of that century. In turn, 90 per cent of all red grape plantings at that time were Grenache, Shiraz and Mourvedre. Grenache was the cornerstone for the production of Tawny Port. It and sweet Sherry were the two most important styles of fortified wine. It was and is a lynchpin in the making of the 100 Year Old Para Vintage Tawny, which is kept in cask until 100 years old, and only then bottled on demand and sold. Vintage Port style may or may not include a small percentage of Grenache; normally it is made from Shiraz, occasionally from the true Portuguese Port varieties.

Particularly in McLaren Vale, but also in the Barossa Valley, Grenache had long had a parallel but minor use in making red table wine (and as the red table wine boom of the second half of the 1960s and first half of the 1970s took hold, so did Riverland's Grenache provide increasing amounts of flagon and cheap bottled wine).

But its presence as a varietal was seldom recognised on the label until d'Arenberg's 1967 Burgundy Shiraz Grenache (now called d'Arrys Original Shiraz Grenache) hit the national headlines by winning seven trophies and 25 gold medals. This wine was followed in due course by various offerings of Grenache, either as a varietal or as a blend, as the number of labels in the d'Arenberg stable multiplied promiscuously – there is no question about d'Arenberg's groundbreaking role for the Rhône styles in McLaren Vale in the 1960s and '70s.

In the Barossa Valley it was left to Charles Melton to lift a Grenache Shiraz Mourvedre blend into icon status with his Nine Popes, first made in 1984. As the 1990s rolled by, the once despised old-vine Grenache was rehabilitated, its price rising accordingly. The Vine Pull Scheme, incidentally, was not restricted to Grenache; while a significant amount of old-vine Mourvedre was also lost, only a relatively small percentage of Shiraz was (happily).

As the most recent figures show, the plantings have stabilised, and its future as a quality grape (but not otherwise) is assured.

Australian Regional Styles

SOUTH AUSTRALIA

McLaren Vale

457 ha, 1922 tonnes

Climate: Warm, MJT 21.3°C, E° Days 1680, SH 8.4, Rain 230 mm, Alt 130 m

While there are plantings in the Barossa Valley every bit as old as the oldest of McLaren Vale, and exceptions to prove every rule, I believe McLaren Vale produces Australia's greatest Grenache. My preference comes chiefly through the prism of the wine in the glass, and three (short) years (1990 to 1992) of making a Grenache Shiraz blend merely served to reinforce my preference.

The best examples manage to combine density of aroma, colour, flavour and alcohol without threatening to engulf you. That said, they are most convincing with commensurately rich food such as jugged hare, wild mushroom risotto or ragout of venison (the list goes on). The flavours range from stewed cherry to plum to raspberry, all with a background of spice and earth.

Best producers

Angove Family Winemakers*, Bekkers, BK Wines, Chapel Hill, Clarendon Hills, D'Arenberg*, Geoff Hardy, Hardys, Haselgrove, Hewitson*, Lloyd Brothers, Ministry of Clouds, Oliver's Taranga Vineyards, Parous, Rudderless, SC Pannell*, Serafino, Two Hands, Ulithorne, WayWood Wines*, Wirra Wirra*, Woodstock*, Yangarra Estate*

Barossa Valley

698 ha, 3328 tonnes

Climate: Warm, MJT 21.4°C, E° Days 1571, SH 8.6, Rain 199 mm, Alt 270 m

It is here, more than in McLaren Vale, that the display of varietal schizophrenia occurs. On the one hand there are some wines with very similar varietal structure and flavour to those I have attributed to McLaren Vale. On the other hand, there are also many wines that are strangely light in colour, and with an overwhelming confectionery/jammy character and flavour. These wines are usually attributed to old, dry-grown vines, but there is a dynamic happening here which I neither understand nor like.

I should add that these characters usually appear most strongly in unblended varietal wines, rather than in the Grenache Shiraz Mourvedre blends.

Then there is the Australian living treasure of the Seppeltsfield 100 Year Old Vintage Tawny (Port has now been dropped from the name in deference to the EU and Portugal). It has been produced since 1878 from a varying blend of Grenache, Mataro and a little Shiraz; it is a true vintage wine, not a solera; it is sold only when 100 years old, when it is taken from cask for the first time; and Seppeltsfield has every vintage from 1878 to the present still in cask, although there are only tiny amounts of the pre-1900 vintages remaining.

Research has shown that the baumé (sugar concentration) peaks when the wines reach 50 to 75 years of age, at between 12° and 17° baumé; that acid peaks at 50 years, between 6 and 11 grams per litre, and like the baumé, then stabilises; and that the alcoholic strength will vary according to the humidity and atmospheric conditions of storage. This concentration takes place as over two-thirds of the original volume of wine is lost by evaporation – the so-called angel's share. A pretty big share. The consequence is a wine of extraordinarily intense flavour; a tiny sip lingers for minutes. The only international wines in the same echelon are Madeiras that are 100+ years old and Tokaji Essencias of similar age. Rutherglen's Rare Muscadelle (Topaque) and Rare Muscat come close.

Best producers
Table wine: *Eperosa, Grant Burge, Hemera Estate, Hentley Farm, John Duval, Kalleske*, Kellermeister, Laughing Jack, Massena Vineyards*, Purple Hands*, Schwarz Wine Company, Spinifex, Teusner, Tim Smith, Torbreck, Turkey Flat, Two Hands, Yalumba, Yelland & Papps*
Fortified wine: *Penfolds, Seppeltsfield**

Clare Valley
65 ha, 237 tonnes

Climate: Warm, MJT 21.4°C, E° Days 1493, SH 8.9, Rain 248 mm, Alt 450 m

For reasons I understand even less than in the case of the Barossa Valley, old-vine Clare Valley Grenache seems more likely to produce the light-coloured confectionery style than the Barossa Valley style. Here, too, blending with Shiraz and Mourvedre works wonders. Kilikanoon is one producer able to produce a single-vineyard Grenache of great quality.

Best producers
Byrne Vineyards, Claymore, Kilikanoon*, Tim Adams

Chapter 13

Second Tier Red Varietals

Barbera

World: 24 178 ha. Australia: 104 ha, 489 tonnes, 101 growers/makers

General Background

DNA profiling shows that Barbera is not related to the other varieties of Piedmont, almost certainly proving that it was not born there.[1] Moreover, there is no credible reference to the grape before 1798; even more cogently, it only assumed its present importance when wholesale replanting of vineyards took place in the wake of phylloxera. This all gives it third place on Italy's list of most planted red varieties (after Sangiovese and Montepulciano), according to the national census of 2010. In turn, 60 per cent of its total plantings are in Piedmont. Its yield needs to be controlled, as does the amount of new oak used in its elevage. Makers such as Elio Altare show the very high quality that can be obtained if these disciplines are observed. Its principal home away from home is California, with 7000 hectares recorded in 2008. Argentina, too, has meaningful plantings of 800 hectares in 2007.

Australian Background

It has been grown in Australia for 50 years, but has not caught the imagination of the alternative variety gang, nor of those ubiquitous sommeliers who drink, sleep and dream about all things Italian, especially red wines. Its plantings, which are primarily dotted around New South Wales and South Australia, have stalled at the 2012 level of 104 hectares. Its flavour profile runs variously through plum, blackberry, red berry and raspberry, earthy tannins more obvious in the black fruit spectrum, the acidity often high.

---

[1] Jancis Robinson, Julia Harding and Jose Vouillamoz, *Wine Grapes*, Ecco/HarperCollins, 2012, p. 85 and Ian D'Agata, *Wine Grapes of Italy*, University of California Press, 2014, p. 188.

Barbera

Best producers
Barossa Valley: Massena Vineyards*, Yelland & Papps; Granite Belt: Boireann*, Golden Grove Estate*; Hunter Valley: Broke's Promise, Catherine Vale Vineyard, Margan Family; King Valley: Chrismont, Dal Zotto; McLaren Vale: Chalk Hill, Coriole, Zonte's Footstep; Mudgee: di Lusso Estate

Cabernet Franc

World: 53 042 ha. Australia: 552 ha, 2897 tonnes, 395 growers/makers

General Background

DNA shows that Cabernet Franc is the parent of Cabernet Sauvignon, Merlot and Carmenere; its own ancestors are believed to be long extinct.[2] Its 53 042 hectares are spread across 25 countries, France having the lion's share of 36 948 hectares.

In some parts of the world, including one of its original two strongholds, the 'left bank' of the Gironde in Bordeaux, Cabernet Franc is in retreat (with 12 396 hectares), while in

---

2   Robinson, Harding and Vouillamoz, *Wine Grapes*, p. 153.

Cabernet Franc

other places it is in the ascendant. In the left bank communes of Haut Medoc and Graves, it is ranked as an insurance grape, along with Merlot; like Merlot, it ripens at least a week before Cabernet Sauvignon, but growers have increasingly replaced Cabernet Franc with Cabernet Sauvignon. The same is not true in St Emilion and Pomerol, where it continues to be the variety of choice to be blended with Merlot. While it is fashionable to regard the grape as inherently less noble than either Merlot or Cabernet Sauvignon, Château Cheval Blanc (with 65 per cent Cabernet Franc in its make-up) does for Cabernet Franc what Château Pétrus does for Merlot (with 95 per cent Merlot).

Its principal use as a straight varietal (in Bordeaux it is invariably blended) is in the Loire Valley (with 30 105 hectares), and in particular in Chinon and Bourgueil. Here it makes a light- to medium-bodied, fragrantly savoury and fresh red wine, its length coming from its fruit and acidity rather than tannins. It is also very popular in northern Italy, variously used as a straight varietal or, more commonly, in a blend. It would seem, however, that the distinction between Cabernet Franc and Cabernet Sauvignon is considered by many Italian winemakers unimportant when it comes to labelling their wine.

Australian Background

Cabernet Franc starts to make the statistical records in Australia in the middle of the 1980s. In 1989, 166 hectares were planted, but of this total, half (85 hectares) were still to come into bearing. By 1993 there were 453 hectares (54 hectares still not in bearing), but after reaching 693 hectares in 2008, it has fallen back to 552 hectares in 2012.

Thanks, it would seem, to a Californian confusion between Cabernet Franc and Merlot, the same confusion existed in Australia in the 1980s, with what was supposedly Merlot being subsequently identified as Cabernet Franc. Plantings are dispersed across Australia, but the variety is seldom shown on the front label, for most Cabernet Franc is used in multi-varietal Bordeaux blends. Only in the southern regions of Western Australia (Margaret River and Great Southern) does the variety produce wines of distinctive quality; Kangaroo Island is an outlier.

Best producers
Barossa Valley: Hemera Estate, Redgate; Denmark: Silverstream*; Kangaroo Island: The Islander*; Limestone Coast Zone: St Mary's; Margaret River: Cape Grace, Hay Shed Hill*, Woodlands Estate*; Orange: Ross Hill*; Rutherglen: St Leonards; Yarra Valley: Jamsheed, Rochford

Chambourcin
World: 1155 ha. Australia: 30 ha (estimate), 78 growers/makers

General Background

Chambourcin is a complex, privately bred hybrid (not to be confused with a cross) which became available in 1963 and quickly became popular in the cooler/wetter parts of Muscadet at the eastern end of the Loire Valley. It is now on the wane in France, albeit still with 758 hectares.[3] Like all hybrids, it is strongly resistant to the mildews; it is also highly productive, and produces a remarkably intensely coloured wine. The United States has 311 hectares, concentrated in the northeastern part of the continent in cool, wet conditions similar to those of Canada (which has 54 hectares).

Australian Background

The first advocate of Chambourcin in Australia was Cassegrain, whose vineyards, in the Hastings Valley region on the north coast of New South Wales, are subject to high summer humidity and rainfall. It was a success, and a number of the other producers who are likewise situated in coastal regions of New South Wales which offer little scope for

---

[3] ibid., p. 218.

conventional *Vitis vinifera* red varieties took note. The wines made in Australia have the spectacular purple-crimson colour one expects, and on first entry into the mouth have a considerable volume of red berry fruit flavour; the problem is the wine is extremely short, with virtually no finish or aftertaste. Perhaps in recognition of this, some producers have elected to produce a vintage Port style, others to turn it into a sparkling wine.

Best producers
Hunter Valley: 201, Tamburlaine, Travertine; McLaren Vale: d'Arenberg; Shoalhaven Coast: Cambewarra Estate, Coolangatta Estate

Dolcetto

World: 6333 ha. Italy: 6128 ha. Australia: 154 ha, 43 growers/makers

General Background

This variety was first mentioned in 1593 in Dogliani, Piedmont, and it is there that it has DOCG status today, notwithstanding that plantings in Piedmont are in retreat, and its best quality wine comes from Alba – but then this is Italy. Its defining qualities are

Dolcetto

deep colour, a markedly soft, fruity flavour, low acidity, and pronounced tannins. It has lost ground to Barbera, in particular, but is often blended with it. Uniquely, in La Morra there is a vineyard over 100 years old, still ungrafted and protected from phylloxera by the sandy soils (not all the soils in La Morra are sandy). Its total world plantings in 2010 were 6333 hectares (down from 7450 hectares in 2000); other than Italy, there are small plantings dotted here and there in the United States (42 hectares), Argentina (6 hectares) and New Zealand (2 hectares).

Australian Background

Australia's plantings come courtesy of numerous small growers, with most of the wine blended. Varietal wines are fresh and cherry-flavoured, and should be slightly chilled to make up for the low acidity.

Best producers

Adelaide Hills: Yacca Paddock; Barossa Valley: Massena Vineyards*; Grampians: Best's; Hunter Valley: Catherine Vale Vineyard; King Valley/Alpine Valleys: Route du Van*; Langhorne Creek: Geoff Hardy, Heartland; Macedon Ranges: Mt Franklin Estate*; Pyrenees: Warrenmang

Durif

World: 3557 ha. Australia: 417 ha, 4142 tonnes, 133 growers/makers

General Background

In the 1970s the ampelographer Pierre Galet identified Petite Syrah as Durif; subsequent DNA fingerprinting has shown that California has in fact four different vines travelling under the Durif name: Durif itself; Shiraz; Peloursin; and a Peloursin/Durif cross. The last is doubly strange, because Durif was bred in France in the 1880s by Dr Durif, from a cross of Syrah and Peloursin.[4]

While briefly popular in France, it has now disappeared, leaving California (2865 hectares) with a jumbled mix of the various manifestations I have described above. Apart from Australia, Mexico (133 hectares), Chile (104 hectares), South Africa (31 hectares) and Brazil (7 hectares) have the other producers.

---

4   ibid., pp. 316–17.

Durif

Australian Background

The principal home of Durif in Australia is North East Victoria, where the majority of the producers are situated, with Morris leading the way. The wine produced by Durif is invariably full-bodied, and always high in alcohol. It is very much in the genre of the huge dry red wines traditionally made in North East Victoria, and seems uniquely suited to Ned Kelly country. In more recent times, it has been extensively planted in the Riverland, where its robust structure and colour partially compensate for high yields. Plantings have increased steadily since 2003.

Best producers

AT Richardson, All Saints Estate*, Baileys of Glenrowan*, Brown Brothers*, Calabria Family, Campbells, Ciavarella, Cofield, Eldorado Road*, Golden Grove Estate*, Kalleske*, Morris Wines*, Pfeiffer, Pinelli, Quarisa, St Leonards, Scion Vineyard, Stanton & Killeen, Warrabilla*

Gamay

World: 31 927 ha. Australia: 15 ha (estimate), 22 growers/makers

General Background

Gamay is an ancient Burgundian variety, born before the fourteenth century, its parents Pinot Noir and Gouais Blanc. It was repeatedly excoriated, first – and at great length – by Philip the Good in Dijon on 31 July 1395.[5] Not content with describing Gamay as 'a bastard', Philip the Good also ordered its removal and destruction. Six hundred years ago it was apparent first that Gamay yielded far more grapes per hectare than Pinot Noir; and second, that the wine was inferior. However, then and now it is uniquely suited to Beaujolais, which has over 18 000 hectares of the variety, and almost no Pinot Noir, Chardonnay or Pinot Blanc. Good Beaujolais is all about pleasure: brilliantly coloured, yet translucent; vibrantly aromatic; bursting with juicy fruit flavours; and finishing crisp and clean. It is widely grown in the Loire Valley, producing a wine which you might get if you were to make a 50/50 mix of good Beaujolais and water.

Gamay

---

5   ibid., pp. 384–85.

Switzerland, which has 1521 hectares, often blends Gamay with Pinot Noir to produce a wine which the Burgundians (who also produce it) call Passetoutgrains – a 50/50 blend which can in fact be a very enjoyable wine. Lesser quantities are spread around the world, none significant.

Australian Background

Quite why Len Evans chose to plant a block on magnificent red soil adjacent to his house in the Hunter Valley with Gamay I do not know, even though I asked him the question dozens of times. The climate of the Hunter Valley is no more suited to Gamay than it is to Pinot Noir, and the end-points are either Rose (not bad) or red wine (dull and uninteresting except for the name on the label). The best results come from the cooler parts of Victoria, the best producers likewise.

Best producers
Beechworth: Sorrenberg*; Central Victoria Zone: Brave Goose; Gippsland: Bass Phillip*; McLaren Vale: Scarpantoni; Margaret River: Marq; Mornington Peninsula: Eldridge Estate of Red Hill*; Rutherglen: Pfeiffer*; Yarra Valley: De Bortoli*

Mourvedre | Monastrell

World: 69 748 ha. Australia: 729 ha, 6094 tonnes, 274 growers/makers

General Background

Mourvedre now ranks as the second most widely planted red variety in Spain (where it is known as Monastrell) with its 58 406 hectares, after Grenache (Garnacha), with 70 140 hectares. It was introduced into France twice in the sixteenth century, once with the name 'Mourvedre', once as 'Mataro', in each case reflecting the name of the town from whence it came. The variety was born in Spain, where it was named Monastrell as early as 1386, and by 1460 was one of the most important varieties in Valencia.[6]

It was the dominant variety in Provence until phylloxera, but its late ripening habit led to other varieties taking its place in the replanting process, to the point where its only significant hold was in the Bandol region. However, it made a major comeback, plantings increasing from 900 hectares to 5600 hectares between 1968 and 1988, rising to 9363 hectares in 2010. Wherever it is grown, it produces a wine high in alcohol and, in particular, tannins, which makes it an ideal variety for a blend, but limits its role as a single varietal.

---

6   ibid., pp. 646–47.

Australian Background

Mourvedre has had three names in this country: historically Mataro in the Barossa Valley, more recently Mourvedre, and historically Esparte at Great Western. The stronghold of Mourvedre has been South Australia, and in particular the Barossa Valley and McLaren Vale. Just as in Europe, most of the Mourvedre is used in combination with Shiraz and Grenache (notably with Charles Melton's Nine Popes and Penfolds Old Vine Shiraz Grenache Mourvedre), but a few brave souls have successfully made it as a single varietal, avoiding the tannin trap. Hewitson Old Garden Mourvedre, the oldest planting in the world, with vines planted in 1853, is outstanding.

Best producers

Barossa Valley: Deisen, Hewitson*, John Duval*, Kaesler, Landhaus Estate*, Sons of Eden*; Clare Valley: Atlas*; Eden Valley: Torzi Matthews; Granite Belt: Boireann*, Golden Grove Estate*; Great Southern: Paul Nelson; Heathcote: PHI*, Syrahmi*; McLaren Vale: d'Arenberg*, Dodgy Brothers, Geoff Merrill*, Haselgrove*, Samuel's Gorge*, Ulithorne*, Yangarra Estate*; Nagambie Lakes: McPherson, Mitchelton, Tahbilk

Nebbiolo

World: 5992 ha. Italy: 5536 ha. Mexico: 180 ha. Australia: 108 ha, 70 tonnes, 124 growers/makers

General Background

A truly ancient variety, described as early as 1226–28, with references in the thirteenth and fourteenth centuries showing it was already one of the most widely planted varieties in Piedmont. DNA analysis shows its parents are long since extinct, and that three clones have developed over the centuries.[7]

Nebbiolo is one of Italy's oldest varieties. Ian D'Agata writes, 'Apparently, Pliny the Elder referred to it as nubiola, the Latin word for "fog" (nebbia) as Nebbiolo ripens late in the season.'[8] Robinson suggests that this is less likely than the word's use referring to the natural white bloom that appears on the skin of the grapes as they approach ripeness. To be fair, D'Agata also mentions this as the source of the name. Both agree that the modern name made its appearance in documents written in the second half of the thirteenth century. The grape's family tree shows eight parent–offspring relationships between

---

7 ibid., pp. 701–06.
8 D'Agata, *Wine Grapes of Italy*, p. 354.

Nebbiolo

Nebbiolo and local varieties from Piedmont and Valtellina.[9] (As an aside, Nebbiolo and Viognier are first cousins.)

Robinson and D'Agata also agree that many centuries of propagation have resulted in three clones (or biotypes) that are morphologically different, but have identical DNA. They are:

- Nebbiolo Lampia, the most common
- Nebbiolo Michet, a virused form of Lampia (fan-leaf virus)
- Nebbiolo Bolla, now decreasing in importance.

Several factors make the history (and present) even more complicated. First, Nebbiolo Rose is not a clone of Nebbiolo, but a separate variety, locally called Chiavennasca in Valtellina, where it may well have originated. Next, Picotendro/Picoutener/Picotèner (in Val d'Ossola) and Spanna (in the Novara and Vercelli areas) are synonyms for Nebbiolo in active use, especially Spanna.

---

9   George Kerridge and Allan Antcliff, *Wine Grape Varieties*, CSIRO, 2000 p. 60.

It is an enigmatic variety, grown in only a handful of areas in northwestern Italy, where it is an early-budding, late-ripening grape, with an exceptionally long hang-time. So the first question is: why haven't Italian growers tried warmer regions further south? The answer may partly lie in the observation that Nebbiolo has characteristics in common with the early-ripening Pinot Noir.

In my view such characteristics only appear once the powerful tannins of Nebbiolo have been softened by age, and then only if the wine is not front-end loaded with tannins in the first place. Over the past 30 years there has been a debate in Italy about the old methods of vinification of Barolo (the greatest evocation of Nebbiolo) and Barbaresco, the traditional style that uses extended maceration on skins post-fermentation, and years in oak thereafter. The modern style dramatically shortens both periods, aiming to decrease the tannin load.

The greatest Barolos I have tasted, which had miraculously taken on a Pinot-like perfume and elegance, were a group of Conterno wines going back to the glorious '37 vintage purchased by Vanya Cullen directly from Italy many years ago. So there are no absolute answers to the where and the how. Before moving on to Australia, the names of some of the best producers are Giacomo Conterno, Gaja (Barbaresco), Bruno Giacosa, Pio Cesare, Ceretto, Bartolo Mascarello, Giuseppe Mascarello, Giuseppe Rinaldi, Vietti and Elvio Cogno.

Australian Background

Since the beginning of this millennium, Nebbiolo has started to come of age in Australia. As a sign of my confidence in its future, I have retained it in second tier importance, even though its plantings are modest. The total Australian plantings may seem paltry, but they are the third largest in the world after Italy and Mexico.

In 1974 two highly successful engineers, Italian-born Carlo Salteri and Franco Belgiorno-Nettis, established Montrose Winery in Mudgee. A few years later they appointed Italian-born and trained Carlo Corino as winemaker. He promptly planted 1.5 hectares of Barbera, 1 hectare of Nebbiolo, and 0.65 hectares of Sangiovese. He blended Barbera and Nebbiolo in 1981 and '82, and I was taken by their fresh, scented aromas and fruit flavours – and not fazed by the tannin levels when the wines were only two years old.

It kept a tenuous presence in Australia until Peter Godden returned from Piedmont, where he had worked in 1995 and '96, undertaking the vintage with Vietti, and joined the Australian Wine Research Institute. Together with partner Sally Macgill (of Red + White wine distributor) he established 35 cuttings, progressively building a sufficient nursery plantation to plant 1 hectare of Nebbiolo in 2001 and to thus found their one-variety winery, Arrivo. In 1995 Garry Crittenden of Dromana Estate began to develop an Italian range of varieties under his distinctive 'i' label, sourcing the grapes from Italian vignerons in the King Valley. Nebbiolo was – in principle – one of the wines under that label.

But in the 1996 bible *Wine Grape Varieties in Australia*, by George Kerridge and Allan Antcliff, published by the CSIRO, Nebbiolo is only mentioned in a list of the varieties at CSIRO's Merbein nursery vineyard. By 2005, the CSIRO-published *Vines for Wines* (by George Kerridge and Angela Gackle) did have an entry for Nebbiolo, saying in conclusion, 'In Australia, around 17 vineyards list plantings, but the total planted area is very small.'[10] The 2012 planting figures from the ABS show that 43 hectares were planted in 2011, which demonstrates the surge of interest in the variety, and also explains the apparent anomaly of 70 tonnes from 122 hectares. In the interests of full disclosure, I should add that the 2012 plantings are virtually the same as those of 2004, having fallen in the intervening period.

The breakthrough in quality came in the period 2004 to 2014. It is striking that most of the best wines come from cool to temperate regions of moderate to marked continentality. It also seems that (modest) increasing vine age may be playing a role. The key change has been the management of tannins, in earlier years harsh and unbalanced, now (in the best wines) integrated and balanced. The colour of the best wines has also improved.

Best producers
Adelaide Hills: Arrivo*, Fletcher*, Ngeringa, SC Pannell*; Beechworth: Giaconda; Bendigo: Glenwillow; Gippsland: Moondara; Granite Belt: Symphony Hill*; Heathcote: Jasper Hill*, The Hairy Arm; Hilltops: Freeman Vineyards, Grove Estate*, Ravensworth*; Langhorne Creek: Casa Freschi*; Macedon Ranges: Mount Towrong; McLaren Vale: Primo Estate*; Pyrenees: AT Richardson*

Petit Verdot

World: 7237 ha. Spain: 1661 ha. France: 896 ha. Australia: 1204 ha, 20 074 tonnes, 304 growers/makers

General Background
Petit Verdot was most probably domesticated from a wild vine population in the Atlantic Pyrenees, and was first mentioned under its present name in 1736.[11] A late-ripening variety wherever grown, it was widely planted before phylloxera. In the second half of

---

10 Robinson, Harding and Vouillamoz, *Wine Grapes*, p. 790.
11 ibid., p. 790.

Petit Verdot

the twentieth century its area in Bordeaux fell to 338 hectares, but warmer vintages in the new millennium have seen an increase in plantings, with the 1885 Classed Growth Châteaux in particular benefiting from the added richness the variety brings to the typical Bordeaux blend.

Late ripening is not a problem for California and, while plantings are not significant in area (853 hectares), the variety is spread thinly across Bordeaux (or Meritage) blends, consumers apparently being fascinated by the idea of 2 or 3 per cent in a blend.

It is found in many countries around the world. Spain (1661 hectares) has the largest plantings, followed by Italy (659 hectares), South Africa (648 hectares), Chile (576 hectares) and Argentina (501 hectares).

Australian Background

Here the variety has come from nowhere in a relatively short time, and we now have the second-largest area of plantings in the world, after Spain. Producers such as Mount Mary in the Yarra Valley have been growing it since inception as a small part of a Bordeaux-based blend (Mount Mary calls its Cabernet blend Quintet), but an increasing number of winemakers are releasing single varietal wines. Pirramimma had early success; the

Riverland/Riverina exponents are doubtless simply content with its ability to produce both colour and tannin irrespective of an average yield of 17 tonnes per hectare.

Best producers
Adelaide Plains: Ceravolo; McLaren Vale: Haselgrove*, Pirramimma; Margaret River: Clairault | Streicker, Xanadu*; Mudgee: Gartelmann; Perth Hills: Millbrook; Riverina: Yarran; Swan Valley: Faber Vineyard*, John Kosovich, Upper Reach

Pinot Meunier

World: 11 267 ha. France: 11 088 ha. Australia: 50 ha (estimate), 60 growers/makers

General Background

Technically, Pinot Meunier is a clone of Pinot Noir (see page xii), but the wine it produces is very different. It is best known as the third grape in Champagne, its wine developing more quickly than Chardonnay and Pinot Noir, and thus helping non-vintage blends. The major and intriguing exception is Krug, which in fact has a high percentage (20–25 per cent) of Pinot Meunier in its Grande Cuvee, a wine not released until it is six years old and noted for its longevity. All except 179 hectares of the world total plantings of 11 267 hectares are in France, almost all in Champagne.

Pinot Meunier

Australian Background

As in France, the principal use of Pinot Meunier is in sparkling wines, although even here it is a relatively new arrival on the scene. The exception (as with many lesser-known varieties) is Best's at Great Western: it has Pinot Meunier that is over 150 years old, which it uses to make a red table wine, sometimes blended with Pinot Noir, and sometimes released as a straight varietal. Those who use it to make a table wine (other than Best's) are not always certain what they should do with it: use it to make a Rose, blend it with Pinot Noir, or release it as a straight varietal. Best's, because of its magnificent storehouse of old vines, certainly leads the field. Australia's plantings are an estimate, with no official figures available, and are increasing.

Best producers
Table wines: *Best's*, Murdoch Hill, Rahona Valley, Spring Vale Vineyards*
Sparkling: *Barringwood Park*, Brown Brothers, Centennial Vineyards, Clover Hill*, Domain Chandon*, Dominique Portet, House of Arras*, Jansz Tasmania*, Seppelt*

Ruby Cabernet

World: 5734 ha. Australia: 769 ha, 11 331 tonnes, 30 growers/makers

General Background

This variety was bred by Dr HP Olmo at UC Davis in 1949, by crossing Carignan with Cabernet Sauvignon. The object was to produce a high-yielding vine with strong colour that retained some Cabernet characteristics. It was also expected that the variety would perform well in hot regions. While the colour and the yield met expectations, the quality of the wine was rustic at best, and after a surge of popularity in the 1960s its Californian plantings have fallen to 2425–2431 hectares, not far in front of South Africa's 2220 hectares.

Australian Background

Plantings and tonnage have fluctuated wildly since 1996, when 644 hectares produced 11 770 tonnes. By 2002 the area had increased to 2780 hectares, producing 49 119 tonnes. Then the wheels fell off: by 2006 the area had fallen to 1468 hectares, by 2008 it had declined to 1142 hectares, and by 2012 to 769 hectares, yielding 11 331 tonnes. The average of 15 tonnes per hectare, second only to Petit Verdot, is the reason it still remains in production: for use in low-cost, low-quality wine, blended with more appealing varieties (with Petit Verdot likely to be part of the formula). There is no 100 per cent varietal wine worth mentioning.

Sangiovese

Sangiovese

World: 77 709 ha. Australia: 575 ha, 5073 tonnes, 293 growers/makers

General Background

Sangiovese's 71 619 hectares dominate the regions of central Italy, most notably Tuscany, Brunello di Montalcino and Nobile di Montepulciano. Like Barbera, it is an ancient variety, but its austerity and geographical origin are the subject of much scientific discussion and argument. If you are into cryptic crosswords, and have a scientific background, you will find D'Agata's discussion of its origins fascinating.[12] To summarise, both he and Robinson cautiously conclude that it is possibly of southern Italian origin.[13] On the subject of parentage, Robinson is more confident than D'Agata that it is a natural cross between Ciliegiolo and Calabrese di Montenuovo.

The emergence of the so-called Super Tuscans over the past 30 or so years has turned on the blending of a percentage of Cabernet Sauvignon (and more recently Merlot) into

---

12 D'Agata, *Wine Grapes of Italy*, pp. 428–30.
13 Robinson, Harding and Vouillamoz, *Wine Grapes*, pp. 942–43.

the wine. Blending itself is nothing new to Tuscany: Chianti has long depended on the blending in of Canaiolo (to soften the tannins of Sangiovese) and other less meritorious varieties to increase production.

Australian Background

The first commercial trial outside nurseries (with vines from the University of California, Davis) was, of all places, in the Kalimna Vineyard in the Barossa Valley, but no wines were made or released from that source. In the late 1970s Italian-born and -trained Carlo Corino planted some Sangiovese at Montrose Winery in Mudgee (then owned by an Italian engineering company). The next move was by Coriole in 1985, but once again, interest faltered.

While Sangiovese was caught up in the rise of interest in all top-quality Italian wines imported into Australia, it proved a difficult variety to grow and to make. Winemaker interest grew as the result of a massive research program in Tuscany seeking to identify the best clones (out of hundreds), and coincidentally or otherwise, Sangiovese turned the corner around 2005, just after the first edition of this book was published.

As each year since has passed, so has the general quality of Sangiovese improved. Colours are bright and don't lose hue so quickly; the range of fruit (usually in the cherry group) has gained more substance; and, best of all, the tannins are in balance with the fruit. This isn't to say there is no more improvement to be had: there is, but it will be built on a real foundation.

Best producers

Adelaide Hills: Ngeringa; Barossa Valley: Penfolds; Beechworth: Castagna, Fighting Gully Road*; Canberra District: Ravensworth*; Clare Valley: Coates*, Kirrihill*, Pikes, Shut the Gate, Stone Bridge; Gippsland: Nicholson River*; Granite Belt: Boireann, Jester Hill; Heathcote: Foster e Rocco, Galli Estate, Greenstone Vineyard*; King Valley: Chrismont, De Bortoli*; McLaren Vale: Coriole*, Dodgy Brothers, Hugh Hamilton*, Mt Billy, Serafino; Pyrenees: Mitchell Harris; Mornington Peninsula: Stumpy Gully; Upper Goulburn: Sedona Estate*; Yarra Valley: Buttermans Track*

Tempranillo

Tempranillo

World: 323 561 ha. Spain: 207 677 ha. Australia: 712 ha, 3422 tonnes, 333 growers/makers

General Background

Tempranillo is Spain's best grape. Either on its own or as the dominant partner in a blend it is responsible for Spain's most famous red wines. It is ironic that in Spain it is called Tempranillo in Rioja, in Ribiera del Duero it is known as Tinta del Pats, in Valdepenas as Cencibel, and in Portugal as Tinta Roriz. (These are the best known synonyms; there are literally dozens of others.) Ironic, because it has spread so quickly that there are very few clones, and its genetic make-up is thus very consistent. The most that DNA analysis comes up with is a parent–offspring relationship with Albillo Mayor from Ribiera del Duero.[14]

---

14 ibid., pp. 1042–43.

Australian Background

Having observed the vine growing in Spain over many years, having tasted individual components destined to be blended and released as Rioja, and having encountered Cencibel over a decade ago (made by Don Lewis of Mitchelton in Valdepenas) at the International Wine Challenge in London, I long harboured a desire to grow and make the wine. For a variety of reasons, including Murphy's Law, I did not achieve that aim, and have instead merely observed the efforts of others. They are a growing band, and Tempranillo is here to stay.

Best producers

Adelaide Hills: Heirloom Vineyards*, La Linea*, Nepenthe; Alpine Valleys: Mayford*; Alpine Valleys/Heathcote: Tar & Roses; Barossa Valley: Kalleske, Quattro Mano*; Beechworth: A Rodda*; Blackwood Valley: Nannup Ridge; Canberra District: Capital, Mount Majura*; Clare Valley: Wines by KT; Fleurieu: Hewitson; Geographe: Willow Bridge Estate*; Granite Belt: Golden Grove Estate*, Summit Estate, Symphony Hill; Margaret River: Hay Shed Hill, Marq, Rosabrook, Woody Nook; McLaren Vale: Angove Family Winemakers, Hither & Yon, Willunga 100; Mornington Peninsula: Tuck's Ridge*; Orange: Centennial Vineyards; Padthaway: Landaire; Perth Hills/Frankland: West Cape Howe*; Rutherglen: Pfeiffer, Stanton & Killeen*; Tasmania: Clarence House; Yarra Valley: Tokar Estate

Zinfandel | Primitivo | Tribidrag

World: 32 745 ha. Italy: 12 234 ha. United States: 19 857 ha. Croatia: 65 ha. Australia: 104 ha, 492 tonnes, 87 growers/makers

General Background

The fact that the correct name for Zinfandel – as it is best known in Australia – is not Primitivo but Tribidrag is the ultimate wine trivia question. If you look for Robinson's chapter on Zinfandel, you'll find it on page 1085, headed Tribidrag[15] (along with seven separate, unpronounceable synonyms). The reason is that the variety was born in Croatia, the missing link between it and Primitivo/Zinfandel a planting of what was locally called Crljenak Kastelanski. At this point I suggest those seeking more information on the tongue-twisting, mind-numbing place names and supposedly (but often incorrectly) linked varieties go to the source. I cannot resist spoiling one discovery of a variety in the Tribidrag family tree: it is called Grk.[16]

---

15 ibid., pp. 1085–90.
16 ibid., p. 1088.

Zinfandel | Primitivo | Tribidrag

The variety is called Primitivo in Puglia, where in 1990 there were 17 000 hectares. There were only only 795 hectares 10 years later – the result of the EU Vine Pull Scheme.[17] Much of the production had in fact been illegally used in wines/blends from further north in Italy. As Puglia's wines have become better known, the plantings have recovered to 12 234 hectares.

From a viticultural viewpoint, it is unique. Any given bunch at harvest time may have bright green, totally unripe berries spotted throughout, without rhyme or reason, and more than likely a similar number of raisined berries. Conventional methods of assessing ripeness are virtually useless; the most successful makers rely on a sixth sense they have developed through observing the vine and making the wine for many years.

It might be seen as appropriate, therefore, that Sutter Home, with encouragement from none other than Darrell Corti (a charming Sacramento-based wine expert and judge), developed Blush, the slightly pink, more or less dry and largely tasteless wine which swept across America like a tidal wave in the 1980s. Mercifully, Blush has no counterpart

---

17   ibid., p. 1089.

in Australia, and is never likely to: it is truly one of the nastiest forms of wine to have been made in the last 2000 years.

Australian Background

Cape Mentelle pioneered plantings in Australia as a direct consequence of David Hohnen spending time in California before he returned to Australia and founded Cape Mentelle in 1970. It's been around for a long time: the small number of producers suggests it's not about to rise above the pack. One further statistic is that apart from Italy and California, only Tunisia (337 hectares) and Australia have more planted than Croatia, which itself has a disproportionately small area given its fatherhood status.

Best producers

Barossa Valley: Groom, Massena Vineyards*; Clare Valley: Wilson Vineyard; Eden Valley: Irvine*; Heathcote: Buckshot Vineyard*; King Valley: Wood Park; McLaren Vale: Haselgrove*, Kangarilla Road*, La Curio; Margaret River: Cape Mentelle*; Murray Darling: Stefano de Pieri

Chapter 14

Lesser Red Varietals

Aglianico

World: 9962 ha. Australia: 5 ha (estimate), 15 growers/makers

Aglianico's home (and only home) is southern Italy, which (contrary to speculation about Greek origin over several centuries) is also its birthplace. Robinson summarises it as a 'High quality, late-ripening, tannic and ageworthy southern Italian red.'[1] Its quality epicentre is the volcanic soil of Taurasi, Mastroberardino the best – and best known – producer, not afraid to let the power of the wine loose. Italy has all but 53 hectares of the global total, Argentina the only other producer of any significance.

Fifteen Australian producers have planted Aglianico, all in warm to hot regions. For those who believe there will be significant increases in growing season temperatures over the next 20 to 30 years, and a decrease in available water, the variety has considerable attraction. However, for the control of tannins, which seem to accentuate acidity, a gentle hand in the winery is needed.

Producers
Amadio, Beach Road, Calabria Family, Chalmers*, Fighting Gully Road, Geoff Hardy, Hither & Yon, La Curio, Scott Wines*

---

[1] Jancis Robinson, Julia Harding and Jose Vouillamoz, *Wine Grapes*, Ecco/HarperCollins, 2012, p. 11.

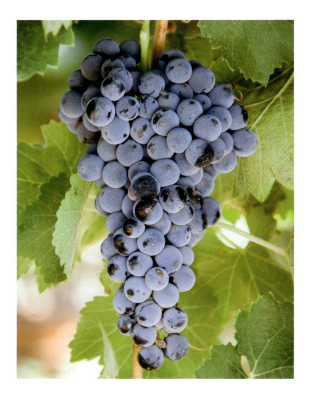
Aglianico

Aleatico

World: 333 ha. Australia: 2 ha (estimate), 3 growers/makers

Described by Jancis Robinson as a 'bizarre Italian red grape variety', simply because it makes a red wine with many of the characteristics of Muscat Blanc a Petits Grains. In particular fostered by Dr Thomas Fiaschi, the Italian-trained doctor who achieved prominence both as a surgeon and hospital administrator with Sydney Hospital and as a vigneron in Mudgee. Italy has all the recorded 333 hectares, the Australian plantings so small they escape detection.

Producers

di Lusso Estate, Freeman Vineyards (blend), Tizzana

Alicante Bouschet

World: 38 371 ha. Australia: 3 ha (estimate), 10 growers/makers

This is a cross of Grenache and Petit Bouschet (the latter itself a cross), bred between 1865 and 1885 by Henri Bouschet (its full name is indeed Alicante Henri Bouschet), and is one of a small group of grapes known as 'teinturiers'. France's plantings are in steep decline, with 4957 hectares (2010) compared to 15 769 hectares in 1988. By contrast, Spain's plantings increased from 16 000 hectares in 1990 to 22 250 hectares in 2008, Portugal likewise increasing.

These grapes have not only red skins, but red flesh, and even when cropped at levels up to 12 tonnes per acre can still produce a deeply coloured, if somewhat flavourless, wine. Rockford has produced an Alicante Bouschet from grapes grown in the Adelaide Plains since the word go. It is made in the fashion of a supercharged Rose, fresh, crisp and aromatic, with a light palate and crisp finish.

Producers
Forester Estate, Rockford*, Taminick Cellars, Vinden Estate

Ancellotta

World: 4774 ha. Australia: <1 ha, 1 grower/maker

Italy's 4340 hectares are cultivated in the province of Reggio Emilia, and used mainly for the production of concentrated musts to reinforce the colour of lighter red wines. Argentina has 302 hectares, and Brazil has 99 hectares, used mainly in blends to provide colour, although there is one deeply flavoured fresh varietal example in Brazil. The 19 hectares in Valais in Switzerland are used to add colour to Pinot Noirs.[2] Water Wheel in Bendigo is – or has been – its only producer.

Aranel

World: 5 ha. Australia: <1 ha, 2 growers/makers

This is a cross between Garnacha Roja (a pinkish grey-berried colour mutation of Garnacha) and a variety not even commercially cultivated, made in 1961 by the great French ampelographer Paul Truel. It was officially authorised in 1967 and has been recommended for the south of France since 1992, but plantings are still a microscopic

---

2   ibid., pp. 42–43.

5 hectares. It's said to have both fruity and floral aromas, with good levels of sugar and acid.[3]

Bastardo | Trousseau

World: 3431 ha. Australia: <1 ha, 5 growers/makers

Trousseau is a variety from Jura in France, but has been cultivated in Spain and Portugal for at least two centuries under different names, including Bastardo, Merenzao and Verdejo Negro. It is not known how it reached the Iberian Peninsula, but DNA studies have confirmed that Trousseau (under the name Merenzao), Chenin Blanc and Sauvignon Blanc are siblings, and that Trousseau has a likely parent–offspring relationship with Savagnin.[4]

In Australia it has always been known as Bastardo, and the plantings go back for an uncertain but reasonable time. It was grown in South Australia as Cabernet Gros, but the name was (correctly) challenged as incorrect by Francois de Castella.[5] Its description as a Port-style variety in Australia is at odds with its European reputation as the producer of powerful, ageworthy red table wines.

Canaiolo Nero

World: 1069 ha. Australia: <1 ha, 5 growers/makers

Yet another ancient Tuscan grape; it is small wonder that so many varieties, both white and red, were at one stage mandatory inclusions in Chianti, rivalling Châteauneuf-du-Pape. Indeed, Robinson records that Canaiolo was more popular than Sangiovese in central Italy until the eighteenth century.[6] It is still one of the major components of the 20 per cent of other local red varieties that may be blended with Sangiovese in Chianti and Chianti Classico's DOCG. Some Tuscan producers have begun making wines from 100 per cent Canaiolo.

D'Agata points out that prior to the sixteenth century most of the wine made was largely Canaiolo Nero, not Sangiovese.[7] Then, in 1873, Bettino Ricasoli, inventor of the original Chianti blend, decided that the best Chianti possible was 7/10 Sangiovese, 2/10 Canaiolo Nero and 1/10 Malvasia Bianca Toscana Lunga. Canaiolo's fall from grace followed the

---

3   ibid., p. 47.
4   ibid., pp. 1093–94.
5   EW Boehm and HW Tulloch, *Grape Varieties of South Australia*, South Australian Department of Agriculture, 1967, p. 77.
6   Robinson, Harding and Vouillamoz, *Wine Grapes*, p. 183.
7   Ian D'Agata, *Wine Grapes of Italy*, University of California Press, 2014, p. 220.

phylloxera devastation, as it did not adapt well to grafting onto American rootstocks. This was exacerbated by the lack of virus-free grapevine material. Next, it's a late ripener with thin-skinned berries, making it vulnerable to rain. Recent clonal selections have significantly improved its reliability, with better colour, more intense aromas, and flavours of balsamic and spicy red fruits.

Collector Wines, in the Canberra District, uses it as part of a four-varietal blend, with Sangiovese, Colorino and Mammolo.

Carignan | Mazuelo

World: 75 715 ha. Australia: 25 ha, 18 growers/makers

Agatha Christie would have revelled in the history of this variety, and the plethora of different names used from the ancient past through to the present, including Cinsaut and Graciano, both of which have been confused with it. Its dozens of synonyms in Spain and elsewhere in Europe suggest, says Robinson, that 'It is a very old variety that was dispersed a long time ago.'[8] Yet the etymology of its two principal names is clear: Mazuelo

Carignan | Mazuelo

---

8   Robinson, Harding and Vouillamoz, *Wine Grapes*, p. 616.

from the village of Mazuelo de Muño, in Castilla y Leon, Cariñena from the eponymous town in Aragon. Simple? Well, not quite. Cariñena was prominent in Catalunya, but was appropriated for the name of the Denominación de Origen, so the authorities now call the grape Samsó to avoid confusion. Sensible? Well, not quite, because Samsó is also a synonym for Cinsaut.

The first obvious question is why was it spread so widely, with 75 715 hectares planted in 18 countries? The answer is its generous yield, up to 200 hectolitres per hectare (30 tonnes per hectare), which it achieves while retaining high acidity, strong colour and super-abundant tannins. Given its Spanish birth, why did France have 53 155 hectares planted in 2009, nine times as much as Spain? The answer is that nearly 80 per cent of the total vineyard area in Languedoc-Roussillon was covered by the variety, which is used as the major component of blends that in many cases use names not linked to any variety. With EU incentives to increase quality and decrease quantity, its plantings are decreasing daily. Australia's winemakers have used a kid-gloves approach, their combined plantings not recorded in the ABS or the Anderson statistics. Since 2003, the area indicated above is likely to have declined. Some Australian growers have, however, reported the size of their planting.

Producers
Cascabel*, Chateau Tanunda, Elderton, Hewitson, Kabminye, Seppeltsfield, Smallfry (all but Cascabel use it as a blend component)

Carmenere

World: 11 389 ha. Australia: 2 ha, 9 growers/makers

This is an old variety from the Gironde; DNA parentage has recently established that it is a natural cross between Cabernet Franc and Gros Cabernet, the latter an odd variety in the Gironde and often confused with Cabernet Franc.[9] Further analysis shows it and Cabernet Franc have a high level of consanguinity, and Carmenere is a half-sibling of both Cabernet Sauvignon and Merlot. Small wonder, then, that it has been confused and misidentified in Bordeaux, in Italy, likewise California and, most famously of all, in Chile. The Chileans were not best pleased to find that they had plantings of Merlot that were in fact Carmenere, as well as plantings of true Carmenere, finally recognised as an official variety in Chile in 1998. This led reported areas starting with zero in 1996 to 7183 hectares in 2006, declining to 7054 hectares in 2008. No one in Australia has so far used it to make a single varietal wine, instead employing it in Bordeaux blends.

9   ibid., p. 189.

Producers who have, or have had, plantings include Amietta, Dixons Creek Estate, Macquarie Grove, Olssens of Watervale, Pikes, Preston Peak, Serafino and Yarra Yering.

Carnelian

World: 316 ha. Australia: 2 ha, 5 growers/makers

This is what might be termed a double cross, the first being a Mazuelo/Cabernet Sauvignon cross, in turn crossed with Grenache, created by Professor Harold Olmo in 1949. The purpose was a grape with some of the characteristics of Cabernet Sauvignon (especially its tannins) but suited to warm climates. It can produce large crops that lack flavour, requiring crop-thinning for best results. Originally planted with enthusiasm in California, interest has waned, with only 316 hectares remaining in 2010. Its categorisation as a double cross is also justified by its Australian plantings in the Perth Hills, Manjimup and Margaret River, when it was supplied by a plant nursery as Sangiovese.

Producers include Burch Family, Oakover, Peos Estate, Western Range and WindshakeR.

Cienna

An Australian-bred cross of Sumoll and Cabernet Sauvignon grown commercially by Brown Brothers to make Rose and Moscato styles, thus avoiding the fearsome tannins which result if the grapes are used to make dry red table wine.

Cinsaut

World: 34 745 ha. Australia: <5 ha (estimate), 21 growers/makers

Despite its plantings across 14 countries, Cinsaut (often spelt Cinsault) is a variety in fast retreat wherever it is grown around the world (except Australia). Its stronghold was and remains Languedoc in the south of France; while recommended for a time as a preferable replacement for Aramon and Alicante Bouschet, it has fallen prey to the more desirable Syrah, Merlot, Mourvedre and Cabernet Sauvignon. One of its problems is its propensity to over-crop, and since there is little inducement to control yields in the south of France, predictably weak wine results.

Algeria (7550 hectares) and Morocco (3940 hectares) rank next in importance after France (19 505 hectares), Tunisia (842 hectares) and Turkey (500 hectares) the other significant growers.

It was South Africa's most important variety until the end of the 1960s and, ironically, continues to be vicariously important by virtue of its crossing with Pinot Noir to produce

South Africa's most interesting red varietal, Pinotage. In its own right, 2052 hectares remain in production.

In Australia it has been known as Oelliade (Lindemans used to produce a wine so labelled from Langhorne Creek) and as Blue Imperial, as Morris calls it. While Australia's plantings (somewhat curiously) escape the statistical net, it has been grown for many years in Langhorne Creek, McLaren Vale, the Barossa Valley and Rutherglen, and is the subject of increasing interest by small producers of alternative varieties.

Producers who have, or have had, plantings include Cascabel, Chambers Rosewood, Charles Melton, Chateau Tanunda, d'Arenberg, Grant Burge, Happs, Hewitson, Kabminye, Lake Moodemere, Massena Vineyards, Morris Wines, Smallfry, Spinifex and Yangarra Estate.

Colorino del Valdarno

World: 436 ha (Italy). Australia: 2 ha, 4 growers/makers

This is Italy's answer to Georgia's Saperavi and France's Petit Verdot. It is one of a number of clones and grapes that may have different parentage, but whose names all start with Colorino. It is chiefly grown in Tuscany. Its name is derived from its dark blue berries and

Colorino del Valdarno

its vivid, deep colour. Despite its colour, it is deficient in aroma and flavour, and hence is used only as a blend component in Tuscany. It is used in the region as a 5 per cent to 10 per cent blend with Sangiovese in Chianti, and in Vino Nobile de Montepulciano as an alternative to Cabernet Sauvignon.

Producers
Fighting Gully Road, Greenstone Vineyard, Sabella, Wood Park

Corvina

World: 7496 ha. Australia: 4 ha, 2 growers/makers

Born and bred in Italy in the province of Verona, home of Valpolicella and Bardelino. DNA analysis shows that Corvina has a parent–offspring relationship with Refosco dal Peduncolo and Rondinella.[10] It also shows that Corvina is a grandchild of Marzemino. This in turn explains why Brian Freeman of Freeman Vineyards sourced Corvina and Rondinella from just six cuttings acquired from the CSIRO nursery at Merbein. The wines made by Freeman Vineyards using a blend of Rondinella and Corvina are very slow maturing. The reputation of sour cherry flavour, fresh acidity and a note of bitter almonds is the Italian description, but it has made its way, to a lesser or greater degree, to Australia with the grape. Centennial Vineyards source their grapes (along with Rondinella) from Freeman.

Counoise

World: 408 ha (France). Australia: <1 ha, 2 growers/makers

A low-profile member of the 13-strong band of varieties permitted to be used in Châteauneuf-du-Pape. Château de Beaucastel is the variety's champion, typically using 5 per cent in their Châteauneuf-du-Pape. Australian producers include battely and Yangarra Estate (on an experimental basis).

Dornfelder

World: 8182 ha. Australia: <1 ha, 3 growers/makers

The most successful modern German red grape cross, bred in 1956 from Helfensteiner and Heroldbebe, and authorised in Germany in 1980. Plantings grew rapidly between 2000 and 2006, the area doubling to 8100 hectares, but have now stabilised. It is also dotted across cool parts of Europe and has an outpost in California's Central Coast.

---

10 ibid., pp. 270–71.

Its only Australian plantings are in the northwest of Tasmania at Phil and Robin Dolan's White Rock Vineyard. They obtained 200 cuttings from the Riverland Improvement Scheme just before most of its 100 vines were pulled out. The first vintage of White Rock was 2013, when it made 60 dozen cases and won the Trophy for Best Other Red Wine at the Mornington Peninsula Cool Climate Wine Show, and would have received a gold medal at the 2015 Tasmanian Wine Show if the minimum quantity requirement had been satisfied. (It was judged without knowledge of this issue, and had been submitted for evaluation.) Most recently, 1000 vines have been planted in the Huon Valley (2014) and other trial vintages are underway in 2015. It has excellent colour, and a soft, plush, velvety mouthfeel; lack of tannins is its only issue.

Freisa

World: 1049 ha. Australia: <1 ha, 1 grower/maker

This is one of the oldest and most important varieties of Piedmont. DNA analysis has shown that Freisa and Nebbiolo have a parent–offspring relationship, and that Freisa could have a close genetic link with Viognier.[11] It was highly appreciated in the nineteenth century and included in almost all Piedmontese red wine blends[12], but is less popular today.

It is lighter and more fragrant than Nebbiolo, yet high in acidity and tannins. It is used for a surprisingly wide range of wines; it is permitted as a minor component in Nebbiolo, Barbera or Grignolino as full-bodied dry red wines. Its other uses are in a range of sweet, still, lightly sparkling Frizzante or Spumante styles, most often with controlled residual sugar.

Its one Australian grower is Dell'uva Wines, with 650 vines planted, and more in contemplation.

Graciano

World: 3112 ha. Australia: 13 ha, 33 growers/makers

Graciano has a daunting number of synonyms throughout Spain and the Mediterranean, establishing – if nothing else – that this is an old variety. Confusion has reigned supreme until recently, with both etymology and early DNA studies producing a series of hypotheses, all since proven to be wrong. The cross that gave rise to Graciano occurred in Spain, but the participants are still the subject of debate. Graciano was far more widely planted

---

11 ibid., p. 367.
12 D'Agata, *Wine Grapes of Italy*, p. 295.

Graciano

in Spain before phylloxera (at the end of the nineteenth century), but is on the road to recovery with sharply increasing plantings, especially in Rioja. Its downsides are its low yield and poor bunch set; its upsides are its colour, flowery/spicy fragrance and good acidity even in hot climates. There are small plantings in California and Argentina, but Australia may become a significant outpost. The number of growers, and producers, is a sign of things to come, its spicy wild flower fragrance, red fruits and airy mouthfeel all commendable. The only downside is the risk of stringy tannins if it is over-extracted.

Producers
Cascabel, Geoff Hardy, Mazza Wines, Mount Majura, Paxton, Rudderless, Woods Crampton, Xanadu

Jacquez

World: 1455 ha. Australia: <1 ha, 4 growers/makers

Jacquez and Chambourcin are the only two hybrids grown in Australia used to make wine. A hybrid is a cross with a difference: one parent is from the *Vitis vinifera* group (as are all conventional grape varieties), the other from a non-*vinifera* variety. Jacquez is said to be a member of *Vitis bourquiniana*, described by Robinson as 'a botanically dubious group'.[13] It was almost certainly bred via a seedling in the southern United States in the eighteenth century, chosen because of its resistance to Pierce's Disease (which doesn't exist in Australia) and phylloxera. While there remain 53 hectares in Texas, its stronghold is Brazil, with 1397 hectares (in 2007) used to make juice, jellies and inexpensive, slightly sweet red wines, the latter with no tannins – the usual problem with hybrids.[14]

It appeared in the Granite Belt around 50 years ago, grown by an Italian farmer until his retirement in 2014, when he pulled out the majority of his vineyard, including all of the 1 hectare he had of it. Prior to this, Ballandean Estate, Ridgemill Estate, Riversands Winery (further north in Queensland) and Two Tails Wines in the Northern Rivers Zone of New South Wales had obtained cuttings, and grow (and use) the variety. The variety produces intensely coloured berries and dark-coloured juice, and the wine has distinctive flavours of plum and blueberry on the mid-palate, but, like Chambourcin, lacks tannin structure on the finish.

Producers
Ballandean Estate, Ridgemill Estate, Riversands, Two Tails

Lagrein

World: 718 ha. Italy: 654 ha. Australia: 17 ha, 29 growers/makers

Robinson sets out the results of extensive DNA profiling, establishing the variety is a natural cross between Teroldego and another parent lost in the mists of time before the thirteenth century.[15] It is also:

- a sibling of Marzemino
- a nephew/niece of Dureza (a parent of Shiraz)
- a grandchild of Pinot Noir, and
- a cousin of Shiraz.

This caused Robinson to dryly comment that it is 'very well connected'. Its Italian home is the Alto Adige/Trento regions in the northeast of the country. Having participated in a tasting, some years ago, bringing together the wines of the most notable Italian

---

13   Robinson, Harding and Vouillamoz, *Wine Grapes*, p. 480.
14   ibid., p. 481.
15   ibid., p. 528.

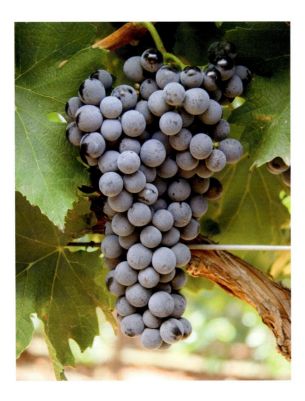

Lagrein

producers and their Australian counterparts, I can say all share a deep, intense crimson-purple colour, equally intense confit black fruit/forest fruits, plus hints of tar and licorice. California has 31 hectares planted in the Paso Robles AVA, the most notable producer Tobin James. The Australian pioneer was Cobaw Ridge.

Producers who have, or have had, plantings include Antcliff's Chase, Bogie Man Wines, Chalmers, Cirami Estate, Cobaw Ridge, di Lusso Estate, Domaine Day, Dos Rios, Fowles, Geoff Hardy, Gisborne Peak, Hartz Barn, Heartland, John Gehrig, King River Estate, Paulmara Estates, Point Leo Road, Regent Wines, Rossifers, Scott Wines, Seppeltsfield, Serafino, Sugarloaf Ridge, Symphony Hill, Tertini and Wines by Geoff Hardy.

Lambrusco

Italy: 13 372 ha. Australia: 2 ha (estimate), 3 growers/makers

Lambrusco comes in many shapes and sizes. Anderson has plantings of nine different varieties (which give rise to the Italian total), Robinson has 12.[16] It has various manifestations: as Rose, dry red, off dry red, sweet red Frizzante and sparkling.

---

16   ibid., pp. 530–38.

Lambrusco Maestri

In a rare situation, all these varietals were believed to be the progeny of locally domesticated wild grapes in Italy, particularly in Piedmont and Emilia-Romagna, and recent genetic evidence has confirmed the assumption.

There are 61 hectares in Argentina (two varieties), and only a handful of plantings in Australia, notably by Chalmers, its importer and grower (along with Parish Hill and Trentham Estate).

Lambrusco Salamino

World: 5003 ha. Australia: <1 ha, 1 grower/maker

This is the most widely planted Lambrusco variety, and makes the most substantial wines. Its strongholds in Italy include Modena and Reggio Emilia, and to a lesser extent the provinces of Mantovo, Bologna and Ferrara. The wine can be dry or sweet, but is always intensely coloured, with fruity aromas; in the best wines, a high level of tannin is offset by fresh acidity. In Australia Lambrusco of any type has an undeservedly poor reputation, mainly because it was used to denote a style, with red grapes of various kinds

Lambrusco Salamino

used. With the EU Wine Agreement in place, this no longer occurs. Parish Hill is its one producer in Australia.

Mammolo

World: 841 ha. France: 773 ha. Australia: <1 ha, 4 growers/makers

This is a very old Tuscan variety, described as early as 1600, and was taken to Corsica either between 1077 and 1284 (during the rule of the Republic of Pisa) or between 1284 and 1768 (during the rule of the Republic of Genova). DNA profiling shows a possible parent–offspring relationship with several old Tuscan varieties. Further DNA profiling has shown that Mammolo is identical to two Corsican varieties, Sciaccarella and Malvasia Montanaccio. Once widely grown in Tuscany, plantings began to decrease in the 1960s as the focus switched to Sangiovese and away from the cocktail of red and white varieties. There were only 52 hectares remaining in 2010. It has a much more important role in Corsica, being one of the main varieties in all red and Rose wines bar one. It is an unusual grape, producing relatively pale wines combining significant alcohol levels with fresh acidity and a bouquet of spice and red fruits, but it ages rapidly.

Mammolo

Although it has kept a low profile in Australia, Thorn-Clarke has co-fermented 5 per cent of Mammolo with Nebbiolo, and Noorinbee Selection Vineyards has also made a blend. Yet another entrant, Collector Wines, blends it with Colorino Nero, Canaiolo and Sangiovese under the catchy name of Rose Red City.

Marzemino

World: 1091 ha. Italy: 1090 ha. Australia: <1 ha, 3 growers/makers

A very old variety from northern Italy (predating 1409) which has been shown by DNA profiling to be a sibling of Lagrein, with one common parent (Teroldego) but different second parents, in each case not known. While the Italian plantings are not large, it is grown in many parts of Trentino and elsewhere in northern Italy, variously used in still or sparkling wines, dry, off-dry or sweet. As a still wine it has red and black cherry and raspberry aromas, with some black cherry/sour cherry notes on the finish. Australia is its only (minuscule) home away from home.

Producers
Chalmers, Chrismont, Michelini

Mencia

World: 10 658 ha. Australia: <1 ha, 2 growers/makers

Mencia is believed to have originated in northwest Spain, although it had a low profile until the arrival of phylloxera.[17] The two countries which have significant plantings are Spain and Portugal (in the latter it is called Jaen). There are 8204 hectares recorded in Spain and 2454 hectares in Portugal. Plantings are increasing as growers are finding its versatility; while making a highly aromatic and fruity Rose, the rediscovery of old vineyards with low yields on deep schist soils has led to some dense, concentrated examples. Oliver's Taranga Vineyards and d'Arenberg are Australia's two producers.

Mondeuse

World: 306 ha. France: 300 ha. Switzerland: 4 ha. Australia: 2 ha, 5 growers/makers

A very interesting variety native to the Jura region of France, where the plantings have rebounded from a low of 200 hectares in recognition of the potential quality of this aromatic, strongly structured and deeply coloured wine. The DNA analysis has shown it to be either a half-sibling or grandparent of Syrah, which has helped its cause.

It was brought to Australia in the wake of phylloxera by Francois de Castella, and planted at the Rutherglen Research Station. Thereafter it has not moved outside the region. It was originally grown and made by Brown Brothers in a blend with Shiraz and Cabernet Sauvignon, and now is made by Buller, likewise blended with Shiraz. It is a powerful wine, with distinctive juicy/peppery flavours. Producers include Brown Brothers, RL Buller and Chambers Rosewood.

Montepulciano

World: 34 947 ha. Italy: 34 660 ha. Australia: 49 ha, 26 growers/makers

Montepulciano is the name of both a grape variety and a region in Tuscany, but it is Sangiovese that is the variety in the Vino Nobilo de Montepulciano DOCG. If this were not confusion enough, the variety is used in the Montepulciano di Abruzzo DOC.

It is a workhorse grape planted across central Italy, the best wines rich, and deep in colour, with ample tannins making them ideal for blending with softer varieties. California had 30 hectares in 2008, Argentina 85 hectares, and Australia 49 hectares – 33 hectares in bearing, and a further 16 coming into bearing (2012).

---

17   ibid., p. 625.

Montepulciano

The variety performs well in the disparate regions in which it is grown in Australia, with nutmeg/cinnamon/spice/pepper/coffee/mocha nuances described in various of those regions, the common denominator being plum, red berry and blackberry fruits with fine tannins. Most assuredly a variety to watch, especially in warm regions.

Producers

Altamont Wine Studio, Bird in Hand*, Brown Brothers, Cirami Estate, First Drop Wines*, Kangarilla Road, Kimbolton, Kirrihill, Lonely Vineyard, McGuigan Wines (Barossa Valley), Mr Riggs Wine Company*, Serafino, Tenafeate Creek, Tscharke*, WayWood Wines*

Muscardin

World: 17 ha. Australia: <1 ha, 1 grower/maker

An extremely rare variety that probably originated in Châteauneuf-du-Pape – the only place in France in which it is grown today[18], although the producers who use it are some of the best known in Châteauneuf. In Australia, Yangarra Estate is establishing a small planting on a trial basis.

Negroamaro

World: 11 462 ha. Italy: 11 460 ha. Australia: 2 ha (estimate), 6 growers/makers

There are two distinct clones in Puglia, the second the earlier-ripening Negroamaro Precoce. Robinson and D'Agata have a fundamental difference on the spelling of the name: Jancis Robinson spells it as one word; Ian D'Agata is insistent it is two words, Negro Amaro. (They also disagree on the etymological origins of the name, she going for Italy, he for Greece.) The wine is deeply coloured and rich, but develops quickly.

Negroamaro

---

18 ibid., p. 678.

Australia is the only country other than Italy to have embarked on commercial production of the wine. Producers include Mudgee Wines, Parish Hill, Tallavera Grove and Torzi Matthews.

Nero d'Avola

World: 16 596 ha. Australia: 33 ha, 19 growers/makers

This is still technically called Calabrese in Italy, and is Sicily's most widely planted red variety, although you have to choose between Robinson, with 19 304 hectares in 2008, D'Agato, with 18 000+ hectares in 2010, and Anderson, with 16 595 hectares in 2010. Some of the confusion arises from the census base: is it just Sicily, or is it the whole of Italy? There are four official clones, but Alesio Planeta, of leading Sicilian producer Planeta Estate, is reported as saying there are hundreds of clones.[19] Robinson more prosaically says a recent DNA survey showed a high degree of genetic diversity in Sicily, with several distinct clones intermixed with other distinct and undetermined varieties, possibly from seedlings, in the vineyards surveyed.[20]

Nero d'Avola

---

19 D'Agata, *Wine Grapes of Italy*, p. 216.
20 Robinson, Harding and Vouillamoz, *Wine Grapes*, p. 723.

D'Agata sketches the rise and fall, then rise again, of the variety, and concludes that it is 'capable of making very good, sometimes great, wines, and can take its place among Italy's noble (or almost noble) varieties'.[21]

Originally used mainly as a blend component to provide colour and richness, this variety now stands in its own right, its origin almost certainly the town of Avola on the south-eastern end of the island. It has no need of the progressively cooler, higher slopes of Mount Etna, as it already underwrites the appeal of the best Sicilian wines. DNA studies show there is considerable genetic diversity, with distinct clones, all pointing to the age of the variety.[22]

Apart from small plantings in California, Turkey and Malta, its home away from home is Australia. Here its flavour spectrum is similar to that found in Sicily, with red and black cherry/raspberry/strawberry flavours, and fine-grained tannins. All the indications are that it will continue to gain traction in Australia. It has gained momentum with 17 producers, the plantings spread far and wide.

Producers
Beach Road, Bird in Hand, Brash Higgins*, Chalmers, Coriole, Eldorado Road*, Fox Gordon*, Geoff Hardy*, Golden Grove Estate*, Hither & Yon, Mount Horrocks, Scott Wines

Pinotage

World: 6404 ha. Australia: 5 ha, 5 growers/makers

This cross was bred in South Africa in 1925 by Abraham Izak Perold, who thought he was crossing Pinot Noir with Hermitage, hence the name. In fact, the supposed Hermitage was Cinsaut, a perpetual cause of frustration in wine trivia games. Opinions within South Africa, and without, have long been polarised. When the late Len Evans first visited South Africa and tasted the Pinotage wines, he was caustic in his dismissal. When I first visited the country, and likewise tasted Pinotage for the first time, I castigated South African winemakers for not taking the wine more seriously. It seemed to me that part of the problem was over-extraction and the use of poor-quality oak. Well handled, it can produce a wine with attractive red fruits in its lighter-bodied manifestation, moving to darker fruits and more depth in its full-bodied side. Small plantings in California, Brazil, New Zealand, Oregon, Washington State, British Columbia, Zimbabwe and Israel have followed, as have scattered small plantings in Australia. Two wines produced from

---

21 D'Agata, *Wine Grapes of Italy*, p. 218.
22 Robinson, Harding and Vouillamoz, *Wine Grapes*, pp. 723–24.

Pinotage

it are sourced from a planting in the Upper Yarra Valley, established by an expatriate South African. On the face of it, it might be expected to do better in a warmer region.

Anderson reports global plantings of 6404 hectares, 6240 hectares in South Africa (and 75 hectares planted in Brazil, 6 hectares in Canada, 74 hectares in New Zealand, and 9 hectares in the United States). He shows zero for Australia, simply because the plantings are too small, but its five makers are in the Granite Belt (Queensland), New England (northern New South Wales), the Riverland (South Australia) and the Yarra Valley (Victoria) – a Catholic spread, if ever there was one.

Producers
Oak Works, Ravens Croft, Ten Men, Thick as Thieves, Topper's Mountain

Refosco dal Peduncolo Rosso

Refosco dal Peduncolo Rosso

World: 1082 ha. Australia: <1 ha, 3 growers/makers

Robinson says that ampelography and DNA profiling have identified six varieties in the Refosco family, not unlike the Muscat group.[23] It has yet to gain much traction in Australia, and, if it were to do so, would create dilemmas for varietal labels. There are only 620 hectares in Italy (2000), mainly in the Friuli and Veneto areas. Its very late ripening in these relatively cool regions suggests that it may respond well in warmer parts of Australia. In Bendigo it is crimson black in colour when picked between 12.5° and 13.5° baumé, and the flavour is full and strong – huge berry flavours with very firm tannins.

Producers

Bendigo: Blanche Barkly; Heathcote: Vinea Marson

---

23 ibid., pp. 877–81.

Rondinella

World: 2481 ha. Australia: <1 ha, 2 growers/makers

Like Corvina, Rondinella's home is in Verona, where it is regarded as a lesser blending partner in Valpolicella and Bardelino. Its name did not appear until 1882, but DNA analysis shows it to be the offspring of Corvina and another unknown, and possibly extinct, variety.[24]

Producers
Centennial Vineyards, Freeman Vineyards*

Sagrantino

World: 995 ha. Italy: 361 ha. Australia: 10 ha, 19 growers/makers

Notwithstanding suggestions that the grape came from Greece, carried by Byzantine monks in the Middle Ages, Robinson says it is most likely to have originated in central

Sagrantino

---

24 ibid., pp. 906–07.

Italy, perhaps Umbria.[25] The variety had been threatened by extinction in the 1960s, but was rescued by Marco Caprai, who continues to make some of the best wines. The key to Sagrantino, in both Italy and Australia, is management of its tannins: the base cherry-flavoured fruit can be sabotaged by tannin gridlock. Despite this, it has a number of producers in Australia.

Producers

Amadio, Andrew Peace, Angullong, Blaxland Vineyards, Chalmers, Chrismont, Coriole, d'Arenberg, Gracebrook Vineyards, Heathvale, Lou Miranda, Mitolo, Oliver's Taranga Vineyards, Preston Peak, Tallavera Grove, Terra Felix, View Road

Saint Macaire

World: 3 ha. Australia: 2 ha, 1 grower/maker

Robinson comments that little is known about the history of this obscure Bordeaux variety.[26] It was commonly grown in the Gironde in the nineteenth century, but has all but disappeared from France (with less than 1 hectare). There are tiny plantings in California, but only Westend Estate in Griffith has a meaningful quantity, of 2 hectares. Owner/winemaker Bill Calabria is proud of his Saint Macaire, but it's not a particularly friendly wine, with more acid and tannin than fruit.

Sankt Laurent | St Laurent

World: 3664 ha. Australia: <1 ha, 1 grower/maker

St Laurent most probably originates from Austria, where it is best known, and is known to have been cultivated since the nineteenth century at the very least. However, DNA analysis has not located any parents, but has dismissed the theory that it is genetically close to Pinot. It is difficult to grow, but when its various problems are overcome it produces deeply coloured, velvety red wines that have always seemed (to me) to not have sufficient tannins. Others may disagree. Its one producer in Australia is Hahndorf Hill.

---

25 ibid., p. 937.
26 ibid., p. 938.

Saperavi

World: 8130 ha. Georgia: 4751 ha. Kazakhstan: 428 ha. Moldova: 716 ha. Russia: 716 ha. Ukraine: 1514 ha. Australia: 5 ha, 28 producers

A very old variety that originated in southwestern Georgia (the word in fact means 'dyer' in Russian). It has exceptional colour, partly derived from its skin, but also from its pink juice (prior to fermentation). It also holds its acidity well, ripening late in the season. Symphonia in the King Valley used it both as a varietal and in its Quintus, a unique blend of Merlot, Cabernet Sauvignon, Saperavi and Tempranillo. For wine trivia games, Robinson records that four clones have been identified, including Saperavi Grdzelmarcvala and Saperavi Mskhvilmarcvala.[27]

Producers

Ballandean Estate*, Cirami Estate, Clovely Estate*, Gapsted*, Hugh Hamilton*, King River Estate, Massena, Oak Works, Patritti, Symphonia, Ten Miles East, Two Hands

Tannat

World: 5889 ha. France: 2914 ha. Italy: 49 ha, California: 96 ha. Australia: 15 ha (estimate), 31 growers/makers

A deeply coloured, rough and tannic wine, grown in Madiran, France, which was directly responsible for the development of the micro-oxygenation technique. Other countries with significant plantings include Argentina (705 hectares), Brazil (295 hectares) and Uruguay (1815 hectares). Given its colour and tannin, it would not surprise me to see plantings increase in Australia for blending with weaker (and probably highly cropped) varieties. Summit Estate in the Granite Belt and Symphonia in the King Valley have both used it as part of innovative (and high-quality) five-variety blends.

Producers

Boireann*, Coolangatta Estate, Glenguin Estate*, Geoff Hardy*, Just Red, Massena Vineyards*, Pirramimma, Sam Miranda*, Summit Estate*, Topper's Mountain

---

27 ibid., p. 949.

Tannat

Teroldego

World: 839 ha. California: 40 ha. Australia: <1 ha, 4 growers/makers

This is a very old variety from Trentino, in northeast Italy. DNA profiling shows that Teroldego spontaneously crossed at least twice with an unknown and most likely extinct variety to give birth to Marzemino and Lagrein. More surprisingly, DNA reconstruction shows that Dureza, which is a parent of Syrah, is a full sibling of Teroldego. Hence both are grandchildren of Pinot Noir, and Teroldego is thus an uncle/aunt of Syrah.[28]

The Michelini plantings in the King Valley, Victoria, have produced a deeply coloured, high-tannin and high-acid structure. The 2008 vintage won a gold medal and trophy at the 2010 Alternative Wines Show, and the same wine tasted by me in February 2015 was still barely ready to drink, so powerful is its structure.

Producers
Amato Wines, Geoff Hardy, Heartland, Michelini*

---

28 ibid., pp. 1047–48.

Tinto Cao | Tinta Barroca | Tinta Roriz

World: 6172 ha (Tinta Barroca), 369 ha (Tinto Cao). Australia: 10 ha, 21 growers/makers

These are Portuguese varieties of varying degrees of importance. Tinta Roriz is in fact Tempranillo, albeit cultivated for centuries under the Tinta Roriz name. All are grown by Stanton & Killeen for incorporation in its excellent vintage Port styles; likewise, Yarra Yering with its Potsorts. Its 21 producers in Australia, from all parts of the country, grow and/or make Tinto Cao in blends of table wine or fortified wine.

Tinto Cao

Tinta Roriz

Touriga Nacional

World: 10 445 ha. Portugal: 10 175 ha, Australia: 48 ha, 31 growers/makers

The cornerstone of Portuguese Vintage Port which, after centuries of use for this purpose alone, is now also being used in the production of high-quality Portuguese table wines (as a blend component). Deeply coloured, thick-skinned and tannic, a small percentage

Touriga Nacional

in a blend makes a major impact, and a number of excellent blends are made in Australia. Australia's plantings of 48 hectares lead Argentina (14 hectares) and Brazil (12 hectares).

Lindemans used it as a component of the vintage Port styles they were then making, and this is the purpose for which it was used by Stanton & Killeen, and Dr Bailey Carrodus at Yarra Yering.

Best producers
Table wine: *919 Wines, Coates*, De Iuliis, First Drop Wines*, Flowstone*, Heslop*, Mansfield Wines, Mazza Wines*, Mount Majura, Old Plains, Paulmara Estates, Piano Piano, Quattro Mano, St Hallett*, SC Pannell*, Seppeltsfield, Sevenhill Cellars, Stanton & Killeen*, Three Dark Horses, Tscharke, Whispering Brook, Yarra Yering**
Fortified wine: *Seppelt*, Tsharke, Yarra Yering**

Trollinger | Schiava Grossa

World: 3011 ha. Australia: 0.6 ha, 1 grower/maker

If ever a variety has flown under the radar in Australia, it is this one. Not only is it known under the two names above, but it is also known as Black Hamburgh, which I had always believed was a table grape, not a wine grape. It turns out that it is indeed a wine grape, and an important one. Robinson says that the variety used to be cultivated all over Western Europe, and has been involved in both deliberate and natural crosses.[29] Its family tree has it connected with Pinot, Muscat of Alexandria and Riesling (among others) as natural crosses, and Muscat of Hamburg and Muller-Thurgau as deliberate crosses. If there is another edition of this book, unscrambling the Black Hamburgh eggs used in various regions at various times in Australia will be necessary. For the time being, the one producer using the Trollinger name is Hahndorf Hill.

Tyrian

Australia: <1 ha, 1 grower/maker

A CSIRO-bred cross of Cabernet Sauvignon and Sumoll taken into commercial production by McWilliam's. It produces a very deeply coloured wine.

Zweigelt

World: 10 027 ha. Australia: <1 ha, 1 grower/maker

This has the distinction of being the very last of the 1368 varieties in Robinson, making its appearance at page 1117. There it is explained that it is a cross between Blaufrankisch and Sankt Laurent/St Laurent obtained in 1922 by Fritz Zweigelt at the Viticultural Research Centre in Austria. Because of its two immediate parents, it turns out to be a grandchild of Gouais Blanc and Pinot, two of the most influential varieties in the genetics of Western European grape varieties. It is being avidly planted in Austria, where it is the country's most widely planted red variety, with 6511 hectares, the area increased by nearly 50 per cent since 2000. Australia's one producer is Hahndorf Hill.

---

29 ibid., pp. 972–73.

Index

Note: Varieties are shown in **bold**; *italic* page numbers refer to illustrations.

3 Drops, 50, 75
13th Street, 10
201 (winery), 244
919 Wines, 128, 140, 290

A

A Rodda, 25, 259
Abbey Creek, 50, 201
Acacia Winery, 9
Acquitania, 150
Adelaide Hills (region), 22, 49, 61–2, 76, 83, 93, 106, 159, 176, 200, 245, 252, 257
Adelaide Plains (region), 254
Adelsheim, 189
Aglianico, 262, *263*
Akarua, 189
Alain Graillot, 206
Alain Paret, 207
Alana Estate, 14, 69
Albany (subregion), 28, 50, 75, 179
Albert Belle, 206
Aleatico, 263
Alicante Bouschet, 264
Aligote, 110
Alkoomi, 28, 50, 75, 163
All Saints Estate, 95, 97, 108, 228, 246
Allan Scott Wines, 14, 42, 71
Allies, 197
Almaviva, 150
Alpha Domus, 210
Alphonse Mellot, 67

Alpine Valleys (region), 245, 259
Altair, 150
Altamont Wine Studio, 279
Altydgedacht, 68
Amadio, 262, 286
Amani, 173
Amato Wines, 288
Amayna, 68
Amberley Estate, 86
Amelia Park, 62, 74, 162
Amelie Robert Estate, 189
Amietta, 268
Amulet Vineyard, 101, 131, 139
Anam Cara Cellars, 189
Ancellotta, 264
Ancient Oaks Cellars, 9
Anderson, 87
Andre Dezat, 67
Andrew Peace, 286
Andrew Will, 171
Angove Family Winemakers, 135, 218, 238, 259
Angullong, 286
Angus Plains, 219
Annie's Lane, 48, 218
Ansonica see Inzolia
Antcliff's Chase, 274
Anvers, 22
Ara, 71, 188
Aranel, 264–5
Araujo Estate, 148, 209
Aravina Estate, 86
Arboleda, 68
Arete, 76, 83
Argyle Winery, 9, 189
Arinto de Bucelas, 136
Armand Rousseau, 186
Arneis, 111–12, *111*
Arrivo, 252
Arrowood, 209
ArtWine, 117
Arundel Farm, 228
Ashbrook Estate, 103
Ashton Hills, 200
Assyrtiko, 112–13
Astrolabe Wines, 71

AT Richardson, 227, 246, 252
Ata Rangi, 14, 187
Atamisque, 149
Ataraxia Wines, 12
Atlas, 218, 249
Au Bon Climat, 9, 190
Aucerot, 113
Audrey Wilkinson, 20, 103, 223
August & Pierre-Marie Clape, 207
August Kessler, 37
Auntsfield Estate, 71, 188
Aurelio Montes, 11
Austin's, 197, 230

B

Babcock Vineyards, 9, 190
Backsberg, 150
Baileys of Glenrowan, 97, 108, 228, 246
Baillieu Vineyard, 83
Balgownie Estate, 163, 226
Ballandean Estate, 133, 273, 287
Ballarat (region), 198–9
Balnaves, 23, 157, 220
Banks Road, 25
Bannockburn, 25, 197, 230
Bannockburn Heights, 15, 189
Bantry Grove, 20
Barbera, 240–1, *241*
Barnett Vineyards, 171
Barossa Valley (region), 23, 50, 87, 95, 97, 100, 101, 106, 108, 158–9, 176–7, 215–17, 238–9, 241, 243, 245, 249, 259, 261
Barratt, 22, 76, 200
Barrgowan, 230
Barringwood Park, 132, 201, 255
Barwang, 21, 224
Bass Phillip, 24, 198, 248
Bass River, 198
Bastardo, 265
Battely, 270
Battle of Bosworth, 218
Bay of Fires, 30, 83, 201

Beach Road, 116, 120, 135, 262, 282
Beaulieu, 148
Beaux Frères, 189
Beechworth (region), 24–5, 100, 101, 106, 248, 252, 257, 259
Bein, 173
Bekkers, 218, 238
Belgravia, 20, 161
Bell Hill, 188
Bellarine Estate, 179
Bellarmine, 28
Bellbrae, 230
Bellvale, 24, 198
Ben Haines, 95, 227
Ben Hill, 15
Bendigo (region), 163, 225–6, 252, 284
Benjamin Leroux, 186
Benton Lane, 189
Benziger Family, 171
Bergstrom, 189
Beringer Blass, 148, 171
Best's, 227, 245, 255
Bethany, 49
Bethel Heights, 189
Bianchet, 134
Bianco d'Alessano, 136
Biancone, 113–14
Big Rivers Zone, New South Wales, 27
Bilancia, 210
Billy Button, 134, 135
Bimbadgen, 76
Bindi, 25, 198, 229
Bird in Hand, 22, 49, 76, 112, 176, 279, 282
Bird on a Wire, 95, 100
Bisquertt, 68
BK Wines, 22, 200, 218, 238
Blackjack Vineyards, 226
Blackwood Valley (region), 259
Bladen Wines, 71
Blanche Barkly, 284
Blaxland Vineyards, 286

Bleasdale, 83, 219
Bloodwood, 20, 161, 223
Blue Mountain, 10, 191
Bodega Catena Zapata, 149
Bodega El Esko, 149
Bodega Norton, 149
Bodegas Fabre, 149
Boekenhoutskloof, 150, 209
Bogie Man Wines, 274
Boireann, 241, 249, 257, 287
Boland, 12
Bonnacorse, 190
Bonneau du Martray, 6
Bookwalter, 10
Borthwick Estate, 69
Bouchaine Vineyards, 9
Bouchard Finlayson, 12, 192
Bouchard Père et Fils, 6, 186
Bourboulenc, 136
Boynton's Feathertop, 132, 135
Brancott Estate, 71
Brand's Laira, 157, 220
Brangayne of Orange, 76, 161
Brash Higgins, 282
Brash Vineyard, 74
Brave Goose, 179, 248
Bream Creek, 51, 132, 201
Bremerton, 103, 116, 135, 219
Bress, 124, 135, 225, 226
Briar Ridge, 60, 222
Briery Estate, 117
Brightwater Vineyards, 14, 71
Broadley Vineyards, 189
Brockenchack, 49, 219
Brokenwood, 25, 60, 222
Broke's Promise, 241
Brookfields, 13
Brookland Valley, 29, 162
Brothers in Arms, 219
Brown Brothers, 84, 90, 97, 108, 109, 132, 138, 139, 246, 255, 268, 278, 279
Brown Magpie, 197, 230
Bruno Clair, 6
Buckshot Vineyard, 225, 261
Buena Vista, 9

Bull Lane, 225
Buller, 97, 108
Bundalong, 220
Bunnamagoo Estate, 61
Burch Family Wines, 28, 29, 50, 62, 74, 162, 163, 231, 268
Burge Family, 177
Burrowing Owl, 171
Buttermans Track, 257
By Jingo!, 121
Byrne Vineyards, 239
Byron & Harold, 28, 50, 231
Byron Wines, 9, 190

C

Cabernet Franc, 241–3, *242*
Cabernet Sauvignon, *142*, 143–65
   Argentina, 149
   Australian history, 151–3
   Australian regional styles, 156–65
   Australian statistics, 153
   Australian winemaking, 154–6
   Chile, 150
   France, 146–7
   international history, 143–6
   Italy and Spain, 147
   New Zealand, 150–1
   South Africa, 149–50
   United States, 148
Cabriere, 192
Cadence, 148
Cafaro Cellars, 171
Cairnbrae Vineyards, 14
Cakebread, 148
Calabria Family, 246, 262
Calcu, 150
Caledonia Australis, 24, 198
Calera, 9, 191
Calina, 150
Caliterra, 11, 172
Calyptra, 11, 68
Cambewarra Estate, 244
Cambridge, 190

Cameron, 9
Campbells, 97, 101, 228, 246
Canada Muscat, 137
Canaiolo Nero, 265–6
Canberra District (region), 106, 223, 257, 259
Canepa, 68, 150, 172
Cannibal Creek Vineyard, 24
Canoe Ridge, 10
Canta Carolina, 150
Cape Barren, 218
Cape Chamonix, 192
Cape Grace, 86, 231, 243
Cape Mentelle, 29, 74, 162, 231, 261
Cape Naturaliste, 179
Cape Point, 68
Capel Vale, 50
Capercaillie, 20, 222
Capital, 259
Cargo Road, 179
Carignan, 266–7
Carillion, 134, 161, 223
Carmen, 172
Carmenere, 267–8
Carnelian, 268
Carrick, 189
Casa Freschi, 22, 83, 252
Casa Lapostolle, 172
Casa Marin, 68
Casas del Bosque, 68
Cascabel, 267, 269, 272
Caserena Winery, 149
Castagna, 100, 106, 257
Castelli Estate, 28, 93, 163, 179, 231
Castle Rock, 28, 50, 201
Cathcart Ridge Estate, 114
Catherine Vale Vineyard, 241, 245
Cavas del 23, 149
Cave Spring, 13
Caymus, 148
Cedar Creek, 171
Cederberg Private Cellar, 68, 150, 209

Centennial Vineyards, 161, 255, 259, 270, 285
Central Victoria Zone, 179, 248
Ceravolo, 115, 254
Chain of Ponds, 76
Chalk Hill, 158, 218, 241
Chalkers Crossing, 21, 224
Chalmers, 116, 120, 122, 124, 125, 135, 136, 225, 262, 274, 275, 277, 282, 286
Chalone Vineyard, 9, 191
Chambers Rosewood, 97, 108, 119, 140, 269, 278
Chambourcin, 243–4
Chandon de Briailles, 6, 186
Chapel Hill, 158, 218, 238
Chapman Grove, 62, 74
Chapoutier, 205, 206, 207
Chappellet, 148, 171
Chard Farm, 15, 42, 189
Chardonnay, xx, 1–30
    Australian history, 15–17
    Australian regional styles, 19–30
    Australian statistics, 17
    Australian winemaking, 17–19
    Canada, 10
    Chile, 11–12
    France, 3–7
    international history, 1–3
    Italy, Spain and other Europe, 7–8
    New Zealand, 12–15
    South Africa, 12
    United States, 8–10
Charles Melton, 136, 217, 269
Chasselas, 114
Château Bouscaut, 55
Château Carbonnieux, 55
Château Climens, 55
Château Coutet, 55
Chateau de Beaucastel, 235
Chateau de Fonsalette, 235
Chateau de la Charbonniere, 235

Château du Nozet (de Ladoucette), 67
Château d'Yquem, 55
Château Guiraud, 55
Château Haut Brion, 55
Château La Louviere, 55
Chateau La Nerthe, 235
Château La Tour Blanche, 55
Château Lafaurie-Peyaguey, 55
Château Laville Haut Brion, 55
Chateau Los Boldos, 150
Chateau Mont-Redon, 235
Chateau Montelana, 8, 148
Chateau Pato, 222
Chateau Rabaud-Promis, 55
Chateau Rayas/Clos Pignan, 235
Château Rayne Vigneau, 55
Château Rieussec, 55
Chateau St Jean, 148
Château Sigalas-Rabaud, 55
Château Suduiraut, 55
Chateau Tanunda, 267, 269
Chatto, 201
Chehalem, 189
Chenin Blanc, 85–8, *87*
    Australian regional styles, 86–7
    Australian statistics, 88
    general background, 85–6
Chimney Rock, 148, 171
Chinook Wines, 171
Chrismont, 84, 112, 128, 241, 257, 277, 286
Christian Thirot, 67
Christmann, 37
Church Road Winery, 13, 151
Churton, 188
Ciavarella, 113, 246
Cienna, 268
Cinsaut, 268–9
Cirami Estate, 274, 279, 287
Circe, 26
CJ Pask, 151, 172
Clairault | Streicker, 29, 62, 74, 162, 231, 254

Clairette, 114–15
Clare Valley (region), 47–8, 109, 160, 218, 239, 249, 257, 259, 261
Clarence House, 131, 259
Clarendon Hills, 158, 178, 218, 238
Clark-Clauden, 148
Claymore, 239
Clearview Estate, 13, 69
Clemens Hill, 201
Clonakilla, 106, 223, 224
Clos Clare, 48
Clos du Bois, 190
Clos Henri, 71, 188
Clos Marguerite, 71
Cloudy Bay Vineyards, 14, 71, 189
Clovely Estate, 287
Clover Hill, 255
Clusel-Roche, 206
Clyde Park, 25, 197, 230
Coates, 257, 290
Cobaw Ridge, 274
Coche-Dury, 6
Cofield, 228, 246
Coldstream Hills, 26, 165, 196
Colgin, 148
Collector Wines, 21, 223, 266, 277
Colombard, 89–90
Colorino del Valdarno, 269–70, *269*
Columbia Crest, 10, 148, 171
Combier, 206
Comte de Vogue, 186
Comte Senard, 6
Comtes Lafon, 6
Concha y Toro, 11, 68, 150, 172
Conde, 150
Condie Estate, 225
Cono Sur, 150, 172
Constantia Clen, 150
Coolangatta Estate, 244, 287
Coonawarra (region), 22–3, 156–7, 177, 219–20

Cooper Burns, 49
Coppabella, 21
Corbis, 207
Coriole, 87, 116, 158, 218, 241, 257, 282, 286
Corison, 148
Cortese, 115
Corvina, 270
Cosentino Dalla Vale, 148
Coudelet de Beaucastel, 235
Counoise, 270
Coward & Black, 86
Cowra (region), 21
Crabtree Watervale Wines, 109, 160
Craggy Range Vineyards, 13, 151, 172, 187, 210
Craiglee, 106, 228
Craigow, 51
Craneford, 177
Creation Wines, 192
Credaro Family Estate, 29, 62, 74, 231
Creekside, 10
CRFT, 93, 200, 219
Cristom, 189
Crittenden Estate, 26, 112, 139, 197
Crouchen, 137
Cullen, 29, 62, 74, 162
Cumulus, 161, 179
Curly Flat, 25, 198
Cuvaison, 8, 148

D
Dal Zotto, 84, 112, 132, 241
Dalfarras, 164
Dalrymple Vineyards, 30, 201
Dalwhinnie, 227
Dandelion, 219
Daniel Schuster, 15
d'Arenberg, 158, 218, 238, 244, 249, 269, 278, 286
Darling Park, 26
David Franz, 177
Dawson & James, 30, 201

De Bortoli, 26, 61, 93, 131, 165, 196, 230, 248, 257
De Grendel Wines, 68
De Iuliis, 60, 222, 290
De Marcoux, 235
De Martino, 150
De Trafford, 150
de Wetshof Estate, 12
Decero, 149
Deep Woods Estate, 29, 162
Dehlinger, 190, 209
Deisen, 249
Del Bosque, 172
del Rios of Mt Anakie, 25, 95, 230
Delaire Graff, 150
Delas, 205, 235
Delatite, 93
Delegats, 151
Delheim, 150
DeLille Cellars, 148
Dellaire Graff Estate, 68
Dell'uva Wines, 136, 139, 271
Denmark (subregion), 28, 50, 75, 179, 201, 243
Denton Winery, 14
Derwent Estate, 30, 51, 83
Destiny Bay, 151
Deviation Road, 83
Devil's Corner, 51, 201
Devil's Lair, 29, 86, 162
Dexter, 26, 197
di Lusso Estate, 129, 135, 241, 263, 274
Diamond Creek, 148
Didier Dageneau, 67
Diemersdal Estate, 68, 150
Diemersfontein Vineyards, 150
Dindima, 139
Dixons Creek Estate, 268
Dobbes Family Estate, 189
Dodgy Brothers, 249, 257
Dog Point Vineyard, 71, 188
DogRidge Wine Co, 158
DogRock, 227
Dolcetto, 244–5, *244*

Domain Chandon, 255
Domain Day, 117, 274
Domaine Asmara, 164, 225
Domaine Bernard Moreau et Fils, 5
Domaine Blain-Gagnard, 5
Domaine Bosquet des Papes, 235
Domaine Bouchard Père et Fils, 5
Domaine Chandon, 26, 190
Domaine Cotat, 67
Domaine de Bellene, 186
Domaine de Chevalier, 55
Domaine de la Réméjeanne, 235
Domaine de la Romanée-Conti, 5, 186
Domaine de l'Ameillaud, 235
Domaine de l'Arlot, 186
Domaine de Montille, 186
Domaine des Comtes Lafon, 5
Domaine du Pegau, 235
Domaine du Vieux Telegraphe, 235
Domaine Dujac, 186
Domaine Etienne Sauzet, 5
Domaine Francois Jobard, 6
Domaine Gagnard-Delagrange, 5
Domaine Gramenon, 235
Domaine Henri Boillot, 5
Domaine Jean Marc Pillot, 5
Domaine Jean Sipp, 40
Domaine la Barroche, 235
Domaine Leflaive, 5
Domaine Louis Carillon et Fils, 5
Domaine Naturaliste, 74
Domaine Ramonet, 5
Domaine Serene, 189
Domaine Vincent Dancer, 5
Domaine Weinbach, 40
Dominique Portet, 165, 225, 255
Dominus Estate, 148
Dönnhoff, 38

Dopff et Irion, 40
Doradillo, 115
Dornfelder, 270–1
Dos Rios, 124, 274
Dowie Doole, 87, 218
Downing Estate, 164, 225
Dr Burklin-Wolf, 37
Dr Crusius, 38
Dr Loosen, 39
Dr Pauly-Bergweiler, 39
Drouhin Estate, 189
Dry Gully, 189
Dry River Wines, 42, 69, 187, 210
Drylands, 42, 71
du Colombier, 206
Du Coulet, 207
Dubrueil Fontaine, 6
Duckett's Mill, 163
Duckhorn, 148, 171
Ducks in a Row, 116, 124, 135
Duke's Vineyard, 50, 163, 231
Dunn Vineyards, 148
Durand, 207
Durif, 245–6, *246*
Dutschke, 159, 177, 217

E

E Guigal, 205, 206, 207, 235
Eagles Nest, 68, 173, 209
Eagles Trace, 171
Eastern Peake, 199
Echelon, 49
Echelon Armchair Critic, 21
Echeverría, 150
Eden Hall, 49, 159, 219
Eden Road, 21, 223
Eden Valley (region), 23, 49, 106, 159, 176–7, 219, 249, 261
Edna Valley Vineyards, 9, 190
Egon Müller, 39
Ehrenfelser, 138
Eikendal, 150
Ekhidna, 116
Elderton, 49, 159, 217, 267

Eldorado Road, 246, 282
Eldridge Estate of Red Hill, 26, 197, 248
Elephant Hill, 13
Elgin Vintners, 173
Elmswood Estate, 178
Emmanuel Darnaud, 205
Emmerich Knoll, 41
Eperosa, 219, 239
Erin Eyes, 160, 218
Ernie Els, 150
Errazuriz, 11, 150
Escarpment, 187
Esk Valley, 13, 172
Estate 807, 50
Et Fille, 189
Etienne Pochon, 206
Evans & Tate, 28, 74, 162, 201, 231
Even Keel, 223
Evoi, 29
Eyrie Vineyards, 189

F

Faber Vineyard, 103, 231, 254
Fable Mountain Vineyards, 209
Fairhall Downs, 14
Fairview, 12, 209
Farr | Farr Rising, 25, 106, 197, 230
Felton Road, 15, 42, 189
Fenton Estate, 151
Fermoy Estate, 29, 179
Ferngrove Vineyards, 50
Fiano, 115–16, *116*
Fiddlehead, 190
Fidelitas, 148
Fighting Gully Road, 25, 257, 262, 270
Finca Flichman, 149
Finca Sophenia, 149
Fire Gully, 162
First Creek, 20, 103, 222
First Drop Wines, 279, 290
Flagstone, 68, 150
Flametree, 29, 74, 162

Flat Rock, 10
Flaxman Wines, 159
Fletcher, 252
Flora, 138
Flora Springs, 148
Flowers Vineyard, 9, 190
Flowstone, 29, 74, 93, 162, 290
Flying Fish Cove, 162, 231
Flynns, 103, 135, 225
Forbes & Forbes, 49
Forest Hill Vineyard, 28, 231
Forester Estate, 62, 74, 162, 264
Forman Vineyard, 8, 148
Forrest Estate, 14, 42, 71
Foster e Rocco, 257
Four Winds, 223
Fowles, 135, 274
Fox Creek, 178, 218
Fox Gordon, 106, 116, 282
Foxes Island, 14, 188
Foxeys Hangout, 26, 83, 197
Framingham Wines, 42, 71
Francois Crochet, 67
Francois Villard, 207
Frankland Estate, 50, 163
Frankland River (subregion), 28, 50, 75, 259
Franz Hirtzberger, 41
Franz Kunstler, 37
Franz Prager, 41
Fred Loimer, 41
Freeman Vineyards, 252, 263, 270, 285
Freemark Abbey, 148
Freestone, 9
Freisa, 271
Freycinet, 30, 51, 132, 201
Friei Weingärtner Wachau, 41
Fritz Haag, 39
Frogmore Creek, 30, 51, 83, 201
Frog's Leap, 148
Fromm La Strada, 210
Fromm Winery, 14, 42, 188
Furmint, 117
FX Pichler, 41

G
Gainey Vineyard, 190
Gala Estate, 83
Galafrey, 124
Gallagher, 223
Galli Estate, 116, 228, 257
Gallo Family Vineyards, 9
Gallows Wine Co, 179
Gamay, 247-8, *247*
Gapsted, 84, 128, 287
Garagiste, 26, 83, 197
Garbin, 103
Garganega, 117, *118*
Garnacha Tinta see Grenache
Gartelmann, 254
Gary Farrell, 9, 190
Geelong (region), 25, 95, 106, 179, 197, 230
Gehringer Brothers, 171
Gembrook, 196
Gemtree, 218
Geoff Hardy, 116, 238, 245, 262, 271, 274, 282, 287, 288
Geoff Merrill, 158, 218, 249
Geoff Weaver, 22, 49, 76
Geographe (region), 75, 103, 259
Georg Breuer, 37
Georg Mosbacher, 37
Georges Roumier, 186
Gewurztraminer, 91-3, *92*
Ghost Rock, 83, 201
Giaconda, 25, 252
Gibbston Valley, 15, 189
Gibson, 219
Giesen Estate, 15, 42, 71, 188
gilbert by Simon Gilbert, 20, 76
Gilberts, 50
Gillmore, 150
Gippsland (region), 24, 198, 248, 252, 257
Gisborne Peak, 274
Gladstone Vineyard, 69
Glaetzer, 217
Glen Carlou Vineyards, 192
Glen Eldon, 159
Glenelly Estate, 150

Glenguin Estate, 222, 287
Glenrowan (region), 101, 108, 228
Glenwillow, 226, 252
Golden Ball, 25
Golden Grove Estate, 135, 241, 246, 249, 259, 282
Goldie Wines, 151, 210
Goona Warra, 228
Gordon Hills Estate, 161
Gouais Blanc, 118-19
Goulburn Valley (region), 95, 164, 226
Grace Family, 148
Grace Farm, 162
Gracebrook Vineyards, 124, 286
Graciano, 271-2, *272*
Graillot, 225
Grampians (region), 100, 226-7, 245
Grampians Estate, 227
Grand Veneur, 235
Granite Belt (region), 103, 179, 241, 249, 252, 257, 259
Granite Hills, 179, 198, 229
Grans Fassian, 39
Grant Burge, 49, 108, 159, 217, 219, 239, 269
Great Southern (region), 28, 50, 75, 162-3, 201, 230-1, 249
Greater Perth Zone, 86, 108
Grebet & Fils, 67
Greco, 119-20, *119*
Greco Bianco, 119, 120
Greenhough Vineyard, 14, 187
Greenstone Vineyard, 225, 257, 270
Greg Cooley, 48, 160
Grenache, *232*, 233-9
    Australian history, 236
    Australian regional styles, 238-9
    Australian statistics, 236
    Australian winemaking, 237
    France, 234-5
    international history, 233-4

INDEX   297

Greystone, 15, 188
Greywacke, 188
Grgich Hills Cellar, 8, 148
Grillo, 120–1, *120*
Groom, 261
Groot Constantia, 12
Grosset, 22, 48, 62, 137, 160, 200
Groth Vineyards, 148
Grove Estate, 224, 252
Grove Mill, 14, 42, 71
Gunderloch, 38
Gundog Estate, 222
Guthrie, 76

H

Haan, 177
Hahndorf Hill, 76, 83, 286, 291
Hall, 148
Hamelin Bay, 29
Hamilton Russell Vineyards, 12, 68, 192
Handpicked, 197
Hanging Rock, 25, 225, 229
Hans Herzog, 188
Hanzell, 9, 190
Happs, 62, 74, 162, 269
Haras de Pirque, 150
Harcourt Valley, 163, 226
Hardys, 158, 218, 238
Hare's Chase, 217
Harewood Estate, 28, 50, 75, 163
Harlan Estate, 148
Harslevelu, 117
Hart & Hunter, 60
Hart of the Barossa, 159
Hartenberg, 150
Hartford, 190
Hartz Barn, 274
Haselgrove, 218, 238, 249, 254, 261
Haskell Vineyards, 12
Hawkesbridge, 14
Hay Shed Hill, 29, 62, 74, 162, 243, 259

Hay's Lake, 15
Head, 219
Heafod Glen, 86
Heartland, 219, 245, 274, 288
Heathcote (region), 101, 103, 106, 164, 179, 224–5, 252, 257, 259, 261, 284
Heathvale, 159, 286
Heemskerk, 30, 51, 93, 201
Heirloom Vineyards, 49, 83, 219, 259
Helens Hill, 26, 196
Hemera Estate, 95, 159, 177, 217, 239, 243
Henri Bourgeois, 67
Henri Gouges, 186
Henry's Drive, 157, 221
Henschke, 22, 49, 83, 93, 159, 219
Hentley Farm, 49, 159, 217, 239
Henty (region), 27, 199
Herons Rise, 124
Heslop, 290
Hewitson, 217, 218, 238, 249, 259, 267, 269
Heyl Zu Herrnsheim, 38
Hickinbotham of Dromana, 110, 133
Hidden Cellars, 209
Highfield, 14
Highland Heritage Estate, 223
Hillbrook, 179
Hillcrest Estate (South Africa), 68, 173
Hillcrest Vineyard (Yarra Valley), 165, 178
Hilltops (region), 224, 252
Hither & Yon, 259, 262, 282
Hoddles Creek Estate, 26, 131, 196
Hogue Cellars, 10, 171
Hollick, 157
Holm Oak, 30, 112, 201
Home Hill, 133, 201
Honeytree Estate, 115
Houghton, 28, 162, 231

House of Arras, 255
Hugel & Fils, 40
Hugh Hamilton, 218, 257, 287
Huia, 14
Hungerford Hill, 21
Hunter Valley (region), 19–20, 59–60, 103, 160, 221–2, 241, 244, 245
Hunter's Wines, 14, 42, 71
Huntington Estate, 61, 160, 222
Hurley Vineyard, 197
Hyde de Villaine, 9

I

Indigo Wine Company, 106
Indomita, 150
Innocent Bystander, 26, 196
Inzolia, 138–9
Iona, 68
Iron Horse Vineyards, 9, 190
Irvine, 128, 177, 261
Isabel Estate, 14, 42
Island Brook, 86, 179

J

J Confuron-Coteditot, 186
J Rochioli, 9
J Wegeler, 37
Jackson Estate, 42, 71, 188
Jacques-Frederic Mugnier, 186
Jacquez, 272–3
Jamsheed, 243
Jane Brook Estate, 74
Jansz Tasmania, 255
Jasper Hill, 225, 252
jb Wines, 115, 131
Jean Claude Chatelaine, 67
Jean Grivot, 186
Jean-Jacques Confuron, 186
Jean-Louis Chave, 205
Jean-Louis Grippat, 207
Jean-Luc Colombo, 207
Jean-Marc Brocade, 7
Jean-Marie Raveneau, 7
Jeanneret, 218
Jeir Creek, 106

Jericho, 116
Jester Hill, 257
Jim Barry Wines, 48, 112, 218
Joh Jos Prüm, 39
Johannishof, 37
John Duval, 95, 100, 239, 249
John Gehrig, 87, 274
John Kosovich, 103, 108, 254
Johner Estate, 69
Johns Blend, 219
Jones Road, 26, 83
Jones Winery, 127, 228
Jordan (Napa Valley, USA), 148
Jordan Wine Estate (South Africa), 12, 68, 150, 173
Josef Chromy, 30, 51
Josef Högl, 41
Josef Jamek, 41
Joseph Jamet, 206
Joseph Phelps, 148, 209
Josmeyer, 40
Journey, 225
Jules Taylor, 14
Julicher, 188
Juniper Estate, 62, 74, 162, 231
Just Red, 287

K

Kaapzicht Wine Estate, 68, 150
Kabminye, 121, 267, 269
Kaesler, 106, 140, 217, 249
Kahurangi Estate, 42
Kaiken, 149
Kalgan River, 50
Kalleske, 87, 159, 217, 239, 246, 259
Kangarilla Road, 158, 218, 261, 279
Kangaroo Island (region), 243
Kanonkop, 150
Karl Lagler, 41
Karrawatta, 76
Karthäuserhof, 39
Kate Hill Wines, 51
Kathryn Kennedy, 209
Katnook Estate, 157, 177, 220

Kay Brothers Amery Vineyards, 158, 218
Keith Tulloch, 20, 60, 222
Keller, 38
Kellermeister, 239
Ken Wright Cellars, 9, 189
Kenefick Ranch, 171
Kennedy Point, 151
Kent Rasmussen, 9
Kenwood Cellars, 148
Kerner, 121
Kersbrook Hill, 49
Kilikanoon, 48, 160, 218, 239
Kim Crawford, 69
Kimbolton, 279
Kina Cliffs Vineyard, 71
King Estate, 9
King River Estate, 84, 274, 287
King Valley (region), 84, 97, 108, 109, 113, 241, 245, 257, 261
Kingsley Estate, 172, 210
Kirrihill, 218, 257, 279
Kistler Vineyards, 9, 190
Klein Constantia, 68, 150, 209
Kleine Zalze Wines, 68, 150
Knappstein, 48, 160, 218
Knee Deep, 74
Koehler-Ruprecht, 37
Kongsgaard, 8
Kooyong, 26, 83, 197
Kuentz-Bas, 40
Kumeu River, 13
Kusuda, 210
Kyneton Ridge, 198

L

La Anita, 149
La Chablisienne, 7
La Crema, 190
La Curio, 261, 262
La Linea, 259
La Motte, 209
La Vielle Ferme, 235
Laanecoorie, 163
Lagrein, 273–4, *274*

Laibach, 173
Lake Breeze Wines, 108, 219
Lake Chalice, 14
Lake Moodemere, 114, 269
Lake's Folly, 20, 160
Lamborn Family, 148
Lambrusco, 274–5, *275*
Lambrusco Salamino, 275–6, *276*
Lamont's, 231
Lana, 131
Landaire, 135, 221, 259
Landhaus Estate, 249
Lane Tanner, 190
Lane's End, 25, 198
Lange Estate, 189
Langhorne Creek (region), 103, 108, 219, 245, 252
Langmeil, 217
Lapostolle, 11
Lark Hill, 223
Laroche, 7
Larry Cherubino, 28, 50, 62, 74, 116, 162, 201, 231
Laughing Jack, 217, 239
Laurance, 179
Laurel Glen, 148
Lawson's Dry Hills, 14, 42, 71, 188
Leasingham, 48, 160, 218
L'Ecole No 41, 148, 171
Leconfield, 157, 177
Leeuwin Estate, 29, 74, 162, 231
Lemelson, 189
Lenton Brae, 29, 62, 74
Leo Alzinger, 41
Leo Buring, 48, 49
Leogate, 222
Leonetti Cellar, 148, 171
Les Cailloux, 235
Les Chanets, 206
Les Clos Jordanne, 10
Lethbridge, 25, 197, 230
Leyda, 172
Lievland, 209
Lillian, 100

Lillypilly, 109
Limestone Coast Zone, 243
Lindemans, 60, 157, 220
Lintz Estate, 14
Lloyd Brothers, 218, 238
Lobethal Road, 22
Lofty Valley, 22
Logan, 222, 223
Lonely Vineyard, 279
Long Mount, 68
Long Shadows, 148, 171
Lord's Wines, 68
Los Vascios, 150
Lost Valley, 115
Lou Miranda, 286
Louis Latour, 6
Lowburn Ferry, 189
Lower Murray Zone, South Australia, 27
Lucien Crochet, 67

M
M Chapoutier, 227
Mac Forbes, 26, 196
Macedon Ranges (region), 25, 198, 229, 245, 252
McGuigan Wines, 279
McHenry Hohnen, 95, 100, 162
McLaren Vale (region), 22, 87, 108, 158, 178, 217–18, 238, 241, 244, 248, 249, 252, 254, 257, 259, 261
McLeish Estate, 60
McPherson, 95, 164, 249
Macquarie Grove, 268
McWilliam's, 61, 108, 137, 291
Mahi, 14
Main Divide, 15
Main Ridge Estate, 26, 197
Majella, 157, 177, 220
Malevoire, 10
Malvasia, 121
Malvasia Istarska, 122, *122*
Mammolo, 276–7, *277*
Man O' War, 151
Mandala, 178, 196

Mandoon Estate, 103, 162, 231
Manjimup (region), 28, 179
Mansfield Wines, 109, 140, 290
Mantlerhof, 41
Marc Sorrel, 205, 206
Marcassin, 9
Marcel Deiss, 40
Marchand & Burch Wines, 28, 201
Margain Vineyard, 14
Margan Family, 20, 222, 241
Margaret Hill Vineyard, 164, 225
Margaret River (region), 28, 62, 74, 93, 95, 100, 103, 106, 161–2, 178, 231, 243, 248, 254, 259, 261
Marimar Torres Estate, 9
Marisco Vineyards, 14
Markus Molitor, 39
Marq, 29, 128, 135, 248, 259
Marquis d'Angerville, 186
Marsanne, 94–5, *95*
Martin Nigl, 41
Martinborough Vineyards, 187
Marzemino, 277
Massena Vineyards, 239, 241, 245, 261, 269, 287
Matua Valley, 172
Maverick, 217
Max Ferd Richter, 39
Maximin Grünhaus, 39
Maxwell Wines, 108, 218
Mayer, 196
Mayfield, 161
Mayford, 259
Mayhem & Co, 49
Mazuelo see Carignan
Mazza Wines, 272, 290
Medhurst, 26
Meerea Park, 60, 222
Meerendal, 150
Meerlust, 150, 192
Meinert Wines, 68
Melon, 139
Mencia, 278

Merindoc Vintners, 106, 164
Merlot, *166*, 167–79
    Australian history, 173
    Australian regional styles, 176–9
    Australian statistics, 174
    Australian winemaking, 174–5
    Canada, 171
    Chile, 172
    France, 169–70
    international history, 167–9
    New Zealand, 172
    South Africa, 173
    United States, 170–1
Merricks Estate, 229
Merry Edwards, 190
Merum Estate, 28
Metcalfe Valley, 229
Michael Hall, 22, 200
Michel Ampeau, 6
Michel Bouzereau, 6
Michel Ogier, 206
Michelini, 277, 288
Miguel Torres, 150
Mike Press, 176
Miles from Nowhere, 62, 74
Millbrook, 112, 135, 231, 254
Mills Reef, 13, 172, 210
Milton Vineyard, 93
Ministry of Clouds, 30, 238
Miro Vineyard, 151
Mischa, 150
Misha's Vineyard, 189
Mission Estate, 42, 69, 151, 172
Mission Hill Winery, 10, 171
Mistletoe, 20
Mitchell, 48, 160, 218
Mitchell Harris, 257
Mitchelton, 95, 226, 249
Mitolo, 135, 158, 218, 286
Monastrell see Mourvedre
Mondeuse, 278
Mondeuse Blanche, 139
Mongeard-Mugneret, 186
Monichino, 139

Montalto, 26, 83, 197
Montana, 188
Montepulciano, 278–9, *279*
Montes, 68, 150, 172
Montgomery's Hill, 163
Montgras, 150
Montils, 122–3
Mooiplaas, 209
Moombaki Wines, 163
Moondara, 252
Moores Hill Estate, 201
Moorilla Estate, 30, 51, 83, 201
Moorooduc Estate, 26, 83, 197
Moppity Vineyards, 21, 224
Morambro Creek Wines, 157, 221
Morgan Vineyards, 178
Morgenhof, 150
Morningside, 51
Mornington Peninsula (region), 26, 83, 197, 229, 248, 257, 259
Morris Wines, 97, 108, 228, 246, 269
Moscato Giallo, 123–4, *123*
Mosquito Hill, 131
Moss Wood, 162, 179
Mount Alexander, 163
Mount Anakie, 114
Mount Avoca, 179, 227
Mount Barker (subregion), 28, 50, 75, 179, 201
Mount Benson (region), 23
Mt Billy, 257
Mount Cathedral Vineyards, 179
Mt Difficulty Wines, 15, 189
Mount Eyre Vineyards, 116
Mt Franklin Estate, 245
Mount Horrocks, 48, 160, 218, 282
Mount Langi Ghiran, 227
Mount Lofty Ranges Vineyard, 49, 200
Mount Majura, 223, 259, 272, 290

Mount Mary, 26, 165, 196
Mount Maude, 42
Mount Pleasant, 60, 113, 123, 222
Mount Riley Wines, 71
Mount Sutherland, 209
Mount Towrong, 252
Mount View Estate, 60, 222
Mountford, 15
Mourvedre, 248–9
Moutere Hills, 14
Mr Riggs Wine Company, 279
Mud House, 188
Mudbrick Vineyard, 13
Muddy Water, 42, 188
Mudgee (region), 20, 61, 109, 160, 222, 241, 254
Mudgee Wines, 281
Mulderbosch, 12, 68, 150
Muller-Catoir, 37
Muller-Thurgau, 124
Munari, 226
Muratie, 209
Murdoch Hill, 22, 76, 200, 255
Murdoch James Estate, 69
Murray Darling (region), 261
Muscadelle, 96–8, *97*
Muscardin, 280
Muscat Blanc a Petits Grains, 107–8
Muscat of Alexandria, 109

N
Nagambie Lakes (region), 100, 249
Nannup Ridge, 259
Narkoojee, 24, 198
Nautilus Estate, 71, 188
Neagles Rock, 218
Nebbiolo, 249–52, *250*
Nederburg Wines, 68, 150, 173
Negroamaro, 280–1, *280*
Neil Ellis Wines, 12, 68
Nepenthe, 22, 76, 200, 259
Nero d'Avola, 281–2, *281*
Neudorf Vineyards, 14, 42, 187
Nevis Bluff, 15

New South Wales *see* specific regions, e.g. Mudgee
Newton Forrest, 151
Newton Johnson, 12, 192
Newton Vineyards, 148, 171
Neyers, 209
Nga Waka Vineyard, 14, 42, 69
Ngatarawa, 13, 42, 172
Ngeringa, 106, 252, 257
Nicholson River, 257
Niebaum Coppola, 171
919 Wines, 128, 140, 290
Noble Red, 225
Northstar, 171
Northwest Victoria Zone, Victoria, 27
Nosiola, 124–5
Nugan Estate, 61

O
O Fournier, 68, 150
Oak Cliff Cellars, 209
Oak Works, 283, 287
Oakdene, 25, 230
Oakover, 268
Oakridge Estate, 26, 112, 165, 178, 196
Obsidian, 151
Occam's Razor, 225
Ocean Eight Vineyard, 26, 83, 197
Oceans Estate, 179
Ochota Barrels, 93, 200, 217
Old Plains, 290
O'Leary Walker, 48, 218
Oliver's Taranga Vineyards, 116, 158, 218, 238, 278, 286
Olssens of Watervale, 268
Onannon, 24
Ondenc, 125–7
Opus One, 148
Orange (region), 20, 76, 95, 106, 179, 223, 243, 259
Orange Mountain, 76, 106
Orange Muscat, 139
Oranje Tractor, 75

Orlando, 217, 221
Oyster Bay, 71

P

Padthaway (region), 23, 157, 220–1, 259
Pahlmeyer, 171
Palliser Estate, 14, 69, 71, 187, 210
Palmara, 132, 138
Palomino, 140
Paradigm Hill, 83, 197, 229
Paradise IV, 230
Parellada, 140
Paringa Estate, 26, 83, 197, 229
Parish Hill, 275, 276, 281
Parish Lane, 179
Parker Coonawarra Estate, 23, 157, 177, 220
Parous, 238
Pask, 151, 172
Passage Rock, 210
Passing Clouds, 226
Patina, 20, 161
Patrick Jasmin, 206
Patrick Piuze, 7
Patritti, 103, 137, 218, 287
Patz & Hall, 9
Paul Blacnk, 40
Paul Cluver, 12, 68, 192
Paul Conti Wines, 86, 108, 231
Paul Jaboulet Aîné, 205, 206, 207
Paul Nelson, 249
Paul Osicka, 164, 225
Paulett, 48
Paulmara Estates, 274, 290
Paxton, 158, 218, 272
Pedro Ximenez, 127
Peel (region), 231
Peel Estate, 86, 231
Pegasus Bay, 15, 42, 188
Pemberton (region), 28, 100, 179
Penfolds, 21, 22, 49, 157, 159, 217, 220, 239, 257

Peninsula Estate, 151
Penley Estate, 157
Penny's Hill, 158, 178
Peos Estate, 28, 268
Pepper Bridge Winery, 148, 171
Pepper Tree, 20, 60, 134, 222
Peregrine, 42, 189
Perez Cruz, 150
Perth Hills (region), 231, 254, 259
Petaluma, 22, 48, 83, 157
Peter Jakob Kuhn, 37
Peter Lehmann, 49, 108, 134, 217
Peter Michael Winery, 9
Petit Manseng, 127–8
Petit Meslier, 128
Petit Verdot, 252–4, *253*
Pewsey Vale, 49
Pfeiffer, 97, 108, 228, 246, 248, 259
PHI, 196, 249
Philip Shaw, 76, 161, 223
Philip Togni, 148
Piano Piano, 290
Picolit, 128–9, *129*
Pierre Barge, 206
Pierre Gaillard, 207
Pierre Morey, 6
Pierre Sparr et Ses Fils, 40
Pierre Yves Colin-Morey, 6
Pierro, 162
Pike & Joyce, 83, 200
Pikes, 48, 160, 218, 257, 268
Pimpernel, 196
Pinelli, 246
Pinot Blanc, 130–1, *130*
Pinot Grigio see Pinot Gris
Pinot Gris, *78*, 79–84
  Australian history, 80–1
  Australian regional styles, 82–4
  Australian statistics, 81
  Australian winemaking, 82
  international history, 79–80
  international styles, 80

Pinot Meunier, 254–5, *254*
Pinot Noir, *180*, 181–201
  Australian history, 192–4
  Australian regional styles, 196–201
  Australian statistics, 194
  Australian winemaking, 195–6
  Austria and Germany, 191
  Canada, 191
  France, 184–6, 191
  international history, 181–3
  New Zealand, 186–9
  South Africa, 192
  United States, 189–91
Pinotage, 282–3, *283*
Pipers Brook Vineyard, 51, 83, 93
Piquepoul Blanc, 140
Pirramimma, 178, 254, 287
Pisa Range, 189
Pizzini, 84, 112, 132, 134
Plan B, 86
Plantagenet, 28, 163
Poacher's Ridge Vineyard, 163, 179
Point Leo Road, 274
Politini, 117
Pondalowie, 163, 226
Ponzi Vineyards, 189
Poole's Rock, 20
Pooley Wines, 51, 201
Poonawatta, 49, 159, 219
Porongorup (subregion), 28, 50, 75, 201
Port Phillip Estate, 26, 112, 197, 229
Portsea Estate Scorpo Wines, 197
Pressing Matters, 51
Preston Peak, 268, 286
Preveli, 74
Primitivo see Zinfandel
Primo Estate, 90, 108, 117, 158, 218, 252
Printhie, 20, 161, 223

Prosecco, 131–2, *131*
Provenance, 197, 230
Puertas, 172
Pulenta Estate, 149
Punch, 26, 165, 196
Punt Road, 178
Puriri Hills, 13
Purple Hands, 239
Pyramid Valley, 188
Pyren Vineyard, 227
Pyrenees (region), 179, 227, 245, 252, 257

Q

Quails Gate, 10
Quarisa, 246
Quartz Hill, 227
Quartz Reef, 189
Quattro Mano, 259, 290
Quealy Balnarring Vineyard, 83
Quebrada de Macul, 150
Quilceda Creek, 148
Qupe, 209

R

Radford, 49
Rahona Valley, 255
Ravens Croft, 283
Ravensworth, 223, 252, 257
Ravine Vineyard, 10
Raymond Trollat, 207
Rebholz, 37
Red Edge, 164, 225
Red Hill Estate, 26
Red Rooster Winery, 10
Redbank, 117
Redgate, 29, 243
Refosco dal Peduncolo Rosso, 284, *284*
Regent Wines, 274
Reichsgraf Von Kesselstatt, 39
Reinhold Haart, 39
Remhoogte, 173
Remi Jobard, 6
René Muré, 40
Rene Rostaing, 20

Rene and Vincent Dauvissat, 7
Rex Hill, 189
Reynella, 158, 218
Richard Hamilton, 158, 218
Richmond Plains, 71
Ridge Vineyards, 148
Ridgemill Estate, 273
Ridgeview, 20
Riesling, 32, 33–51
    Australian history, 43–4
    Australian regional styles, 47–51
    Australian statistics, 45
    Australian winemaking, 45–7
    Austria, 40–1
    France, 39–40
    Germany, 36–9
    international history, 33–6
    New Zealand, 42–3
    North America, 42–3
Riglos, 149
Riposte, 93, 200
Rippon Vineyard, 42, 189
Riverina (region), 61, 108, 109, 254
Riversands, 273
Riversdale Estate, 30
Riwaka River Estate, 71
RL Buller, 278
Robe (region), 23
Robert Channon, 103
Robert Johnson Vineyards, 177
Robert Mondavi, 148
Robert Oatley Vineyards, 29, 50, 162, 201, 222, 231
Robert Sinskey Vineyards, 171
Robert Stein, 160, 222
Robert Weil, 37
Robinvale, 121
Rochford, 165, 196, 225, 243
Rochioli, 190
RockBare, 158
Rockburn Wines, 189
Rockcliffe, 28, 201, 231
Rockford, 108, 159, 217, 264

Roger Sabon, 235
Rohrlach, 177
Rondinella, 285
Ros Ritchie, 93
Rosabrook, 29, 259
Rosemount Estate, 116, 218
Rosily Vineyard, 62, 74
Ross Hill, 76, 161, 223, 243
Rossifers, 274
Roulot, 6
Roussanne, 99–100, *99*
Route du Van, 245
Rowanston on the Track, 229
Ruby Cabernet, 255
Ruca Malen, 149
Rudderless, 238, 272
Rudi Pichler, 41
Rust en Vrede, 173, 209
Rustenberg, 12, 68, 150
Rustic Prayer Rock Vineyard, 209
Rutherglen (region), 87, 95, 97, 101, 108, 228, 243, 248, 259
Rutherglen Estates, 116
Rutini Wines, 149
Rymill, 157, 220

S

SA Prüm, 39
Sabella, 270
Sacred Hill Wines, 13, 151, 172
Saddleback Cellars, 148
Sagrantino, 285–6
Saint Clair Estate, 14, 42, 71, 172, 188
St Clement Vineyards, 8, 171
St Hallett, 49, 217, 290
St Helena Wine Estate, 15
St Huberts, 100, 165
St Laurent *see* Sankt Laurent
St Leonards, 108, 228, 243, 246
Saint Macaire, 286
St Mary's, 243
Saintsbury, 9, 190
Salena Estate, 136
Salomon Undhof, 41

Saltram, 49, 159
Sam Miranda, 112, 287
Samuel's Gorge, 249
San Pedro, 150
Sandalford, 103, 231
Sanford Winery, 9, 190
Sangiovese, 256-7, *256*
Sanguine Estate, 164, 225
Sankt Antony, 38
Sankt Laurent, 286-7
Santa Alicia, 150
Santa Barbara Winery, 190
Santa Carolina, 11, 68
Santa Rita, 68, 150, 172
Saperavi, 287
Sauvignon Blanc, *64*, 65-76, 77
    Australian history, 71
    Australian regional styles, 74-6
    Australian statistics, 72
    Australian winemaking, 72-3
    Chile, 68
    France, 66-7
    international history, 65-6
    New Zealand, 69-71
    Northern Italy, Austria and Slovenia, 67
    South Africa, 67-8
Savaterre, 25
Savina Lane, 116
Saxenburg, 68, 173
SC Pannell, 218, 238, 252, 290
Scarpantoni, 248
Schiava Grossa *see* Trollinger
Schloss Gobelsburg, 41
Schloss Reinhartshausen, 37
Schonburger, 132
Schossgut Diehl, 38
Schwarz Wine Company, 87, 239
Scion Vineyard, 139, 246
Scorpo, 26, 83
Scotchmans Hill, 25, 197, 230
Scott Paul Wines, 189

Scott Wines, 22, 83, 116, 117, 262, 274, 282
Screaming Eagle, 148
Sedona Estate, 179, 257
Seifried Estate, 42
Selaks Dryland Estate, 14, 71
Selene, 148
Semillon, 52, 53-62, *63*
    Australian history, 55-6
    Australian regional styles, 59-62
    Australian statistics, 57
    Australian winemaking, 57-8
    France, 54-5
    international history, 53-4
Seppelt, 199, 227, 255, 290
Seppeltsfield, 97, 108, 239, 267, 274, 290
Serafino, 158, 218, 238, 257, 268, 274, 279
Seresin Estate, 14, 42, 71, 188
Serrat, 26, 196
Seven Hills Winery, 148
Sevenhill Cellars, 290
Seville Estate, 26, 165, 196, 230
Seville Hill, 178
Shadowfax, 25, 198
Shafer Vineyards, 148, 171
Shannon, 173, 192
Shaw + Smith, 22, 49, 76
Shaw Family, 158
She-Oak Hill, 225
Shea Wine Cellars, 189
Shedleys, 133
Shingle Peak, 14
Shingleback, 158, 218
Shiraz, *202*, 203-31
    Australian history, 210-12
    Australian regional styles, 215-31
    Australian statistics, 213
    Australian winemaking, 213-15
    France, 205-8

    international history, 203-4
    Italy and Spain, 208
    New Zealand, 210
    North America, 209
    South Africa, 209
Shirvington, 218
Shoalhaven Coast (region), 244
Shut the Gate, 257
Sidewood Estate, 76
Siduri, 190
Siegerrebe, 132
Signorello Vineyards, 8
Sileni Estate, 13, 69, 172
Silent Way, 25, 198
Silvaner, 133
Silverado, 148
Silverstream, 243
Simi Winery, 9
Simon Bize et Fils, 186
Simonsig, 12, 150
Singlefile, 28, 75, 163, 201
Sirromet, 103, 179
Sittella, 86, 109
Skillogalee, 48, 160, 218
Smallfry, 95, 267, 269
Smith & Hooper, 178, 221
Snake + Herring, 28
Snoqualmie Vineyards, 171
Sonoma-Cutrer Vineyards, 9
Sons & Brothers, 161
Sons of Eden, 49, 219, 249
Sorrenberg, 248
Soter Vineyard, 189
Soumah, 106
South Australia *see* specific regions, e.g. McLaren Vale
Southern Highland Wines, 109
Southern Highlands (region), 109
Spencer Hill Estate, 14
Spier, 173
Spinifex, 217, 239, 269
Spottswoode, 148
Spring Mountain, 8
Spring Vale Vineyards, 255

Spy Valley, 14, 42, 71, 188
Staete Landt, 71
Stag's Leap Wine Cellars, 148, 171
Staniford Wine Co, 28
Stanton & Killeen, 97, 108, 246, 259, 289, 290
Stargazer Wine, 51, 201
Stark-Condé Wines, 150, 209
Steele Wines, 209
Steenberg, 68
Stefani Estate, 101
Stefano de Pieri, 124, 261
Stefano Lubiana, 51, 83, 179, 201
Stella Bella Wines, 62, 74, 106
Stellenzicht, 150, 209
Stephen Ross, 9
Stimson Lane, 10
Stoller Family Estate, 189
Stone Bridge, 257
Stonecroft, 13
Stoneleigh, 71
Stoney Rise, 30, 201
Stonier, 26, 197
Stony Hill, 8
Stonyridge Vineyard, 151
Stormflower, 86
Strandveld, 209
Strathbogie Ranges (region), 24
Stumpy Gully, 257
Sugarloaf Ridge, 274
Sumac Ridge, 171
Summerfield, 227
Summit Estate, 259, 287
Sunbury (region), 106, 228
Sunset Valley Vineyard, 71
Sutherland Estate, 165
Sutton Grange, 116
Swan Valley Wines, 86, 120
Swan Valley/Swan District (region), 86, 103, 108, 109, 231, 254
Swanson, 209
Swinging Bridge, 20
Swings & Roundabouts, 86
Symphonia, 84, 128, 287

Symphony Hill, 103, 252, 259, 274
Syrah see Shiraz
Syrahmi, 225, 249

T

Tahbilk, 95, 100, 164, 226, 249
Talboit, 9
Tallavera Grove, 103, 222, 223, 281, 286
Talley Vineyards, 9, 190
Tamar Ridge, 51, 83, 201
Tambo Estate, 24, 198
Tamburlaine, 20, 76, 95, 103, 161, 244
Taminga, 133
Taminick Cellars, 101, 228, 264
Tannat, 287, *288*
Tapanappa, 22, 178, 221
Tar & Roses, 259
Tardieu-Laurent, 205, 207, 235
TarraWarra Estate, 26, 95, 100, 178, 196
Tasmania (region), 30, 51, 82–3, 93, 179, 200–1, 259
Tawse, 10
Taylors, 48, 160, 218
Te Awa, 151
Te Kairanga, 14, 187
Te Mania, 187
Te Mata, 13, 69, 151, 172, 210
Te Motu Vineyard, 151
Te Whare Ra, 42
Te Whau Vineyard, 151
Tekena, 68
Tempranillo, 258–9, *258*
Tempus Two, 222
Ten Men, 227, 283
Ten Miles East, 287
Ten Minutes by Tractor, 26, 197
Ten Sisters, 71
Tenafeate Creek, 279
Terindah Estate, 230
Teroldego, 288
Terra Felix, 286
Terra Sancta, 189

TerraVin, 188
Terrazas de los Andes, 149
Terre à Terre, 178, 221
Tertini, 112, 274
Teusner, 239
T'Gallant, 83
The Alchemists, 62, 74, 179
The Foundry, 209
The Hairy Arm, 228, 252
The Hitching Post, 190
The Hogue Cellars, 148
The Islander, 243
The Lake House, 28, 75, 201, 231
The Lane Vineyard, 22, 176
The Old Faithful Estate, 218
The Partners, 50
The Settlement Wine Co, 127
The Story Wines, 100, 227
Thelema Mountain Vineyards, 150, 173
Thick as Thieves, 13, 112, 283
Thierry Alleman, 207
Third Child, 51
13th Street, 10
Thomas Wines, 60, 222
Thompson Estate, 29, 74, 162
Thorn-Clarke, 159, 217
Three Dark Horses, 290
3 Drops, 50, 75
Three Wishes, 30
Tim Adams, 48, 239
Tim Gramp, 127
Tim Smith, 106, 239
Tinklers Vineyard, 222
Tinta Barroca, 289
Tinta Roriz, 289, *289*
Tintara, 158, 218
Tintilla, 20
Tinto Cao, 289, *289*
Tizzana, 263
Tokar Estate, 165, 259
Tokara, 12, 68, 150
Tollot-Beaut et Fils, 186
Tolpuddle, 30, 201
Tomboy Hill, 199
Tomich, 22, 76

Tongue in Groove, 188
Toolangi, 26, 196
Topper's Mountain, 128, 283, 287
Torbreck, 217, 219, 239
Torres Estate, 190
Torzi Matthews, 101, 249, 281
Touriga Nacional, 289–90, *290*
Tower Estate, 60
Traminer *see* Gewurztraminer
Trapiche, 149
Travertine, 244
Trebbiano, 101
Trentham Estate, 133, 275
Trevor Jones, 217
Tribidrag *see* Zinfandel
Trimbach, 40
Trinity Hill, 13, 151, 172, 210
Trollinger, 291
Trousseau *see* Bastardo
Truchard Vineyards, 9, 171
Truffle Hill, 179
Tscharke, 279, 290
Tuck's Ridge, 26, 197, 259
Tulloch, 103, 222
Tumbarumba (region), 21
Turkey Flat, 100, 127, 159, 217, 239
Turners Crossing, 129, 163, 226
Two Hands, 49, 219, 238, 287
201 (winery), 244
Two Rivers, 103
Two Tails, 273
Tyrian, 291
Tyrrell's, 20, 60, 222, 225

U

Ulithorne, 238, 249
Umamu Estate, 74, 162
Upper Goulburn (region), 24, 93, 179, 257
Upper Reach, 231, 254

V

Valdivieso, 150, 172
Vasse Felix, 29, 62, 74, 162
Vavasour Wines, 14, 71, 188
Veenwouden, 173
Velo, 201
Ventisquero, 150
Verdejo, 133–4
Verdelho, 102–4, *102*
Verduzzo Friulano, 134
Vergelegen, 12, 68, 150, 173, 209
Vergenoegd, 173
Vermentino, 134–5
Victoria *see* specific regions, e.g. Yarra Valley
Victory Point, 162
Vidal Estate, 13, 151, 172, 210
Vidal-Fleury, 206
Vieux Donjon, 235
View Road, 286
Villa Maria, 13, 71, 151, 172, 188, 210
Villa Mount Eden, 9
Villard, 11, 68, 172
Villiera Wines, 68, 150
Viña Carmen, 11, 150
Viña Casablanca, 11, 68
Vincent Paris, 207
Vincent Pinard, 67
Vinden Estate, 264
Vinea Marson, 106, 284
Viñedo Chadwick, 150
Viognier, 105–6, *106*
Viu Manent, 68
Vlader Estate, 148
Volker Estate, 148
Von Basserman-Jordan, 37
Von Buhl, 37
Von Hövel, 39
Von Schubert, 39
Voss Estate, 187
Voyager Estate, 29, 86, 162, 231

W

Wagener-Stempel, 38
Waipara Hills, 42, 188
Waipara Springs, 188
Walla Walla, 171
Walter Hansel, 190
Warner Glen Estate, 74, 162
Warner Vineyard, 25
Warrabilla, 108, 228, 246
Warrenmang, 227, 245
Warterkloof, 68
Warwick Billings, 200
Warwick Estate, 12
Water Wheel, 264
Waterford, 150
Watershed Wines, 74, 162, 231
Waterton Vineyards, 51
WayWood Wines, 218, 238, 279
Wedgetail Estate, 178
Weingut Bründlmayer, 41
Weingut Hiedler, 41
Weingut Hirsch, 41
Weingut Malat, 41
Weingut Proidl, 41
Weingut Schmelz, 41
Wendouree, 160, 218
West Cape Howe, 28, 75, 163, 231, 259
Westend Estate, 286
Western Australia *see* specific WA regions, e.g. Margaret River
Western Range, 268
Westlake, 217
Whinstone Estate, 139
Whispering Brook, 290
White Rock Vineyard, 271
Whitehaven, 71
Wignalls, 75
Willakenzie Estate, 189
Willem Kurt, 135
William Fevre, 7
Williams Selyem, 190
Willoughby Park, 28, 50, 75
Willow Bridge Estate, 75, 86, 259
Willunga 100, 259
Wilson Vineyard, 48, 261
Windance, 74
Windows Estate, 29, 62, 74
WindshakeR, 268
Wines by Geoff Hardy, 274

Wines by KT, 48, 259
Winslow, 42
Winzerhof Dockner, 41
Wirra Wirra, 22, 49, 158, 218, 238
Wise, 103
Witchmount Estate, 228
Wither Hills Estate, 71, 188
Wittmann, 38
Wolf Blass, 22, 217
Wood Park, 261, 270
Woodgate Wines, 179
Woodlands Estate, 29, 162, 243
Woods Crampton, 49, 272
Woodstock, 218
Woodward Canyon, 10, 148
Woody Nook, 162, 259
Wooing Tree, 189
Woollaston, 187
Wrattonbully (region), 177–8, 221
Wynns Coonawarra Estate, 157, 220

X

Xabregas, 231
Xanadu, 29, 162, 254, 272

Y

Yabby Lake, 26, 83, 197, 229
Yacca Paddock, 245
Yal Yal Estate, 26
Yalumba, 106, 135, 157, 159, 217, 219, 239
Yangarra Estate, 136, 139, 140, 158, 178, 218, 238, 249, 269, 270, 280
Yann Chave, 205, 206
Yarra Valley (region), 26, 93, 95, 100, 106, 164–5, 196, 229–30, 243, 248, 257, 259
Yarra Yarra, 165
Yarra Yering, 106, 165, 196, 230, 268, 289, 290
YarraLoch, 112
Yarran, 225, 254
Yealands Family Estate, 14, 71
Yelland & Papps, 100, 135, 239, 241
Yering Station, 26, 100, 165, 196, 230
Yeringberg, 95, 100, 106, 165, 196, 230
Yilgarnia, 75, 179
Yonder Hill, 173
Yves Cuilleron, 206, 207

Z

Zaca Mesa Winery, 9
Zema Estate, 157, 220
Zillikin, 39
Zind-Humbrecht, 40
Zinfandel, 259–61, 260
Zonte's Footstep, 241
Zweigelt, 291

Acknowledgements

As ever, the foundation of this book is the cooperation and goodwill of all of the winemakers of Australia, who freely give of their time and receive no reward for doing so, other than my heartfelt thanks. There is, however, one person who deserves special recognition in this context: Kim Chalmers of the eponymous wine business, which focuses on making hitherto unavailable varieties available for Australian growers, having first evaluated their potential worth (and making seven or more wines of various varieties). She supplied the first round of photographs taken by Dr Stefano Dini and Adam Hobbs of One Idea at the Chalmers Nursery Vineyard, and has been a constant source of information, always responding quickly to my questions. For his part, Adam Hobbs provided most of the photographs in this book; photography took place between 2014 and 2015. Additional photography came courtesy of Randy Caparoso and Kevin Miller.

When the first edition of *Varietal Wines* was published in 2004, Jancis Robinson MW gave permission for me to publish all of the synonyms for each of the 84 varieties profiled in that edition. Since then she has been the lead author of *Wine Grapes*, which, as the footnotes throughout this book indicate, has revolutionised our understanding of the origins of and relationships between the 1368 wine grape varieties profiled in that book. Since then, too, the number of grape varieties in this book has risen to 130, although that number is still (as was the case in 2004) circumscribed by the prerequisite of commercial production in Australia. While I have continually referred to *Wine Grapes*, I have not used the synonyms in this book for space reasons. My thanks to Jancis Robinson remain undimmed.

Then there is the team at battleship headquarters, Paula Grey and Beth Anthony, with a cumulative 40 or so years working for me without complaint, even tolerating the Bermuda Triangle of my desk, where documents and the like can disappear without trace five minutes after being given to me or placed in the relevant paper tray.

Finally, there is the *sine qua non* of my relationship with Hardie Grant Books. I have been incredibly fortunate since this started to crystallise almost 10 years ago (it seems like yesterday), my only regret being that it wasn't 20 or more years ago – an unreal regret because there always has to be a time and a place for the stars to come so perfectly into alignment. Rihana Ries has been infinitely patient in steering the book through the edit stage, Sarah Shrubb the skilled copyeditor. My special thanks to each of them.